Point
Counterpoint II

Point Counterpoint II

New Perspectives on People + Strategy

RICHARD VOSBURGH, PH.D. I ANNA TAVIS, PH.D. I MARC SOKOL, PH.D.

Published by HR People + Strategy
1800 Duke Street, Alexandria, VA 22314
www.hrps.org

Published in association with the Society for Human Resource Management.

ISBN: 978-1-586-44418-1

eISBN: 978-1-586-44420-4

Kindle: 978-1-586-44421-1

CONTENTS

CONTENTS continued

113

82

Credit: Bill Browning

New Perspectives on People + Strategy

This book is the second in a series originated with *Point Counterpoint* in 2012 which addressed the five knowledge areas of HR: Strategy and Planning; Leadership Development, Talent Management, Organization Effectiveness, and Building a Strategic HR Function. This book contains 16 sets of Point Counterpoint debates addressing five key topics at the intersection of people and strategy:

- The Future of HR
- Leadership and Talent Development
- Performance and Potential Management
- Organizational Design
- Organizational Purpose and Health

The book is intended to serve several audiences, including:

- VPs of HR in organizations that want to easily lead lunch-and-learn sessions for the continued professional development of their HR team
- Professors in college programs focused on strategic HR issues, with the Learning Guides providing the instructional design
- HR professionals committed to their own continuing development (including SHRM certification credits)

Each set of articles has a Learning Guide for the development of teams in organizations (think: "lunch and learn" sessions) or students in classrooms (think: a complete syllabus and facilitated lesson plan). Our intent is to make it easy for both an HR leader in an organization and an academic in the classroom to facilitate significant conversations on essential issues that have no clear black and white answers. For each Point/Counterpoint, the Learning Guide is structured as follows:

- **Discovery Questions.** What are you dealing with in your organization today that relates to this content area?
- **Selected Facts.** What new facts that were presented got your attention?
- **Key Discussion Points.** What were the key points being made in this presentation?
- **Review of Solutions.** Identify two to three "big ideas" worthy of exploring in your organization.
- **Identifying the Paradox.** How is it that a solution appropriate for yesterday's organization is no longer valid? Consider how very different perspectives might be correct given different situations.
- **Learning Outcomes.** What one new piece of information did you learn that will be important to you in the future?

More than 90 authors, consultants, academics, and practitioners contributed and many of our profession's strongest thought leaders are represented in *Point Counterpoint II*, including John Boudreau, Allan Church, Daryl Conner, Jay Gailbraith, Eva Sage-Gavin, Robert Hogan, Aaron Hurst, Amy Kates, Greg Kessler, Bob Rosen, Noel Tichy, among many others.

The *People + Strategy* journal Perspectives: Point/Counterpoint column was started with an understanding that in the strategic arena of HR, there often is "no one right answer," and that proper solutions evolve from the straightforward presentation of facts and various points of view. It is in this context that we offer *Point Counterpoint II.*

Richard M. Vosburgh, Ph.D.
HR People + Strategy Board
Chair, 2016–2017

Richard M. Vosburgh, Ph.D., has 40 years of human resource and organizational development experience and is president of RMV Solutions since retiring as senior vice president and chief human resource officer at KEMET Electronics Corporation. Previously, he was senior vice president, HR, at MGM Resorts International and has held VP HR positions at Hewlett-Packard, Volkswagen, Hyatt, Campbell Soup Company, Gallup, and PepsiCo. He is the author of numerous journal articles and three books.

HR's Learning Acceleration Course

Anna A. Tavis, Ph.D.
Perspectives Editor
People + Strategy Journal

Anna A. Tavis, Ph.D., is a clinical associate professor of leadership and human capital management at New York University and a researcher, writer, speaker, and global educator focused on the Future of Work. She is also a senior lecturer and director at the Workforce Innovation Lab at Latin American Business School. Anna has held senior HR positions at Motorola, United Technologies, and AIG. She is a senior fellow with the Conference Board and the former executive editor of the *People + Strategy* journal.

Most of the questions confronting HR today are not new. Where do we stand as a profession? Are we changing fast enough? What do we need to do to stay current? What is the future of HR?

These existential questions underlie the issues addressed in our collection of Perspectives, which consist of points and counterpoints—professional debates—presented here. This volume is designed to provide a launching pad for HR professionals to navigate the fast-moving, disruptive world of work. It will also help you learn to develop an informed point of view while grappling with today's paradoxes.

Every one of us has participated in discussions about HR's relevance and competence, if not outright survival. In the end, most of us would agree that HR collectively confronts the challenge of professional identity. We have called ourselves many names—from administrators to business partners, talent managers, credible activists, and advisors to the business. You name it, we have heard it before. As professionals, we have undergone a fair amount of public scrutiny and self-reflection in recent years and arrived at a much clearer vision of what our unique professional agenda must represent. It is challenging and energizing. As an array of trend reports and academic studies continue to point out, HR's increasingly strategic importance in organizations is only going to increase.

The real challenge HR faces today is not one of survival but one of accelerated learning. Are we learning fast enough? Are we unlearning what does not matter? Will we be able to meet the expectations that business places on us?

There is an ongoing debate in the HR profession about what matters most for HR's learning. Some might argue that HR is a trade and therefore it is to be learned through a hands-on apprenticeship with the business. Others would say that it is a science and would turn to psychology, neuroscience, sociology, and other disciplines to equip themselves with scientific tools and methods to know what it takes to work with people. Yet a third group may claim that it is an art, as all applications are different and require a creative, innovative, customized approach.

We have committed to figuring out in these Perspectives what HR's learning should look like, both in content and in method. HR needs to do three things well on its path to success:

- Commit to fast, ongoing learning.
- Practice.
- Review, reflect, and adjust.

All three of these learning stages are essential. We must have a ton of practice, be grounded in science, and master the art of marrying the two.

These Perspectives will not replace your rigorous academic study, nor will they be a substitute for your professional certification. Rather, they will support your learning no matter where it takes you. Engaging with your colleagues or going through the points and counterpoints on your own will help you model how complex decision-making is done in a manageable and accessible way. *Point Counterpoint II* will provide you and your team with the context to practice decision-making at the intersections of practice, science, and personal reflection.

You are in for a unique learning journey.

The Power of Paradox to Deepen Perspective

Among the questions for reflection that follow each contribution in this volume is an opportunity to identify the underlying paradox. We believe these questions can deepen appreciation of and readiness to discuss important issues.

Paradox usually begins when we focus on the tradeoff of a set of contrasting values, such as whether centralization or decentralization is a better approach to organizing. Proponents of each side tend to get locked into seeing only the benefits and upside of one view, and only the cost and downside of the opposing view. In reality, each side has benefits and costs, an upside and a downside. Too much emphasis on the benefits of one side often leads to fostering the downside and cost of that same side. This isn't always easy for proponents of either side to recognize, just as we see organizational leaders stuck in one view when they debate colleagues who are just as stuck holding an opposing view.

In simplest terms, the essence of learning from paradox is to take an "either/or" dilemma and develop the capacity to reframe it as a "both/and" set of perspectives. This allows us to be a force for collaboration, to more effectively facilitate opposing views, and to get both sides to higher ground.

As an educational practice, it's easy enough to see this dynamic when two people or groups are asked to do the following:

1. Ask Group 1 to make a list of all the benefits of being active, and then a list of all of the potential costs or negative effects of too much rest. At the same time, ask Group 2 to make a list of all of the benefits of rest, and then a list of all of the potential costs or negative effects of too much activity.
2. Have Group 1 present its view on why being active is better than inactive, starting with the upside of being active, then following with the downside of too much rest or inactivity. Group 2 should then present its view, beginning with the upside of rest, and then following with the downside of too much activity. As you and everyone listen to each group, you can see the roots of how we get polarized into one side or another of different perspectives.
3. We know, of course, that too much activity without rest has a downside, just as too much rest without activity has a downside. The opportunity is to see the benefits of both activity and rest.
4. Now have someone from Group 1 and Group 2 repeat out loud the benefits of activity and rest, this time alternating one benefit of activity and then one benefit of rest. As you and everyone else listen to the complementary nature of activity and rest, you can easily see how we get maximum value when we frame the activity and rest debate in "both/and" rather than "either/or" terms.
5. To add to perspective, ask both groups to identify early warning signs of too much activity at the expense of rest, or too much rest at the expense of activity, and what they advise we do as we encounter those early warning signs. Close by asking them to describe the benefit of keeping both in balance.

The same process can be applied to others issues that seem to be paradoxes: centralization vs. decentralization; skills for the present vs. the future; being employee-centric vs. customer-centric; thinking global vs. local, and so forth. To learn more about paradox, read Johnson, B. (1996). *Polarity Management: Identifying and Managing Unsolvable Problems*. Amherst, MA: HRD Press.

Marc B. Sokol, Ph.D.
Executive Editor
People + Strategy Journal

Marc B. Sokol, Ph.D., is an organizational psychologist, consultant, executive coach, writer, and speaker on workplace dynamics. He has worked in both the public and private sectors, with leaders and companies across North America, Europe, Asia, Australia, and Africa. The founder of Sage Consulting Resources, Marc is coauthor of two books. He is also on the advisory board of the University of Maryland's Masters of Professional Studies in Industrial Organizational Psychology. Prior to being named executive editor of *People + Strategy*, Marc served as Perspectives editor.

PART 1:
THE FUTURE OF HR

The Future of Work

By Marc Sokol

Perhaps you know the William Gibson saying, "The future is already here; it's just not very evenly distributed." Some people really do get to the future sooner than others, and we would be wise to learn from them.

In our lead Perspective, **Eva Sage-Gavin and Kaye Foster-Cheek** describe the future of work and human resources—a future that has arrived for some of us and, in time, will involve all of us. This is not just their opinion, but reflects a consensus of experts across our profession. They summarize five major trends that will increasingly impact all companies in the coming decade.

In the commentaries that follow, you can read examples of how the world of HR is evolving and how the future has indeed arrived. **John Boudreau** reminds us that the lead Perspective isn't just forecasting trends; it's about changing how we see and define the world of work— and that can fundamentally change everything we do in human resources.

Eric Severson reports how retail companies are already thinking big as they take the lead addressing the expectations of Millennials. As employees and as customers, Millennials will have more and more impact on the workplace. Eric illustrates how human resources leaders and their companies can make a profound difference.

Tom Gaunt sees a different implication from the lead Perspective, alerting us to ways that networking increases the capacity of companies to form agile teams, while also advancing the careers of individuals.

Bob Black, a seasoned P&L executive, closes out the set of commentaries with an observation that the story here is not just about some aspirational future for human resources, but rather it's also about running a business and should be a priority for every executive.

If you have been wondering how hu-

It's about changing how we see and define the world of work—and that can fundamentally change everything we do in human resources.

man resources can embrace the future, and even shape what work looks like in the coming decade, then this installment of Perspectives is for you.

Marc Sokol, Ph.D., is Perspectives editor.

POINT

The Transformation of Work: Will HR Lead or Follow?

By Eva Sage-Gavin and Kaye Foster-Cheek

The pace of change and demands of the workplace require traditional HR roles to proactively evolve and transform. An increasingly connected world—fueled by rapid advances in technology—is driving massive workplace change.

These changes present new challenges and opportunities for HR leaders. A unique collaboration of professionals, The Future of HR project was chartered to envision what work will look like in 2025. This open-source project received sponsorship from the National Academy of HR, HR People + Strategy, University of Southern California's Center for Effective Organizations, and PricewaterhouseCoopers. Fortune 500 CHROs, Silicon Valley HR leaders, HR thought leaders, and academics have collaborated virtually over the last year and identified five emerging roles for HR practitioners that, if embraced, will keep our profession at the helm of change.

Five Emerging Roles for HR Practitioners

1. Trend Forecasting and Change Leadership

Business and HR leaders need to anticipate trends and then proactively lead change so organizations can thrive in the new world of work. One critical skill will be the ability to analyze diverse sources of data and develop insights, providing "sense making" with strategic recommendations that can guide CEOs, boards, and organizations—in advance of a trend's impact. As important, HR must shift its mindset from change *management* to change *leadership* and foster truly agile leadership.

2. Talent Sourcing and Community Building

Talent management will extend beyond our current view of company to include those who will come together to deliver work outside a regular employment relationship, such as e-lancers, contractors, and partners. Sourcing and recruiting must evolve to develop relationships over an extended period of time, leveraging global talent pools, and using crowdsourcing or technology-enabled channels.

HR leaders have the opportunity to serve as connectors, orchestrators, and brokers of a constantly evolving talent marketplace, bringing unique and innovative solutions to best match the demand and supply of skills and capabilities.

3. Organization and Performance Architecture

Diverse forms of "employment" and new ways of collaborating will challenge traditional approaches to how organizations have inspired and rewarded people to deliver results. Business practices will need to truly optimize talent and create less hierarchical, non-employment relationships. Organizations will need to apply a market segmentation approach to develop highly personalized "deals" for individuals that are still considered fair and equitable across a global framework.

4. Culture and Community Activism

We will continue to shift away from legacy, company-centric views of the world and toward views that consider an ecosystem of stakeholders, including customers, vendors, and current and future "employees," be they freelancers, partners, or shareholders. Company brand and reputation management strategies will shift from being externally focused to engaging employees and the larger talent ecosystem, as companies realize that these employees and extended influencers are the best brand ambassadors.

While corporate social responsibility

How Business Practices May Shift From Today to 2025

Fueled by the **Five Forces of Change**, we anticipate that the specific Drivers for Success related to each Capability will undergo a significantly transformation over the next ten years. While the degree of change will vary based on industry, geography and competitive pressure, some organizations are already facing and addressing these shifts. The following pages provide a description of what these changes may look like.

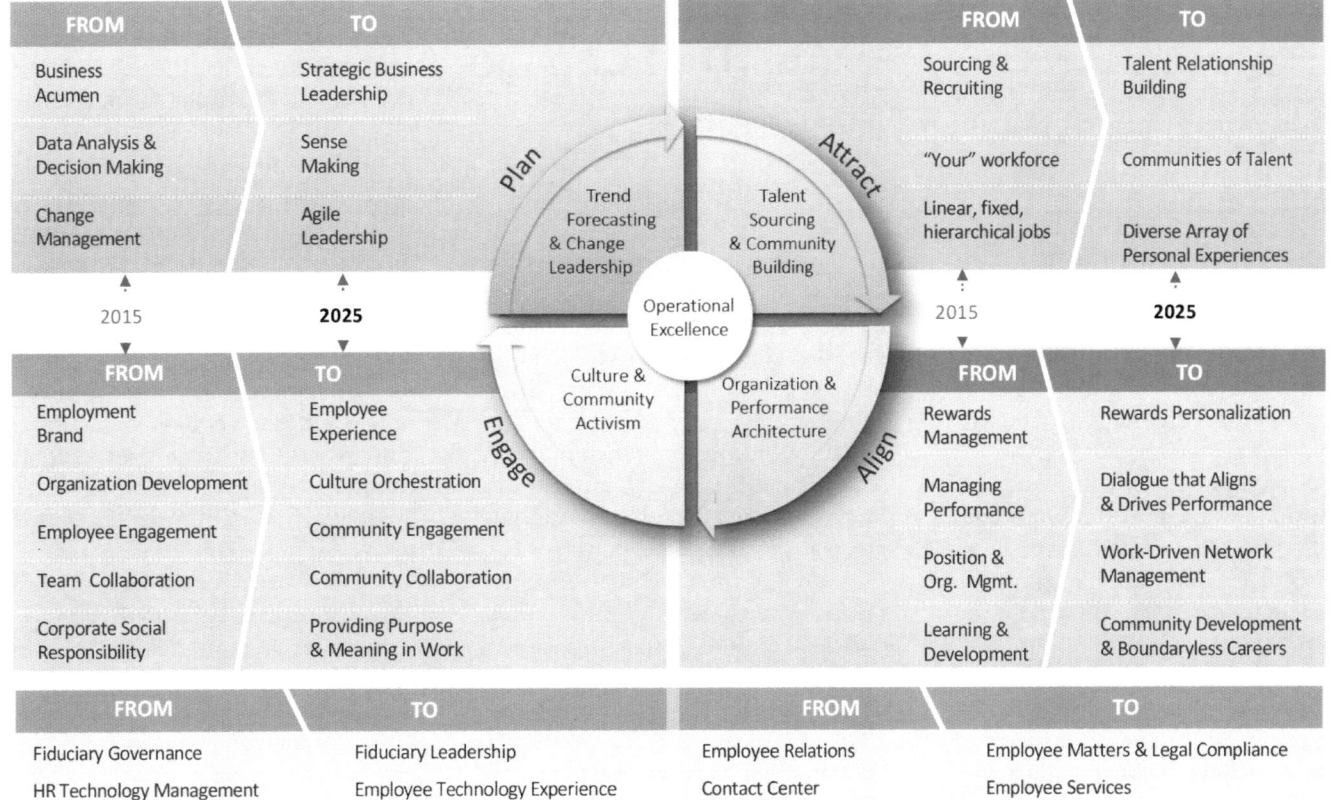

FROM	TO
Business Acumen	Strategic Business Leadership
Data Analysis & Decision Making	Sense Making
Change Management	Agile Leadership

2015 → 2025

FROM	TO
Sourcing & Recruiting	Talent Relationship Building
"Your" workforce	Communities of Talent
Linear, fixed, hierarchical jobs	Diverse Array of Personal Experiences

2015 → 2025

FROM	TO
Employment Brand	Employee Experience
Organization Development	Culture Orchestration
Employee Engagement	Community Engagement
Team Collaboration	Community Collaboration
Corporate Social Responsibility	Providing Purpose & Meaning in Work

FROM	TO
Rewards Management	Rewards Personalization
Managing Performance	Dialogue that Aligns & Drives Performance
Position & Org. Mgmt.	Work-Driven Network Management
Learning & Development	Community Development & Boundaryless Careers

Circle labels: Plan · Attract · Align · Engage · Operational Excellence · Trend Forecasting & Change Leadership · Talent Sourcing & Community Building · Organization & Performance Architecture · Culture & Community Activism

FROM	TO
Fiduciary Governance	Fiduciary Leadership
HR Technology Management	Employee Technology Experience

FROM	TO
Employee Relations	Employee Matters & Legal Compliance
Contact Center	Employee Services

will remain critically important, employees want to bring their whole selves to work in a very different way. They want to share their knowledge and skills beyond simply building houses or serving the less advantaged in limited volunteer engagements. They want their personal contributions outside and at work to serve a greater good, and they want to constantly experience personal growth. They want to craft employment to leverage their strengths, while also enabling them to have an impact on social capital priorities they consider important. In anticipation of this trend, HR needs to lead the shift of community activism focus from "nice to do" to being essential for talent attraction and retention.

5. Operational Excellence

The influence of technology will increasingly present options for work to be deconstructed and delivered by diverse talent pools anywhere and anytime. This will change the landscape of human capital contracting and service delivery as we contend with new practices, regulations, and governance. Private and public partnerships will emerge to shape new global ways of working, with transparency and equity as key themes by which these efforts are evaluated. HR is positioned to navigate the establishment of new structures and policies that enable and ensure equity of access to opportunities across the globe.

So Now What?

Challenging times offer an opportunity to flip our perspectives and throw away calcified assumptions. It is an understatement to say that we are on the precipice of a sustained period of change. This is an inflection point for our profession, and we have a choice: We can play it safe, making small adjustments to our own organizations. Or we can take up the real challenges and become leaders that leave a legacy, having made deep and significant changes to our profession and the global workplace.

This is the time to think *big*. We need to understand the shifts ahead and respond with bold and proactive strategies. Providing leadership to this future workplace is not without risk, just like those that CEOs, CFOs, and other

> HR is positioned to navigate the establishment of new structures and policies that enable and ensure equity of access to opportunities across the globe.

top executives bear. And if we do not provide leadership on the new world of work, who will?

Eva Sage-Gavin is vice chairman of the Aspen Institute's Skills for America's Future Advisory Board and the former CHRO and head of corporate affairs at Gap Inc.

Kaye Foster-Cheek is a senior advisor to the Boston Consulting Group (BCG) and former CHRO at Onyx Pharmaceuticals and Johnson & Johnson.

COUNTERPOINT

Work and Community: Two Words That Change Everything

By John Boudreau

Eva Sage-Gavin and Kaye Foster-Cheek propose revolutionary ideas. What may be less apparent is how their model provides a bridge from today to tomorrow, and through two simple word substitutions.

The outside words in their model look familiar enough: HR has long embraced the need to plan, attract, align, and engage workers, supported by HR service delivery. Yet, inside the circles, greater distinctions emerge, and two in particular illustrate just how much may change.

From Employment to Work

"Employment" is pervasive in HR. Our plans relieve employment gaps, we attract employment candidates, we

align employee performance, and we increase employee engagement. But what if you assumed that your work will not be done by your employees? The trend toward organization and performance architecture to include an extended workforce outside traditional company boundaries means just that. Can your HR operating models and strategies handle it? Most fall short.

Sage-Gavin and Foster-Cheek's framework encompasses the work that will continue to be done by employees, but only as one option. The future work and workplace also reside beyond traditional employment, such as creative work done by volunteer gamers, or software development done by freelancers on a cloud platform. Iconic organizations like Disney, Siemens, Apple, IBM, and Visa have avoided employment competition by loaning and borrowing employees from each other. Why shouldn't you?

Look again at their framework and you see that detaching work from employment fundamentally changes every HR concept. What does it mean to plan, attract, align, and engage volunteers, freelancers, or contractors? Put simply, winning organizations in the future will lead the work, not only the employees.

From Organization to Community

Consider how ideas like organization design, accountability, effectiveness, change, and management evolve when you simply substitute the word "community" for the word "organization." Traditional organization and management now become agile and boundaryless community building. Sage-Gavin and Foster-Cheek's framework reminds us that in a community transparency often trumps secrecy, democracy often trumps authority, and networks often trump hierarchies.

Indeed, even the Future of HR consortium that they acknowledge is itself a model of getting work done beyond employment and organization. For more than two years, prominent and creative executives and other leaders have devoted hundreds of hours to this work. Why? Each of them is motivated to give back to a profession that has given them so much, and they know that this profession must accelerate to meet its

future potential. So they work beyond their day jobs to design this "future of HR" community collectively.

Two Simple Words

With two simple words—work and community—Sage-Gavin and Foster-Cheek describe a future that can be either wonderful or awful, or even both. On one hand, it can devolve into a winner-take-all and commoditized work world that serves few and exploits many. Or it can evolve into a sustainable ecosystem of empowerment across many varieties of work, of transparency and boundary-less opportunities, and all freed from the exclusive reliance on traditional concepts of employment and organization.

The ultimate path will depend on those who are willing to lead the transformation of work, and the profession that supports them. As duly noted, it is time to think *big*.

***

John W. Boudreau is professor at the Marshall School of Business and research director of the Center for Effective Organizations, University of Southern California.

Employers Can No Longer Stand on the Sidelines

By Eric Severson

It was a watershed moment. In March 2015, nearly a dozen Fortune 500 CEOs—including leaders of Apple, Salesforce.com, Gap Inc., and the world's largest employer, Walmart—publicly denounced legislation in Indiana and Arkansas that they believed discriminated against the Lesbian, Gay, Bisexual, and Transgender (LGBT) community.

Such corporate activism on a controversial social issue would have been unthinkable a decade ago. Yet in a world where Millennials make up a growing percentage of the workforce,

taking a stand on community issues is no longer taboo for companies; in fact, it's fast becoming a necessity. As a generation, Millennials are social activists—and they expect their employers to be too. According to the *2013 Cone Communications Social Impact Study*, a majority of Millennials make critical decisions, such as where to shop or which stocks to invest in, based on a company's corporate social responsibility reputation. Of critical importance to HR leaders: 78 percent of Millennials said company reputation for social responsibility influences where they choose to work.

According to Deloitte's *2014 Millennial Survey*, by 2025, 75 percent of the global workforce will be Millennial. That means "culture and community activism," one of the five critical skills identified in the Future of HR Project, will be more important than ever

Leading from the Front

For Millennials, social activism isn't something reserved for one's personal life or an all-employee volunteer outing. It's about *how* a company does business every day, Millennials expect businesses, not government, to take the lead on social change. "The biggest 'aha' for us in the whole study," said Scott Beaudoin, author of the Cone report, "was that although trust in business is still low, Millennials see business as the only solution for a better future. They've given up on government."

A poignant recent example of this phenomenon involves the minimum wage. After President Obama unsuc-

> For Millennials, social activism isn't something reserved for one's personal life or an all-employee volunteer outing. It's about *how* a company does business every day.

cessfully lobbied Congress to increase the federal minimum to $10.10, Gap Inc. decided to lead on the issue by announcing it was raising its minimum wage to $10.00. Walmart, IKEA, Target, TJX, and others soon followed, announcing their own minimum wage thresholds. This single issue illustrates the power of business to significantly improve the quality of life for millions of Americans—just by changing a single business practice.

Co-Creating a Better Community

As the lead Perspectives authors observe, "employees want to share their knowledge and skills beyond simply building houses or serving the less advantaged in limited volunteer engagements. They want their personal contributions outside and at work to serve a greater good, and they want to constantly experience personal growth."

According to a 2014 study commissioned by MSLGROUP, 69 percent of Millennials want business to make it easier for them to get involved in creating social change. One example of this co-creative approach was at Gap Inc., where we collaborated with our 74 per-

cent female workforce to advocate for pay equality. On Equal Pay Day 2015 (April 14), while the company spoke out for pay equality at press conferences and in blogs, over 100,000 employees were encouraged to wear red to work (symbolic of women being "in the red" globally when their average earnings are compared with men's) and to post pro-pay equality messaging on social media.

A World Without Borders

The Millennial world is getting smaller—and less siloed. Having grown up in a digital world where physical proximity was irrelevant and boundaries blurred, Millennials expect the workplace to be like their Facebook page—a mashup of all of the interests in their lives, including work, home, family, friends, hobbies, and causes.

Demographers tell us that Millennials don't see the world in dichotomies the way their predecessors did (work vs. life, commerce vs. social responsibility, global vs. local). Instead, they focus on synergies and convergences, bringing together the diverse aspects of their lives. At Gap Inc. this meant we stopped focusing on work-life *balance* and instead focused on work-life *integration*. It's also why we encouraged employees to join us in advocating for social change both globally (for example, worker safety in Bangladesh) and locally (for instance, a local breast cancer awareness walk for store employees in Minnesota).

Who Better Than Human Resources?

Corporations have enormous power to create positive change in the communities where they do business. Given their substantial brand equity, marketing savvy, and human and financial capital, they are poised to be the change agents of the 21st century. And Millennials, as the primary consumers of the future, will hold them accountable for doing so. But who will lead business into this largely unexplored territory? Who better than human resources—the ones with "human" right in our name? Let's own it.

Eric Severson is senior vice president, global talent solutions, at Gap, Inc.

How Networking Transforms the Future of Work

By Tom Gaunt

The authors posit that in the future work is going to be done not by traditional employees alone, but rather by a workforce of employees, e-lancers, contractors, and partners. Implicit in this is the notion that teams will form, drawing from a diverse pool of talent for a particular purpose. Once that objective is met, the team will disband and others will form in its place.

To succeed in this environment, companies must encourage their people to develop strong professional networks. These networks can be leveraged to identify changes in the market that represent opportunities or threats and can help rapidly identify talent necessary to accomplish their objectives. This leads to better performance for individuals and companies.

While this may seem to be intuitively obvious, this idea meets with a surprising amount of resistance. I have been asked, "Why would I want to help someone build a network so they can get a new job outside of my company?" I view that as a "calcified assumption," one that implies that networks pose only the downside risk of helping people find a new job. The real risk is an insular culture that is incapable of rapidly responding to changes in the market. As Reid Hoffman states in his book, *The Alliance: Managing Talent in the Networked Age,* "In a nutshell, network intelligence that leverages the individual networks of your organization's people is the most effective way for your organization to engage with and learn from the outside world."

Many companies would benefit by providing tools and support for all of their employees' networking efforts. For example, my company is focused on helping others respond to a persistent issue that is impacting the culture of their companies. In far too many companies, women are woefully underrepresented on the executive team. We intend to help women harness the potential of their networks to accelerate their careers. Doing so will help these women outperform peers who are not leveraging professional networks. It will also increase their visibility within their own firms, thus helping them accelerate their career success as well.

Most HR systems and practices were designed for a workplace that no longer exists. The new world of work is already being performed by loosely coupled teams. Networked relationships feed those teams, helping groups and individuals become optimized for the job at hand.

Smart people recognize that their networks are critical for success in this environment. Smart companies will support their people in building these networks. Smart HR professionals see the potential.

How smart do you want your company to be?

Tom Gaunt is CEO of NQuotient, as well as an angel investor in several startup companies.

Of course! It's How You Run a Business

By Bob Black

As a business leader, often the question is not, "What would we like to do?" It's, "Can we make it all the way through the journey without losing the support of our stakeholders—while simultaneously delivering increased profits at each footstep?"

The vision provided in the lead Perspective identifies the changes smart business leaders and their organizations need to implement for longer-term success. We need to be significantly more talent centric, more flexible, more virtual—and we need strong HR leadership to get there. That is not just a set of aspirations; it's how we need to run our businesses.

Focus not just on "what," but on "how." For a journey of this magnitude, strong HR leadership is a minimum prerequisite. There are at least four additional requirements of how we must proceed:

- **New mental models for how organizations really work.** Most acknowledge that culture, processes, and relationship networks are at the core of how groups of people work together. Yet most such constructs start with and focus on structure and organizational charts. Our people often struggle with "messiness," even in simple matrix organizational designs. Significant angst goes into detailed clarification of solid, dotted, or duel reporting lines. Everyone wants to know who really "has the D"—the authority for decisions that must be made.

  In contrast, the authors paint a much more biological and flexible organization of the future. This will require a new framing of how organizations really work in a way that all disparate members can be both comfortable and effective.

- **Supporting infrastructure.** The implications of much larger pools of talent, with many willing to work more flexibly and virtually, include discovering answers to questions of how to access, evaluate, and incent them—and ensure economic and social continuity for them. This also has larger implications for change in labor legislation across many markets.

- **Inclusive organizations.** One byproduct of business process outsourcing was the severing of many historically integrated organizational experiences and networks. As organizations become more complex, diverse, and dispersed, there emerges a need to foster new dimensions of connectivity and inclusiveness.

  Ironically, as an organization becomes more fluid, less hierarchical, and far-flung, it needs to become even tighter and more interwoven. This might look like numerous separate nodes, work structures, and legal entities serving many companies but still operating as a single unit with a uniform culture exclusively integrated in your company—a challenging paradox!

- **Bold business leaders.** Leaders who display both the courage to pursue dramatic innovation and the wisdom to understand how to truly partner with HR professionals are critical. Major change entails risk and takes time. This takes courageous business leaders, but they can't and shouldn't expect to do this alone. They need partners who understand the complexity and challenges and who can help develop solutions and guide them when the tough times inevitably hit.

Sage-Gavin, Foster-Cheek, and the members of Future of HR Project are on to something critical here. How can we help them get to this future state more quickly and across a wider field versus just seeing a few marginal experiments along the edges? ⊞

Bob Black, former group president at Kimberly-Clark International, currently serves on several corporate boards and as an advisor to many companies on global business, organizational, and talent issues.

LEARNING GUIDE

The Future of Work

DISCOVERY QUESTIONS

- What are you dealing with in your organization today that relates to this content area?
- What did you pick up on as events and trends that have potential to dramatically change the workplace?
- What companies did you read about that are trying to embrace and lead change in HR practices?
- Which trends noted in the table surprise you the most?
- Which trends do you already see companies making progress on?
- Which changes forecasted by the authors are potentially most disruptive compared to the present state?

SELECTED FACTS

- What new facts that were presented got your attention?
  - Changes in the workplace and workers will lead the role of HR to evolve between now and 2025.
  - In 2015, nearly a dozen Fortune 500 companies publicly denounced legislation they believed discriminated against the LGBT community.
  - According to a 2013 social impact study, a majority of Millennials decide where to shop or invest based on a company's reputation for corporate social responsibility.
  - Seventy-eight percent of Millennials responded in a study that company reputation for corporate social responsibility influences where they choose to work.
  - By 2025, 75 percent of the global workforce will be Millennial.
  - Companies like Disney, Apple, IBM, and Visa have avoided employment competition by loaning and borrowing employees from each other.

KEY DISCUSSION POINTS

- What were the key points being made in this presentation?
- What is meant by the introductory phrase, *"The future is here; it's just not very evenly distributed"*?
- What changes mentioned in this Perspective do you already see in the organizations around you?
- In what ways might employee sourcing be different in ten years from what it looks like today?
- What do you think personalization of rewards could look like?
- What could be the benefit of companies that combine employee learning with community development?
- What is the difference between focusing on employment brand and employee experience?
- One anticipated shift in trend forecasting is to spend less time on trend analysis and more on 'sense making'. What might it look like for HR professionals to be sense making for their clients in the workplace?
- What might look different when a company shifts from fiduciary governance to fiduciary leadership?
- What additional trends can you think of, not included in this Perspectives, may also impact the workplace in the coming ten years?

REVIEW OF SOLUTIONS

- Identify two to three big ideas worthy of exploring in your organization.
- Why is it important to anticipate and plan for trends like the ones described in this Perspectives?
- What trends discussed in this Perspectives would you emphasize to attract, recruit, and retain millennials?
- Where among these forecasted changes do you see HR professionals able to move forward on their own, and where do they need to move forward with the entire company?

IDENTIFYING THE PARADOX

- How is it that a solution appropriate for yesterday's organization is no longer valid?
- Consider how very different perspectives might be correct given different situations.
- What is the challenge of a company being 'boundaryless' and open, but to also protect competitive advantage?
- How can you personalize rewards systems and stay consistent across the organization?
- How can leaders give up control and still retain control in this future state?
- How does the shift in mindset from "organization" to "community" both open up opportunities for companies and create new challenges?

LEARNING OUTCOMES

- What one new piece of information did you learn that will be important to you in the future?
- Identify one thing that you will do differently based on what you learned.
- If the authors are correct, what must companies do differently to prepare for and embrace the future?
- How does this change the way you assess the readiness of an HR department to embrace the future?
- Toward which area of the future do you feel most drawn?

World HR Associations:
Leading the Profession into the Future

People + Strategy Executive Editor Anna Tavis convened HR professionals from around the world to explore the future of HR from a global perspective. While committed to a common vision, HR's impact and influence is delivered differently across time zones and cultures. No doubt questions and thoughtful contemplation will rouse you while reading the contributions of our global partners—and though they do not offer all the answers here, they do point us in the right direction.

By Howard A. Wallack

More than a decade ago, cross-border research by the Society for Human Resource Management (SHRM) revealed that a strong majority of HR professionals believed that to work in the profession some type of recognized credential was necessary. Moreover, an even greater majority—reaching as high as 83.1 percent in Argentina and 80.8 percent in

the United States—believed that a recognized credential was necessary for career advancement in HR (see chart). Those respondents then, and HR practitioners today, continue to get professional certification around the world as a means to advance their careers, demonstrating what Nobel Laureate (economics) Michael Spence has recognized as the "unobservable attributes" of potential employees, such as their education and training, which serve as "signals" to current and future employers of individuals' potential productivity.

Today, an overview of certification efforts internationally in Argentina, Australia, Canada, Germany, Israel, Thailand, and the U.K., as exemplified in the short summaries here that were supplied by the HR associations in those countries, shows great variety in the requirements and steps to get certified

	To work in HR, one must have some type of recognized credentials.			To advance one's career in HR, one must have some type of recognized credential.		
	% Agree	% Neutral	% Disagree	% Agree	% Neutral	% Disagree
Argentina	62.1	20.7	17.2	83.1	9.5	7.3
Canada	61.3	17.0	21.6	68.3	16.9	14.8
Israel	71.1	13.3	15.6	79.1	7.0	13.9
Thailand	56.7	29.8	13.5	57.7	33.7	8.7
United Kingdom	61.1	17.9	21.0	77.9	10.5	11.6
United States	53.6	23.5	22.9	80.8	11.7	7.5

(Source: SHRM/SHRM Global Forum's *The Maturing Profession of Human Resources*, 2004; survey reports for Argentina, Canada, Israel, Thailand, the UK and the US.)

as well as the many competencies that HR professionals need for success. Nonetheless, there are some trends and commonalties.

These various country contributions highlight that terminology referring to the concepts of credential, qualification, certification, and certificate programs are, regrettably, all too frequently used inconsistently. A credential is usually issued by an organization with some authoritative status or power, and is evidence of an individual's knowledge or competence in a given subject. A qualification can be an educational degree or certification, when an individual is required to pass an examination or assessment in order to achieve recognition as a practitioner or professional in a specific activity or function. Certification, however, usually includes both an educational and experiential eligibility requirement, and frequently is pursued after a basic tertiary educational degree has been achieved. Moreover, in addition to a requirement to pass an examination successfully, certification includes adherence to an accepted code of ethics for the field and an obligation to recertification within a specified time frame to maintain certification status. In getting recertified, either through the accumulation of professional education credits or reexamination, a practitioner or professional demonstrates a commitment to life-long learning and maintaining their knowledge and competencies at the forefront of their specialization. On the other hand, a certificate program may be a series of related training elements that cumulatively demonstrate knowledge or be a one-time documentation of attendance at a learning event, which documents exposure to content, though without necessarily measuring understanding, absorption and retention of the information.

First, as the pieces reveal, there is growing collaboration with, or endorsement by, governments of certification efforts. In the U.K. and the two Canadian provinces of Quebec and Ontario (with efforts underway to extend this into more provinces), HR associations and the HR profession are statutorily recognized, conferring increased authority and accountability on certified HR professionals compared to their uncertified peers. Recently, too, in Kenya, *the Human Resource Management Professionals Act* was passed, identifying HR as a profession for which practitioners needed recognized study or credentials and authorizing the national HR association there to define further what those qualifications might be, a process now underway.

In Australia, an independent national certification council has been announced as the credentialing body which will be fully active by 2017, and in Israel the HR association there indicates that their "future goals are to find a way for government to make the accreditation an official requirement for HR management." As we read here, in Thailand, certification needs to be accredited by the Thailand Professional Qualifications Institute (TPQI), and in other countries, such as Bahrain, Malaysia, Singapore, South Africa, UAE, and others, national qualifications frameworks and authorities are currently either monitoring or already guiding certification efforts, not only in the HR profession, but more broadly.

A second trend manifest by these summaries is that frequently the competencies for professional effectiveness are defined *both* functionally and behaviorally *and* at different levels of HR career or responsibility. This reflects both the immense complexity and the different levels and answerability of HR management that exert themselves simultaneously and synergistically as HR professionals accept and confront daily the diverse global and local management challenges that they do each and every day, as well as through their extended career progressions with greater levels of experience, spans of control, and seniority.

Clearly what we see here is that the certification and professionalization of HR is a work-in-progress, with many elements concurrently in play. It is a combination of market forces, governmental scrutiny and pressure, the reliability and universality of methodologies to create competency models, validity of certification schemes and exams, and most importantly the results and return on investment that certified HR professionals achieve, contributing to their organizations' strategic goals and objectives, all of which will ultimately determine the best path to sustained credibility, legitimacy,

and effectiveness for the HR profession.

The third trend we can see is less a commonality than an observation: The link between certification and HR association membership is a choice, but not necessarily a given circumstance. In some jurisdictions, one must have and maintain HR association membership to be certified, whereas in others the achievement of a professional designation is separate and independent of membership, though possibly at a higher nonmember cost. Nonetheless, as these readings attest, across the globe it is the membership-based national HR associations—the institutional bodies uniting, engaging, and representing the profession to the public, to government, and to other stakeholders—that currently drive the move toward broader certification and professionalization of the HR function. In that respect, they are all leading the profession into the future, albeit with differences in tactic and tone.

Howard A. Wallack, M.A., M.Sc., SHRM-SCP, is a former global markets executive at the Society for Human Resource Management (SHRM) where he shares responsibility for SHRM's involvement in the World Federation of People Management Associations (WFPMA) and has accountability for partnership and relationship management in Brazil, Europe, sub-Saharan Africa, and the Asia-Pacific region, excluding China and India.

Professionalism in Human Resource Management: Evolution of a Standard

By Laura Harrison

The concept of certification in HR is a curious one. Unlike some professions, there are no formal or universally ap-

The Profession Map

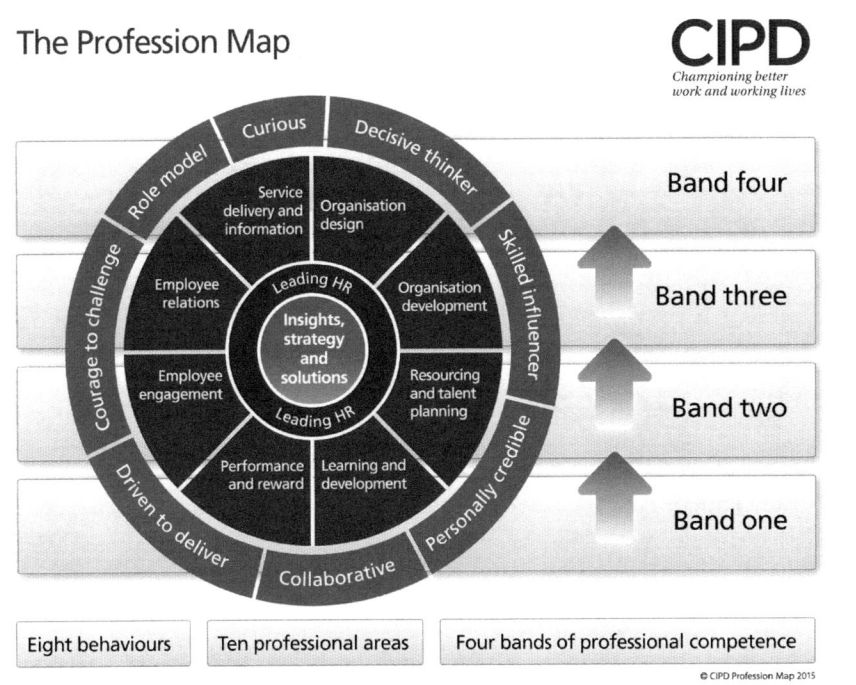

CIPD
*Championing better
work and working lives*

Band four

Band three

Band two

Band one

| Eight behaviours | Ten professional areas | Four bands of professional competence |

© CIPD Profession Map 2015

plied requirements to practice HR. Of course, many employers expect their HR teams to have specialist qualifications, but can a qualification really "certify" someone to practice in a particular field? Most employers look for more than a qualification when recruiting HR practitioners; they look for a symbol of professionalism that indicates an individual's commitment to raising his or her standards of knowledge, capability, and ethical practice. In the U.K., and increasingly in other parts of the world, particularly Southeast Asia and the Middle East, that mark of professionalism comes in the form of chartered membership in the Chartered Institute of Personnel and Development (CIPD). Headquartered in the U.K., with more than 140,000 members worldwide, we're among only a handful of professional bodies in the world that awards HR and L&D professionals with chartered status.

All chartered members of the CIPD must demonstrate that they have the technical knowledge, skills, behaviors and experience outlined in our body of knowledge, the Profession Map.

The Profession Map was first published in 2008, after a large-scale research program involving organizations all around the world, and we've been continually updating it ever since. As well as defining the building blocks of effective people management practice across 10 professional areas or specializations, including L&D and organization design, it also describes eight fundamental behaviors that underpin good HR regardless of your specialty (see chart).

A range of CIPD qualifications help provide individuals with the expert knowledge outlined in the map. They span three levels—foundation, intermediate and advanced—and are taught at hundreds of approved universities, colleges, and private training providers across the world, meaning there's a range of full- and part-time courses and flexible study options that enable students to learn at their own pace and gain credit for their achievements.

These qualifications form the most popular route to professional membership of the CIPD. The foundation and intermediate certificates and diplomas qualify learners for associate membership in the CIPD, while our advanced (Masters level) diplomas provide the underpinning knowledge to apply to become a chartered member or chartered fellow. But a qualification alone doesn't make you eligible for chartered status, nor is a qualification necessary if you can demonstrate that you've developed the relevant knowledge through experience on the job. While a qualification assesses a person's knowledge at a given point of time and certifies that they successfully completed a particular program of study, professional membership also indicates an ongoing commitment to continuing professional development that is far more indicative of a person's professional competence.

With or without a qualification, we assess all our chartered members and chartered fellows against the levels of competence outlined in the Profession Map. The map is flexible, so practitioners can choose what to focus on, depending on their area of work, the level of accountability they have in their role, and their career development ambitions. For example, one professional may find their role requires a far deeper knowledge of resourcing and talent planning, while another will focus much more on employee relations.

The world of work is increasingly diverse and complex, so keeping this body of knowledge relevant is challenging. HR capabilities must advance in line with the rapidly evolving needs and expectations of businesses and employees. To date, we've been able to describe a set of "best" practices across various HR activities. But, "good" HR is increasingly context-specific, and depends on business priorities, the nature of the workforce and organizational culture. The shape and the role of the HR function is changing too, with significant shifts in the focus and scope of responsibilities. Describing a single set of practices amounting to "best practice" HR is therefore increasingly difficult.

This is why we think good HR should be defined in terms of broader principles, like many professions have. In contrast with a rules-based approach to standards, which defines specific practices, the principles-based approach focuses on professional judgement, describing the fundamental professional obligations we should take into account when deciding how to act in practice. It requires an astute awareness of the stakeholders who will be affected by alternative practices, for example, weighing public interest against increased profit margins, even in the absence of regulation.

The need for credible professionals who can foster productive relationships between various stakeholders is becoming more evident every day. Businesses increasingly recognize that effective human capital management is critical to their competitive advantage, and they rely on practitioners who can deeply understand the business context to get the most out of the workforce. At the same time, changing standards of corporate governance are putting a premium on organizations' ability to create long-term shared value for the business, its people, and broader society.

We believe that a principles-based approach to professional standards is key to ensuring HR balances competing stakeholder interests to find win-win solutions for everyone. Ultimately, this will shape the evolution of the HR profession in two ways. Firstly, it will highlight HR's unique role in creating shared value through the sustainable treatment of people. Secondly, the principles will provide a guiding framework for making professional judgments in the context of high uncertainty, thus fostering the development of a professional body of knowledge and a standard of good practice that transcends time, cultures, geographies, and legal boundaries.

The result will be to build trust and credibility in HR, and to put an end to debates about its relevance and value, so that it becomes a recognized profession like medicine or accounting. But our motivation is not to professionalize HR for HR's sake. Our guiding purpose is to champion better work and working lives by improving practices in people and organization development for the benefit of individuals, businesses, economies, and society. In other words, we believe that good people management and development is vital to creating shared value for a range of stakeholders. And ultimately, if we're to live up to that laudable claim, we must professionalize HR.

Laura Harrison is director of people and strategy at the CIPD, the professional body for HR and people development.

Certification Defines HR's Business Value in Canada

By Jason McRobbie

CHRP Overview and Philosophy

The Certified Human Resources Professional (CHRP) designation provides Canadian employers the highest degree of surety in their HR practices, supported by proven expertise, continual learning, and demonstrated commitment, as well as a nationwide community of knowledge and code of ethics.

Established in 1994, the Canadian Council of Human Resources Associations (CCHRA) is a collaborative effort of human resources associations from across Canada, which represent more than 41,000 professionals—21,000 of whom hold the CHRP designation.

CHRP Standards and Process

From its inception in 1996 to present, the CHRP designation has set the standard and served as a catalyst for HR in Canada—one profession, one competency framework and one certification, served by a national body unified by purpose and clarity of process.

As a commitment to a national standard of excellence, the CHRP designation emphasizes the strategic role of HR in business, and is administered across Canada through provincial associations. In order to pursue the CHRP, individuals must become and remain a member in good standing with their provincial association.

Two provinces—Quebec and Ontario—have laws recognizing the HR profession "for the public good." Other provinces are now advocating for similar status with their provincial legislatures. This statutory provision authorizes HR professionals who are members of the HR associations and certified to perform certain functions that uncertified HR professionals cannot.

Four Qualification Pathways

The Standards Advisory Council of the CCHRA recently revised the requirements for candidacy and certification to include four primary paths to obtain the CHRP. All paths require a minimum of a bachelor's degree from an accredited college or university, and three years of professional-level HR experience.

Route one requires a Bachelor's degree in any field or discipline to be supplemented by successful completion of the National Knowledge Exam (NKE), which assesses HR knowledge and skills based on the CHRP Competency Framework (NKE exam prep courses are made available through Captus Online and CCHRM member associations), and an experience assessment validated by the current employer to prove a minimum of three years of professional-level HR within the last 10 years—recently opened up to include teaching experience for full-time HR instructors and international HR experience.

Candidates for certification must register for the NKE two months prior to testing, with results being released one month after, creating a streamlined inflow process of approximately three months. Once becoming a CHRP candidate, individuals have seven years to complete the process.

Routes two and three promote strategic partnerships with post-secondary institutions while allowing greater influence over curriculum by waiving the NKE requirement for individuals holding—in addition to a Bachelor's degree in any field—either a credit-level HR certificate or diploma program accredited by CCHRA or an MBA or Master's degree in HR, respectively.

Route Four permits for inter-provincial transfer of existing designation-holders.

Competency Framework Updated by Professional Practice Analysis

The CHRP Competency Framework details the pathway to the CHRP designation and is built upon the results of the evidence-based process undertaken in the 2013 Professional Practice Analysis (PPA). Conducted by a third-party research firm (Castle Worldwide), the 2013 PPA surveyed or interviewed more than 1,000 HR experts and professionals from across Canada.

Functional Knowledge Base and Enabling Competencies

The resultant 2014 CHRP Competency Framework is based on a dual-competency model, and outlines 44 professional competencies organized into nine functional areas of knowledge, together with five enabling competencies that complete the professional's skill set. It also specifies the proficiency level at which each competency is to be demonstrated and how it will be assessed.

The nine functional areas of knowledge in the CHRP Competency Framework are:

- Strategy
- Professional practice
- Engagement
- Workforce planning and talent management
- Employee and labor relations
- Total rewards
- Learning and development
- Health, wellness, and safe workplace
- Human resources metrics, reporting and financial management

The five Enabling Competencies, now integrated into the experience requirement, are:

- Strategic and systems thinking
- Professional and ethical practice
- Critical problem-solving and decision-making
- Change management and cultural transformation
- Communication, conflict resolution, and relationship management

Maintaining the CHRP Designation and Costs

To maintain their CHRP designation, HR professionals must retain their provincial association memberships and demonstrate that they have achieved 100 points worth of professional development activity over a three-year period.

The CHRP application fee is $60. The NKE registration fee is $275. The Experience Assessment Certification fee is $400. The Experience Assessment Review fee is $100. The annual CHRP dues are $155.)

Jason McRobbie is the editor of *PeopleTalk Magazine.*

HR Credentialing in Australia

By Peter Wilson

There are no regulatory bars to people wishing to work as a practitioner within a human resources division of an Australian company or a public service HR department, or to set up as a sole trader in an Australian HR consultancy.

From time to time, members of the judiciary have refused leave for consultants calling themselves HR practitioners to appear before the courts. Refusals tend to occur in cases where HR practitioners specializing in industrial relations seek leave to appear on behalf of a client but do not possess a law degree. Cases of that order aside, there is no bar in Australia to practicing as an HR employee or a HR private consultant.

The Australian Human Resources Institute (AHRI) is the sole body representing the professional interests of HR practitioners and has been so since the association was established by one of its antecedents in 1943. In those early years, immediate post-war preoccupations did not include certification. AHRI succeeded the Institute of Personnel Management of Australia in 1992.

During 2004 and 2005, AHRI management restructured the member categories and created the post-nominal CAHRI, with the C indicating certified. That move involved an immediate plunge in member numbers, which in turn was followed by a reassurance to members that their classification was safe. The flow was stemmed but the CAHRI credential was retained in a weakened form that required little assessment other than the sighting of a curriculum vitae denoting time spent and/or courses completed.

By 2014, the AHRI board had come to the realization that while the earlier certification move was well intentioned, it was hasty and lacked a process enabling consultation and lead time. It also acknowledged that if HR practitioners were to be respected in business, a credible credentialing mechanism had become a matter of urgency.

A number of steps have since been taken to make HR certification a reality.

The first was to indicate the fundamental principle behind certification. The principle, simply stated, is that Competence = Knowledge + Skills, a proposition I elaborated on in the 2014 ebook *Certification: The Steps Toward Best Practice*, edited by Dave Ulrich.

The second was to pilot and launch a new program called the AHRI Practicing Certification Program (APC) which consists of three knowledge units and one mandatory capstone unit, the latter comprising an organizational capability workplace-based project. Together, they attest to practitioners' capacity to behave as an HR expert and a business partner.

The program is an industry recognized, postgraduate program designed to equip HR professionals with essential prerequisites for advanced strategic HR management. It is work integrated and includes an in-depth examination of the key functions of human resources management as it relates to the business environment, the organization, and the individual. Students may complete the APC on a part-time basis over two years by either workshop or distance learning.

The third was to reassure CAHRI members that their existing credential was to be respected and would be grandfathered when the new arrangement became effective. All new members seeking certification under the new robust framework will be required to take the APC as of January 2017. Upon doing so, they will be entitled to carry the post-nominal CAHRI-CP (certified practitioner). If the member is a practitioner and an AHRI fellow, the post-nominal will be FAHRI-CP.

Finally, an independent national certification council was announced as the credentialing body. Composed of representatives from industry, government, and academia, it will credential the first practitioners to complete the APC and be presented to it in January 2016.

The bar has been set. A communication strategy is under way and includes a campaign to inform the employment market that AHRI certified practitioners are the only practitioners with a credential that attests to their HR expertise and their capability in practice to act as a true business partner.

Peter Wilson is the chairman and national president of the Australian Human Resources Institute. He is also an advisory council member of the *Harvard Business Review* and is adjunct professor in management at the Monash University Business School.

Professionalization of Human Resource Management in Germany

By Katharina Heuer

In Germany, there are several opportunities for studying HR management, either by taking HR classes at a university or acquiring qualification through professional development. In 2005, in collaboration with experts from industry, science, and consulting, the German Association for People Management (DGFP) developed the training program ProPro—Professionalization of Human Resources Management. Meanwhile more than 1,800 participants have completed this training successfully. Through the training program, DGFP has been able to estab-

lish standards for professional human resource management in the market within the last decade. The main idea is that the professional HR management has a sustainable impact on the success of a company. ProPro prepares an individual for the complexity of HR management, brings transparency to its challenges, and highlights all HR areas. To be eligible for ProPro, participants must be in am HR manager position, HR administrator, or HR operator role. ProPro is available for members and nonmembers to participate in. However, nonmembers pay a higher rate. Up until now, every professional who has started the program has finished it successfully.

Primary HR Policy Areas

The program has a strategic approach, practical structure, and modular design. The DGFP concept of integrated and professional HR management is based upon 12 strategic and employee-related HR policy areas that form the HR-political framework of all success-relevant HR activities of a company. These HR policy areas are the basis of the DGFP standards for integrated, professional HR management and are also the underlying structure of the DGFP ProPro Training Courses (see graphic).

Target Group, Learning Methods, and Examination

The DGFP is offering on the one hand the training course "ProPro Professional" for HR functional specialists and on the other hand the training course "ProPro Executive" for heads of HR management.

Over the course of 15 days, attendees use different learning methods, from individual to group work, case studies, role-playing games as well as self-reflection. In addition to that one can use the ProPro Professional Learning Platform, an online tool which allows a very individual and flexible learning. The online tool provides individual and autonomous learning phases. The Professional Learning Platform offers the possibility to prepare the learning content of ProPro in advance or to revert to the content of the modules. The individual modules are taught at lectures. Additionally, they are made available in the form of up-to-date study materials which the participants study during self-learning phases. The final examination consists of an oral and a written exam.

The format of the exam is developed in a target-group specific manner and depends on the specific level of job experience.

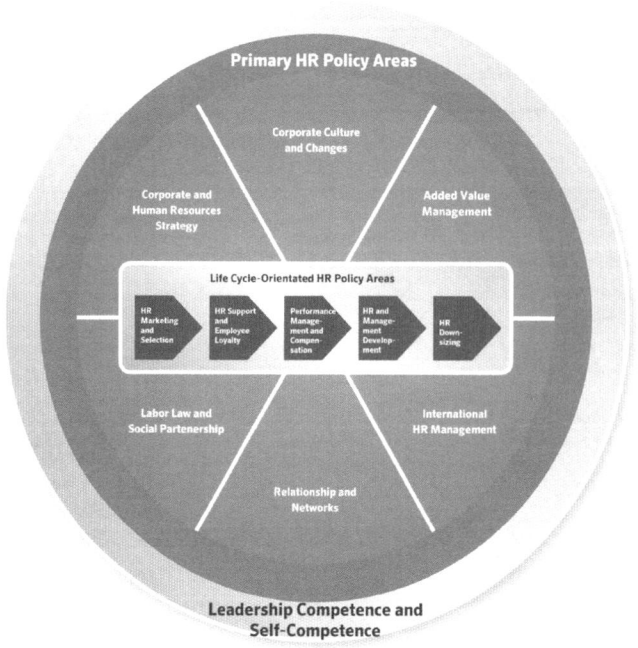

For the target group of HR manager and personnel officer, the final examination consists of an oral and a written part. The participant will prepare as written homework a concept for a subsection of Human Resources Management that he or she will present and discuss during the oral examination. The oral examination takes 20 minutes. For the target group of HR administrator, the written part of the exam is a multiple choice test, which contains 40 questions. The duration of the exam is 90 minutes. The oral examination is a short 10 minute presentation of a HR-topic.

During the final examination, the candidate demonstrates that he or she has understood and mastered the ProPro competence fields, and that the participant is able to apply this knowledge to his or her daily practical work. Candidates have two years to take the program and complete the exam. The DGFP offers five examination dates each year.

The members of the Examination Board are chosen interdisciplinary. The board consists of a scientist, a practitioner, and the specific program manager of the DGFP.

Participants prepare as written homework a concept for a subsection of human resources management that the candidate presents and discusses during the oral examination.

Fit for Future

The issues of HR management are constantly changing; therefore, ProPro also has to change again and again to remain on the cutting edge. An advisory board makes sure that the training is continually being developed and the curriculum is being adjusted.

Katharina Heuer is managing director of the Deutsche Gesellschaft für Personalfuehrüng (DGFP), the German Association for People Management. The DGFP was founded as a nonprofit organization by representatives from the worlds of business and science in 1952. It has more than 2,500 members, ranging from large company groups to small firms. Its mission is to promote human resources management—its practice, research, and teaching—and to be a networking organization for HR communities.

Israel Human Resources Accreditation Program

By Ilan Meshoulam

The Israeli Society for Human Resource Management activities are a reflection of changes in Israel's environment, divided into two major periods.

The first, Independence (1948) to the late 1970s, was characterized by fast growth as well as a continuous state of war. The country was led by strong socialist ideologies of the pioneers. The only union (Histadrut) was a dominant power, economically and politically. It was not surprising that socialism was the leading socioeconomic ideology during the first decades of Israel's existence.

During the 1950s, fast-growing immigration movements drew the country's attention. Absorption, assimilation, and training were major roles undertaken by personnel departments. Internal labor market strategy—the system by which a company looks inside its own organization to find a suitable person for a senior job, before considering candidates from outside the company—was adopted by most large organizations, emphasizing formal and contractual relationships, bureaucratic organizational structures, narrow job designs, and long-term commitment. All were heavily unionized, advocating seniority-based pay.

Labor relations were a major human resource management (HRM) activity, dictated mainly by the union and supported by legislation and regulations. HRM functions focused mainly on administration, recruitment, labor relations, and some aspects of skills and managerial training. In many organizations, HR was not part of the leading management team, but reported to the financial or other operational unit.

The second era began in the late 1970s and exist today. External challenges have caused transformations in Israel's economy and a modernization of its industrial system. New forces helped shape the incremental development of the HRM field.

First was the growth of a high-level technical workforce, a result of the downsizing of technical professions in the defense industry and immigration of Russian scientists in the 1980s. At the same time, the high-tech industry began to gain momentum. Some large U.S. companies opened local branches and new start-ups emerged.

A new government approach of deregulation and privatization of businesses was adopted. New and extremely different demands were made on the HRM profession. Large and complex organizations, an educated workforce, and strong national and international competition have forced the profession to adapt. A fresh HRM of university educated professionals and HR executives at larger organizations have emerged. A new external labor market strategy was adopted by organizations, emphasizing global competition, broad and self-managed positions, individual growth and development, flexible workplaces, and performance-based pay.

The Accreditation Program

As a result of the new demands for a higher level of HR professionalism, the Israeli Society of Management, Development and Research of Human Resources was formed in 2004.

Its first activity was to define society goals. A major goal, which later served as a basis for the accreditation program, was to help raise the level of HR professionalism in Israel by encouraging mutual learning, exposure to HR activities in and outside of Israel, and more.

Two years later a group of members wrote a code of ethics, which became behavioral guidelines to all members. Next, the society moved on to develop an accreditation program, which was launched in 2007.

The first step was to define the knowledge required as a base for accreditation, based on the accreditation methodologies learned during visits with U.S. and U.K. HR societies.

The second step involved approximately 30 individuals, all HR vice presidents from a wide scope of industry and academy, who formed a committee to define the basic principles of the accreditation program, as well as the knowledge base needed for each of accreditation level.

Four levels of accreditation were suggested: accredited, specialist, senior specialist and leading senior specialist.

The third step consisted of teams of senior members formed to define accreditation criteria for each level. For example, the first level allowed for two options: those with at least three years of HR field experience and a B.A. in HR studies, or those with other a B.A. and at least 100 hours additional certificate studies in the field. The criteria for expert level were numerous: six years of work experience and a B.A. not in HR, plus certificate studies; six years with a B.A. in the field; experience of more than three years and a Master's not in the field, plus certificate studies; or more than three years' experience and a Master's in the HR field, could all be accredited.

The fourth step included negotiations with universities and colleges to accept the society's requirements as part of their curriculum. The degree received from those institutions was accepted as a basis for accreditation. Currently, 14 institutions have joined the program.

Our future goals are to find a way for government support to make the accreditation an official requirement for HR management and to enhance professionalism by introducing many activities, including learning meetings at various organizations, conferences, collaboration with universities, an HR excellence competition, and more.

Ilan Meshoulam, Ph.D., is a professor at the University of Haifa and chair of the Israeli Society for Human Resource Management, Research, and Development.

Thailand's HR Accreditation Model

By Suchada Sukhasvasti na Ayudhya

The Original Model

As a driving mission to promote the HR profession in Thailand, the Institute of Human Resource Professional Development (IHPD) under the Personnel Management Association of Thailand (PMAT) has studied, researched, developed HR competencies, and introduced HR Professional Competency Accreditation since 2005.

The original model of HR competency comprised of two major groups of competencies, generic/managerial functional/technical. Specifically focused on the latter competency, PMAT defined that there are human resource management (HRM) and human resources development (HRD) competencies. In HRM, there were four areas of competency: human resource planning; recruitment and selection; labor law and employee relation; and compensation and welfare. HRD competencies comprised of training and development; performance management; organization development; and career development.

In the original PMAT HR accreditation model, there were three levels of HR personnel: HR practitioner, professional HR (PHR), and senior professional HR (SPHR). However, PMAT only offered the PHR accreditation level to eligible HR persons with at least five years of experience or at least three years of experience in HR field and a Master's degree.

The accreditation processes started with application screening, multiple-choice testing, and interview as final test of HR accreditation. Each applicant must fill out a form to be screened by an accreditation committee. Qualified applicants are invited to take a test which encompasses eight HR functional areas, and those who pass go on to the final interview.

The New Model

A decade has passed, and PMAT recognizes an indispensable need to improve the HR competency and accreditation model to catch up with both academic and practical changes. PMAT has an agreement with the Thailand Professional Qualification Institute (TPQI) to develop the Thailand HR Occupational Standard and

> The new HR accreditation model divides HR roles into four groups that align with the Thailand Professional QualificationFramework.

Professional Qualification, which is in the final approval stages.

The new HR competency model has been developed through research and the help of academics, practitioners, professionals, and experts in HR. It is meant to evaluate HR academic knowledge and understanding, HR-related knowledge and technical experience in its application, analytical skill, and the integrative problem-solving skills of the test takers.

The new HR competency model also can be divided into two major sets of competency:
- HR generic competency, for HR professional practice
- HR functional/technical competency, for HR expertise

The new HR accreditation model divides HR roles into four groups that align with the Thailand Professional Qualification Framework:
- HR practitioner
- HR professional
- Senior HR professional
- HR expert

This accreditation process is similar to the original model except that the person must provide a portfolio, there are a different number of criteria a practitioner must meet to achieve each level, and only the HR practitioner is not required to do the interview.

The accreditation organization must be qualified by TPQI's standards and certified by TPQI.

Suchada Sukhasvasti na Ayudhya is past president of the Personnel Management Association of Thailand in Bangkok.

HR in Argentina: Certification Has Yet to Catch On

By Gustavo Aquino

Though the Human Resources Association of Argentina (ADRHA) was founded in 1968, human resource management (HRM), or perhaps a perceived lack of it, has a long history in Argentina. Yet progress, while admittedly slow, is being made. To understand the state of HRM and efforts to standardize practices and credential practitioners, it's important to understand the history of it here, which dates as far back as the Steel Age.

In 1855, when Gustavus Swift founded a meat packing company in Chicago, its rapid development saw Swift factories give rise to HR laboratories where analyzing and synthesizing workflows, assembly lines, union bargaining, welfare policies, and other workplace practices were pioneered.

In 1907, Swift and Company expanded to Buenos Aires (later to Río Gallegos in 1912 and Rosario in 1924) where expatriate managers transferred their knowledge of developing local proto-HR teams trained in time and methods analysis, pay practices, personnel statistics, and policies. HR pioneers came from the very heart of factories, far away from universities. Personnel management was taught among scrap, grease, and smoke, with the goal of developing and implementing measures and techniques to maintain or increase productivity.

In this setting, Alpargatas, the leading textile company in Argentina, brought the first university graduates to its personnel offices: the industrial engineers. These degreed professional brought new and improved methods—and along with them prestige—to the up-and-coming profession.

The installment of the welfare state in Argentina post-WWII boosted labor regulation and legislation. Due to political process, a second diploma was now impacting employment laws and human resources: the Juris Doctorate. As engineers sought productivity, lawyers focused on labor relations and professionalization.

During the 1960s, American companies such as Ford, General Motors, and Exxon brought some concepts, such as motivation and leadership, to the workplace. Trying to cope with Maslow, Herzberg, and Drucker, a third diploma, the Ph.D., was added to list. These professionals wanted not to just study and practice the entire gamut of HR—from leadership and management to organizational psychology—but also to shape it.

The creation of degrees offered by business schools in various HR discipline saw a rise in the number of jobs for those graduates, which spread interest in the degree programs. Universidad Argentina de la Empresa (UADE) introduced its industrial relations major in 1962, and it is still being taught today. The Universidad del Salvador has its own personnel management field of study as well. Today, students here can choose to study HR at more than 40 universities.

HR in Argentina evolved as an open community where you can find HR professionals from diverse backgrounds, including HR degree holders, engineers, lawyers, psychologists, sociologists, educators, and so forth. So far, two World Federation of People Management Association (WFPMA) presidents, Carlos Marcelo Aldao Zapiola (2002–2004), a lawyer, and Horacio Eduardo Quirós (2010–2012), an HR degree holder, have hailed from Argentina. HR as an art and science is practiced widely here.

By the end of the 20th century, groups of colleagues initiated a movement looking for HR labor market regulation. It was supported mainly by HR students and professors and resisted mainly by HR managers at local WFPMA chapters, such as Human Resources Association of Argentina (ADRHA). This remains an ongoing debate. HR graduates and students are still calling for official credentialing, but their opponent now in the HR community is indifference.

> HR graduates and students are still calling for official credentialing, but their opponent now in the HR community is indifference.

Except some specific jobs, mostly in the supply chain, there is no tradition of certification in Argentina, but it seems that the process started and will grow. In the building industry, the Construction Institute of Statistics and Regulation (IERIC) ensures only certified persons are put in specific jobs. ADRHA's President Raúl Massarini manages IERIC.

Labor Ministry promotes these kind of certification processes, focused on blue collar and unionized workers. White collar professions remain open, or with individuals earning degrees rather than obtaining certifications. Some colleagues are certified by international associations in compensations and benefits, training, or coaching, but they are not relevant—at least not yet.

Far away from the American tradition of certified members of professional associations and the European one of government promoted processes, Argentina's labor market remains open and without regulations. Employer expectations of HR professionals here are simply not tied to certification. ■

Gustavo Aquino is an ADRHA member.

LEARNING GUIDE

World HR Associations:
Leading the Profession into the Future

INTRODUCTION

This Point Counterpoint begins by presenting the U.S. perspective on HR certification and then expands that view to include historical and current HR certification processes in countries outside the United States, specifically in the United Kingdom, Canada, Australia, Germany, Israel, Thailand, and Argentina. Experts in each country summarize the detail of the various HR competency models that have been developed and the different processes for becoming certified. The first article provides an overview, based on SHRM's role vis-à-vis the World Federation of People Management Associations (WFPMA).

The countries varied widely in their approaches showing that there is no one universally accepted certification process or organization for the world. The U.K.-based Chartered Institute of Personnel and Development's (CIFD) "Profession Map," first published in 2008, represents their competency model for HR. The Canadian Council of Human Resource Associations (CCHRA) offers the Certified Human Resource Professional (CHRP) designation, with 21,000 of their 41,000 members having attained that status. Their CHRP was published in 2014. The Australia Human Resource Institute (AHRI) offers a Certification (CAHRI) via the AHRI Practicing Certification Program (APC), implemented in 2016. The German Association for People Management (DGFP) developed a training and certification called ProPro in 2005, and 1,800 people have since been certified. The Israeli Society of Management, Development and Research of Human Resources was established in 2004 and introduced their certification program in 2007. The Personnel Management Association of Thailand (PMAT) established the Institute of Human Resource Professional Development (IHPD) and introduced their certification program in 2005. The Human Resource Association of Argentina (ADHRA) was founded in 1968, and the article traces the history of the development of HR, concluding that certification is not currently an expectation for HR professionals there.

DISCOVERY QUESTIONS

- What are you dealing with in your organization today that relates to this content area?
- How would you assess SHRM's certification process, compared to those offered by other countries? Which model best applies to your organization?
- Based on what you learned, how would you advise your organization on HR certification?
- Which HR credential do you believe is best for your organization? Why?
- In your organization, what are some "context variables" that define what "good HR" looks like?
- If your organization is global, what HR certification process would you recommend? Why?
- Which content areas of the various competency models are most needed by your organization? Why?

SELECTED FACTS

- What new facts that were presented got your attention?
  - Eighty-one percent of U.S. respondents believe that to get ahead in HR an advanced credential is needed.
  - A growing number of country governments are involved in HR certification (United Kingdom, Canada, Kenya, Australia, Israel, Thailand, Bahrain, Malaysia, Singapore, South Africa, United Arab Emirates).
  - CIPD has more than 140,000 members worldwide.
  - The CIPD competency model defines eight behaviors, ten professional areas and four bands of professional competence.
  - The CCHRA represents 41,000 professionals; with 21,000 credentialed in their CHRP.
  - The CCHRA CHRP model defines 44 competencies in nine functional areas; along with five enabling competencies.
  - From Israel's independence in 1948 the first driving power in defining HR was the one Union.
  - The Thailand model of HR has four competencies under HR management and another four competencies under HR development.
  - HR in Argentina has a rich history of development and growth, but no common certification standard.

Point Counterpoint II: 1.2

World HR Associations:
Leading the Profession Into the Future

KEY DISCUSSION POINTS

- What were the key points being made in this Perspectives?
- Why is it important for the HR profession to have a recognized credentialing program?
- Discuss the logic and merits of the LBIT competency model in the United States.
- Globally, how does the content of certificate programs vary?
- Why might it be important to have different levels of certification within HR?
- What is the difference between a "credential" and a "certification"?
- What should the role of government in the certification process be?
- What should be the role of membership based national HR associations in certification?
- How do the CIPD and SHRM HR models differ and how are they similar?
- How does the CIPD differentiate between "rules-based" and "principle-based" approaches to certification and do you agree with them?
- Compare and contrast the HR certification approaches of the United Kingdom, Canada, and Australia.
- Which country's certification process requires an organizational capability workplace based project; and what do you think of that?
- What are the pros and cons of the German and Thai approach using oral examinations?
- From the late 1970s until recently, what were the forces that changed Israel's approach to HR?
- In Argentina, how did both engineers and lawyers shape the role of HR historically?

REVIEW OF SOLUTIONS

- Identify two to three big ideas worthy of exploring in your organization.
- Is there one best HR certification?
- How would you assess the quality of certification?

IDENTIFYING THE PARADOX

- How is it that a solution appropriate for yesterday's organization is no longer valid?
- Consider how very different perspectives might be correct given different situations.
- Is one consistent global model of HR needed, or should there be global variations?

LEARNING OUTCOMES

- What one new piece of information did you learn that will be important to you in the future?
- Identify one thing that you will do differently based on what you learned.

Reimagining the Future of Work

By Marc Sokol

We tend to think of organizational change as occurring in great sweeps of activity, followed by periods of stability. Reality is different; many of us don't fully see the real changes around us until they have already become the norm. Yet those who aspire to lead organizational change must find the balance of change and stability, deftly navigate tidal waves of action amidst undercurrents of resistance, and help others find life rafts or learn to swim in new waters.

Social architecture, the subject of this Lead Perspective, sets the stage for how companies can effectively navigate large-scale systems transformation. Luc Galoppin, an organizational change agent who also manages a 40,000-member social network, describes how digital technologies are reshaping the shipping lanes of enterprise-wide systems change, and how virtual communities can become the speedboats of success.

To expand on Luc's perspective, we invited commentary from change agents around the world. American Daryl Conner, whose writing has shaped the thinking of consultants and leaders globally, builds on the Lead Perspective, noting the significance of this point in time. Jennifer Frahm weighs in from Australia, reminding us we still have a long way to go, while Holger Nauheimer, from Germany, places social architecture in the broader context of history, technical change and leadership. Finally, Peter Vermeulen, from Johnson & Johnson, shares with us a view from inside a large global corporation.

If you ever felt it takes too long and is too complex to design and implement new information systems, this issue of Perspectives is for you. If you ever wondered how to better engage your workforce in the midst of change, then this issue of Perspectives is also for you.

Marc Sokol, Ph.D., is executive editor of *People + Strategy.*

POINT

Advice to Change Agents: Skate to Where the Puck Is Going, Not Where It Has Been

By Luc Galoppin

The title of this Lead Perspective plays off hockey great Wayne Gretsky's explanation of his tremendous success. When one looks at how the digital economy is shifting the world of work, it becomes apparent that successful organizations must discover the new balance between hierarchy and community that is called Social Architecture. Organization change practitioners must also update their own methods and tools to capitalize on these trends, tapping into the new potential for collaboration and social media.

What Is Going On?
On May 5, 1835, the first train was riding through Belgium. At that time, nobody could predict that this train would trigger a whole new era of the Industrial Revolution. Today, we see that the Internet has leveraged our economy in the same way the train fueled the Industrial Revolution.

All large companies depend on information systems to enable business processes. Effective systems upgrades can be transformative, while failure to achieve effectiveness can cripple the enterprise. However, the way we run these projects is for the most part still governed by command-and-control, top-down logic. In reality, there is a tension between the authority dynamic of traditional hierarchy on the one hand, and the influence dynamic of collaboration that is becoming the norm in our society since the rise of social media.

As the world changes, many of the rules that brought us here become obsolete. Just as social media has enabled consumers to influence and even define a company's brand, it is increasingly setting the stage for inclusion of the target audience into the design and deployment of new systems. Leadership and workplace dynamics are no longer simply hierarchical, as tribal dynamics of communities now trump top-down management.

Successful projects are those that strike a healthy balance between the compliance imposed by hierarchy, and the co-creation brought about by the communities that connect people. Hierarchy alone can no longer accomplish change.

Gradually everyone is getting acquainted to liking, sharing and crowdsourcing, and a lack of social media sophistication is no longer an excuse for not collaborating. The Internet and social media have radically raised our expectations for inclusion, voice and collaboration. We are in the middle of a paradigm shift. If you were on that train in Belgium in 1835, would you have seen how far it could go?

Here We Are; Now What?

There is a tremendous opportunity to tap into the new literacy of collaboration and to balance it with the existing organization. This is called Social Architecture, balancing authority and influence.

Winning organizations of the future will find a good balance between controlling the outcomes of stable processes with reaching outside of the boundaries of the organization chart in order to connect with customers, suppliers, and other stakeholders. Ultimately, there is no outside.

In practice, this comes down to empowering interconnected layers of communities, projects, task forces and tribes. We do this by assigning roles as opposed to permanent hierarchical positions. Next, people connect based

on those roles, using social media as desired. For instance, imagine the community of warehouse managers created during the global rollout of an ERP package. Warehouse managers from different production sites all over the world are given a warehouse manager "badge" as a project role; they use this designation to find each other, to recognize each other as members of the same "tribe," and assume trust in each other that might have otherwise taken years to foster. This illustrates the productivity advantage of collaboration over compliance.

What's in It for Organizational Change Practitioners?

The rise of social media is changing our organizational DNA, and it takes the lens of social architecture to see how the toolbox of organizational change practitioners needs to be upgraded. For instance, the traditional view of a change leader as a problem-solving expert is under pressure. Now our job as organizational change practitioners is to build platforms for communities to connect, to recognize ambassadors who emerge within and across communities, and to balance their influence with the authority of the surrounding organization. The benefits of leveraging social architecture to help drive systems change include:

- Early prototyping, feedback and error detection that can be accelerated through communication platforms.
- Using platforms to engage stakeholders with each other in meaningful conversations around problems and solutions, and even the overall vision of the desired end state of change.
- Evolving project communication plans to include shared stories that emerge from real user experiences.

Change leaders of the future must display the courage to decrease their level of top-down control and trust the wisdom of virtual communities. As organizations discover that emergent social communities are not a threat to hierarchy, they too will benefit from the balance of influence and authority.

This is exactly where the competitive advantage of the next generation of organizations resides.

Luc Galoppin, a Belgium-based organizational change practitioner, founded the LinkedIn group Organizational Change Practitioners, which has more than 40,000 members. He is the coauthor of *Managing Organizational Change During SAP Implementations*.

Social Architecture: A Balanced Call to Action

By Daryl Conner

When reading this Perspective, I was struck with what an inflection point the professional change community is living through. Most disciplines periodically experience bifurcations, where a clear "before and after" point of reference emerges. Something takes place that separates the eras when practitioners did and didn't have access to certain knowledge or technology. The change execution profession is living through one of these historic junctures; it is the demarcation from pre- to post-awareness of the powerful implications of what is referred to here as "social architecture."

Before the great divide, most successful endeavors involved some version of driving change down into organizations from the sponsor's perch. With the emergence of social architecture, change facilitators are able to leverage both the downward directed power of sponsorship and the upward influence of community—capitalizing on leadership's authority as well as the collective impact of collaboration.

"Hierarchy alone can no longer accomplish change" has been declared by those on the bleeding edge for some time, but until recently, it produced little more than rhetoric and good intentions. Despite all the "engagement-" and "empowerment-"

oriented activities, most implementation plans that have led to significant change have been heavily weighted toward a top-down bias. Future generations of practitioners will look back on this period as one where the profession finally evolved enough to recognize that authority and community aren't mutually exclusive—when leadership directives and social media networking began to be seen as equal partners in the transformational process.

Luc epitomizes this shift by refusing to let the professional change community off the hook with self-congratulations for merely waking up to

> Before the great divide, most successful endeavors involved some version of driving change down into organizations from the sponsor's perch.

this new reality. His statement is a call to action…a rallying cry to actually incorporate the social architecture mindset into the planning and execution of our craft.

This isn't as simple as command and control approaches and social media influence having their respective places in the process; each must be integrated with and balanced by the other. They should be seen as two interdependent ends of a single continuum, creating a range of intervention options that we can draw upon as needed. Future relevancy in our field requires that we embrace the notion that the zone where hierarchy and community intersect offers the greatest possibility for people and organizations to successfully adapt to changing circumstances. The social media genie is out of the bottle, and life as a professional change agent will never be the same.

Daryl Conner is chairman of Conner Partners, a firm that has been active in the human side of change for 40 years.

Social Architecture: Still a Long Way to Go

By Jennifer Frahm

Luc Galoppin has drunk the Kool-Aid, buckets of it. I've been known to sip from the social enterprise cup myself, but I'm more cautious of guzzling from it for a few reasons.

We Are Still Justifying Investments, Rather than Tending to Communities

While moving to a more collaborative hyper-connected organization that eschews command and control may yield benefits with regard to skating where the puck will go, there are ample companies firmly entrenched in command and control, without social architecture, and they are doing just fine. Galoppin says tribal dynamics of communities now trump top-down management, but I can't agree, at least not from what I see in corporate Australia. Yes, there is increasing interest and exploratory activity in social business, but it is far from the norm.

Recent research by Hudson suggests that, while 61 percent of local businesses report using enterprise social networks, only 10 percent consider them to be a great success. My experience with companies using enterprise social networks is that community managers spend their time trying to capture the ROI and business case for extending licenses, and proving potential to their C-suite, rather than actually tending to their communities.

The Change Must Start with Us

Don't get me wrong; I want to believe. I also believe that the success of the social architecture paradigm shift begins with all of us who are practitioners and leaders of organizational change.

Galoppin calls for us to update our own methods and tools, "tapping into the new potential for collaboration and social media." From what I see, our own professional community

may be too time poor or just too lazy to keep abreast of the trends. Only a handful of change practitioners regularly use Twitter, or share fresh thinking and content. Active engagement on LinkedIn also remains limited to a small percentage. Far too many change practitioners don't even have a LinkedIn profile, or know how to use Dropbox, or consider how to use

> How can we champion the use of new tools when we don't use them ourselves?

aspects of gamification, mobile, or the thinking behind MOOCs within their change practices. How can we champion the use of new tools when we don't use them ourselves?

If you are reading this, I have to believe you are interested in where the puck will be. My advice is to put your skates on, gather your colleagues, and start to be the change we wish to see in the companies we support.

Jennifer Frahm, Ph.D., based in Melbourne, Australia, is the founder of Conversations of Change and an experienced change management practitioner.

At the Core, the Revolution Is about Leadership

By Holger Nauheimer

The essence of the Lead Perspective boils down to the question: "Has the world of management changed?" One position could be that actually it hasn't changed significantly. Management is still about achieving results with the available resources—as it has been since the moment when non-family members were appointed to look after the operations of an enterprise. There have been managers for 5,000 years.

The construction of the Egyptian pyramids gave rise to a new profession of people who were technology experts but also able to organize and supervise labor. Since then, we have been seeing management models come and go. No wonder that Sun Tzu and Machiavelli are still frequently cited.

We also know that technology has always been a driver of innovation in the management field. There have been periods of disruptive change in the way organizations and people are managed. Frederick Taylor, for example, described the impact of new ways of manufacturing following the invention of the conveyor belt. The safety elevator, introduced 50 years earlier by Elisha Otis, opened the opportunity

> Our conversations should be about *how* we want people to engage, and not just what they should be doing.

to create large office spaces in cities, which subsequently helped financial and other service institutions to grow exponentially. It took 100 years until another technological revolution, the World Wide Web, fundamentally changed the way we work, organize and relate to each other.

For me, the real revolution that is happening is about leadership in response to the changes around us. For example, I facilitated a meeting of a dispersed team. The team leader, who had joined the team only six months before, was ambitious to increase performance. I provided my thoughts on how to work over distance, including the idea that exchanging personal and private news is as important in virtual meetings as it is in face-to-face meetings. Following my comment, the team members shared with their boss that she had eliminated this very aspect of their collaboration, which was a routine before she had joined and taken over facilitation of the meetings. While her intention was to increase ef-

ficiency, she didn't consider the desire for closeness among the team, which is not satisfied in many virtual teams.

Leaders need to cultivate trust and the spirit of collaboration in the face of change, and for some, this may become even more challenging across new technology. Our conversations should be about *how* we want people to engage, and not just what they should be doing.

Holger Nauheimer, a thought leader on leadership, collaboration, and new ways of working, hosts the annual Berlin Change Days, an international conference for change practitioners.

The Power of Co-Creation

By Peter Vermeulen

For Johnson & Johnson, a company with operations in more than 50 countries and over 120,000 employees, change is not something taken lightly. A few years ago, we started to fully embrace the power of co-creation when designing and deploying major change initiatives within the Human Resources function. We recently rolled out a new set of Leadership Imperatives (i.e., the way we want our leaders to show up), a new Performance Management System, and we are currently in the process of globally implementing a cloud-based human capital system. We are successfully deploying these initiatives for a variety of reasons, but one important enabler has been co-creation as a way we have chosen to engage with different stakeholders from the very beginning of the project.

Co-creation involves both involvement and decentralization in design, moving it from development by a corporate office to development by a true change lead that understands the power of engaging stakeholders in the process. This methodology not only forced us to think differently about how we engage internal and external stakeholders in design and implementation of processes and systems, it also

changed the very nature of engagement between managers, functional experts, partners and employees.

> Co-creation involves both involvement and decentralization in design, moving it from development by a corporate office to development by a true change lead that understands the power of engaging stakeholders in the process.

The advantages have been huge. Take the example of the implementation of Leadership Imperatives, our new set of leadership behaviors. The entire creation and deployment of these leadership behaviors was leader-led, not HR-led. It was incredibly powerful to hear leaders around the world sharing their personal stories regarding how and why they need to show up differently as leaders. The buy-in for this project was so much greater compared to similar efforts in the past. The new set of leadership expectations are now fully adopted and have become part of our performance management system.

I support the Lead Perspective. There is terrific power in embracing new ways to engage different stakeholders. It is a critical success factor for leading change in a complex environment. At the same time, I encourage readers to remember that, while social media can be a great enabler, there are other ways to organize co-creation, such as focus groups and think tanks. The change lead should be empowered to use the techniques and tools that best fit the environment. ▪▪

Peter Vermeulen is vice president, human resources–diversity and talent management, Johnson & Johnson.

LEARNING GUIDE

Reimagining the Future of Work

DISCOVERY QUESTIONS

- What are you dealing with in your organization today that relates to this content area?
- Is your organization more about top-down hierarchy or open collaboration?
- Do you have an example in your organization where collaboration, rather than compliance, provided a productivity advantage?
- When your organization rolls out large scale change, how much of the process is based on top-down hierarchy and how much on bottom-up community?
- What additional ways could social media be used in your organization to assist in the co-creation of new solutions?

SELECTED FACTS

- What new facts that were presented got your attention?
- The first train ran through Belgium on May 5, 1835; What is this a metaphor for?
  › Social architecture is about balancing authority and influence.
  › Effective change leverages both the downward power of sponsorship and the upward influence of community.
  › Social media can support cocreation of new solutions, but so can focus groups and think tanks.

KEY DISCUSSION POINTS

- What were the key points being made in this presentation?
- What is the tension between the authority dynamic of traditional hierarchy and the influence dynamic of collaboration?
- Describe the difference between compliance imposed by hierarchy and co-creation inspired by communities.
- How has social media radically changed our expectations for inclusion, voice and collaboration?
- Itemize Frahm's reservations regarding complete support for Galoppin's social media thesis. What do you think of it?
- Describe the technology innovations that led to changes in management approaches.
- What are some issues in how to create trust within geographically dispersed teams?
- Give an example of a Leader-Led rather than HR-Led initiative, and why it worked well.

REVIEW OF SOLUTIONS

- Identify two-three big ideas worthy of exploring in your organization.
- What one thing could your organization do differently based on this new information?

IDENTIFYING THE PARADOX

- How is it that a solution appropriate for yesterday's organization is no longer valid?
- Consider how very different perspectives might be correct given different situations.
- Change leaders used to be problem-solving experts. How has that role changed?
- How can you discover the right balance between top-down compliance and bottom-up collaboration?

LEARNING OUTCOMES

- What one new piece of information did you learn that will be important to you in the future?
- Identify one thing that you will do differently based on what you learned.

The Role of Strategy and Employee Engagement

By Anna Tavis

As has been our quarterly practice, the Perspectives section of *People + Strategy* joins in the central HR/business/strategy debates to revisit core human capital management assumptions.

We invited **Scott Brooks** and **Jeffrey Saltzman,** two veterans in the employee survey/HR analytics field, to present an alternative view of employee engagement. Employee engagement has been considered for at least the past two decades to be the proverbial strategic imperative of most employee survey initiatives.

To Brooks and Saltzman, engagement does not stand on its own as a goal for organization's human capital effort. To create a meaningful result, they argue, the survey needs to be grounded in business strategy. As strategies vary from business to business, so does employee engagement. It needs to be looked at in an informed, uniquely aligned way. Brooks and Saltzman conclude by saying:

"While important to survey design or HR strategy, the question of how engagement can help is absolutely subordinate to understanding the strategic priorities of the organization. This is where surveys really become potent and connect with the passions of executives."

Based on this set of business-based assumptions, Brooks and Saltzman partnered in creating OrgVitality, a boutique assessment consultancy that challenges market leaders in the business of employee surveys.

Our four panelists hold senior HR roles in various types of business organizations.

Tony Fogel, chief human resources officer of Ciber, steps into the debate with some illustrative cases from his own rich business experience. He concludes, "We still needed an engaged workforce;

we just needed them engaged on the right things in the right way."

Dave Binder, vice president of talent and organizational capability at Pfizer, defines a manager's role in the employee engagement rollout. "Improving engagement presents a unique challenge for managers. Managers are rewarded for taking on a problem, developing and implementing a solution and moving on to the next problem. With engagement, they are expected to personally alter and sustain their behavior over time in the hope that engagement will improve their team's impact at an undetermined point in the future."

Eivind Slaaen, senior vice president of human resources at Hilti Corporation in Switzerland, cautions HR as a function not to get too carried away with engagement as a standalone initiative. So many times, Slaaen argues, we fail as a function to deliver on the appropriate strategic alignment and, deservedly, we do not get the much discussed "seat at the table."

Matt Valenti of Starwood Hotels & Resorts illustrates how his company has "changed the engagement conversation." Valenti writes that at Starwood Hotels "engagement scores are no longer relegated to the annual event of when reports are distributed, and action plans have moved away from 'improve engagement scores.' Action plans have become more holistic with the data informing the how, not defining the what."

In summary, the conversation about employee engagement is changing. In this series, our senior human resources contributors call on their audience to use engagement data as part of an overall holistic approach of measuring organizational vitality, aligning with business strategy, and continuing to focus on execution and management excellence.

Anna A. Tavis, Ph.D., is Perspectives editor and an associate professor at New York University.

Why Employee Engagement Is Not Strategic

By Scott M. Brooks and
Jeffrey M. Saltzman

Employee engagement has a well-acknowledged meaning and impact. It has become core to many surveys and can be found as a critical metric within HR strategies across the globe. But is the measurement, tracking or the setting of an engagement improvement target strategic?

While specific definitions of engagement vary widely, engagement tends to be thought of as passion and commitment in service of an organization's goals that can result in a stronger collective motivation to get things done. In turn, this motivation can lead to higher performance. But let us be clear: a *connection* to business outcomes does not automatically make something *strategic*. The pursuit of higher engagement is like the pursuit of more

> Strategy is not the same as goals or ambition. Making more money, being an employer of choice, having the best place to work, and having a highly engaged workforce are all ambitions.

customers, market share or profit—all good things to have, yet these more properly refer to ambitions rather than strategic choices.

Moreover, we assert that engagement by itself is like motivation without ability.

Characteristics of Strategy

Here are a few characteristics of effective strategies that are generally accepted:

1. Strategy is not the same as goals or ambition. Revenue targets, market share or "being No. 1" can be specific goals or general aspirations. But they are not strategy. Strategies need to suggest how goals will be achieved.
2. Strategies direct choices and action. In suggesting how goals will be accomplished, effective strategies suggest pursuing certain paths over others. Strategies directly address challenges and bottlenecks.
3. Strategies will be unique. They capitalize on factors competitors find costly or impossible to copy. Good strategies will not look like others in the marketplace.

Clearly, there can be other characteristics of effective strategies. These, however, are sufficient to illustrate our points.

Matching Engagement to Characteristics of Strategy

1. Strategy is not the same as goals or ambition.

   Making more money, being an employer of choice, having the best place to work, and having a highly engaged workforce are all ambitions. Ambitions can be crafted into goals, but they are not strategies. Like motivation or money, engagement without direction or ability is easily wasted. Similarly, having an engaged workforce—while an important outcome—is not strategic.
2. Strategies direct choices and action.

   While engagement can be part of a how an organization succeeds, it is only a piece of the solution. At the root of many engagement theories is a kind of wishful thinking that business concerns will resolve themselves if only employees were more engaged. How will we address the changing global marketplace? Engagement. How will we reduce manufacturing bottlenecks? Engagement. How will we reinvent our product offerings? Engagement. This cannot be the solution to any and all business challenges. Different challenges demand different strategies (even HR strategies), or else we suboptimize our impact and

   lose credibility as business people.
3. Strategies will be unique.

   A strength of engagement—its universal applicability—is also a limitation. To maximize the strategic impact of an employee survey, it needs to measure strategic topics. Embrace all the best practices you want, but you cannot copy your way to competitive differentiation. Engagement, it follows, is not a strategic topic. Not by itself. As a topic, it holds no uniqueness for a given organization.

The Role for Engagement

If engagement is not a strategic topic for an organization, can it nevertheless support strategy? Surely. How an organization *uses* its engagement is

> For many in the HR marketplace ... engagement has become an end and not a means. We confuse the tool or the resource with the strategy itself.

where the unique, competitive edge will be found. While important to survey design or HR strategy, the question of how engagement can help is absolutely subordinate to understanding the strategic priorities of the organization. This is where surveys really become potent and connect with the passions of executives.

Making Employee Surveys More Strategic

Science can help. Linkage research can illuminate strategic choices, inform decision-making, and highlight challenges or areas of risk. It can help guide leaders on where to focus limited resources in order to maximize success. Engagement is often a smaller piece of success than people expect. In scientific head-to-head tests, for example, the best predictor of customer loyalty is not engagement, but service climate. Similarly, the best predictor of safety is not engagement, but safety climate.

Other broad measures, such as employee confidence, are better at predicting business success than employee engagement. Employee confidence asks the employees about the business environment in which they are embedded.

Where this leads us is that employee surveys should not be simply about employees. Employees are valuable sources of information about directions and execution—topics that help us understand and improve organizational strategy. The automatic assumption that engagement is the most important topic in a survey is almost certainly suboptimizing the effort. It is important not simply to ask employees about themselves, but to ask them about what they see around them.

Conclusion

For many in the HR marketplace, engagement, unfortunately, has become an end and not a means. We confuse the tool or the resource with the strategy itself. In doing so, engagement has become a shortcut, mono-focus for survey designers and managers who do not start with a business-centric scrutiny of strategy. Surveys, if done appropriately, can help leaders evaluate and shape decisions, clearly identify challenges and enhance an organization's competitive edge.

Making surveys strategic requires focused thinking. It is custom. It is uniquely solved for each organization.

Scott Brooks, Ph.D., is a partner and vice president of employee surveys and organizational research at OrgVitality, based in San Francisco. He is a popular blogger, whose OrgStories posts illustrate where stories and science come together to create more effective organizations.

Jeffrey M. Saltzman is the chief executive officer of OrgVitality and an associated fellow at the Center for Leadership Studies, School of Management, at Binghamton University. He has extensive experience in diverse settings, consulting financial services, retail, media, high technology, service companies, not-for-profits and government agencies on how to improve organizational performance. Based in New York, he has traveled and worked extensively in Europe, Latin America and Asia-Pacific.

Strategy Leads; Engagement Contributes

By Tony Fogel

"Why Employee Engagement Is Not Strategic" will appear a provocative title to many HR professionals. Employee engagement has been a ubiquitous strategic objective in HR strategy presentations since at least the mid-'90s, but it has its origins going back much further to the early days of industrial and organizational psychology research. Scott Brooks and Jeff Saltzman accurately point out that, while important, employee engagement is not strategic. So why is the concept so often a part of HR strategies?

Employee engagement, as a driver of employee productivity and an essential element of effective human capital management, is axiomatic. The issue is that HR professionals and business leaders often mischaracterize employee engagement and, by doing so, take attention away from the strategic dialogue they should be having with leadership or the board. I have seen far too many HR leaders and leadership teams get wrapped around the axle of employee engagement and other traditional HR topics when they should be focused on strategic choices and desired outcomes. Brooks and Saltzman adeptly point out that, "Engagement unfortunately has become an end and not a means." The distinction contained in Brooks and Saltzman's thesis is not merely academic; it is fundamental to clear-minded strategic thinking.

If HR professionals have input into and understand their organization's strategic imperatives, if they are aligned on desired outcomes and clear that business concerns will not be resolved simply because employees become more engaged, they will be positioned for truly strategic dialogue. But what does strategic HR dialogue look like? This is the elephant in the room of why employee engagement is not strategic.

Much has been written on the topic of strategic HR, and the subject cannot be given justice here. But, at its core, it has to do with integrating people, strategies, processes and systems to achieve the organization's long-term, desired outcomes. In essence, HR strategy will be about enabling the company to harness its people for maximum competitive advantage. If HR leaders are working with their leadership teams to ensure adequate human resources are in place at the right time with the right skills to deliver desired results, and if these same HR leaders are mindful of workforce trends and macro issues, they are more likely to put employee engagement in its proper place.

With strategic outcomes in mind, we can set goals for enabling employee engagement and maximize the relevance and benefit of an employee survey. I was

> Much has been written on the topic of strategic HR … At its core, [Strategic HR] has to do with integrating people, strategies, processes and systems to achieve the organization's long-term desired outcomes.

part of an acquisition integration team that was presented employee survey data showing a highly engaged work force. Unfortunately, the business was experiencing a year-over-year decline in profit. We dealt with this conundrum by setting clear strategic priorities to arrest the decline, and then we surveyed our employees to help us identify obstacles and gaps to achieving our objectives. We still needed an engaged workforce; we just needed them engaged on the right things in the right way.

Tony Fogel is senior vice president and chief HR officer at Ciber, a global IT consulting company that helps companies and governments build, implement and manage IT systems and business processes.

Executing Engagement Strategy Creates the Real Value

By Dave Binder

Scott Brooks and Jeff Saltzman correctly point out that focusing on engagement in and of itself is not necessarily strategic. However, business leaders are notoriously imprecise about how they articulate and label strategies, goals and objectives (not to mention vision and mission). For example, it is not uncommon to see a revenue target called a strategy. Similar to a survey-based engagement measure, a revenue target is a desired outcome influenced by a variety of factors. More important, as Brooks and Saltzman note, is whether organizations have an integrated approach to people and culture that is closely aligned to and driven by the business. In this context, engagement is a potential enabler or driver of business success.

Today's competitive business environment coupled with Wall Street's short-term expectations drive leaders on a constant search for that next competitive edge. As a result, even companies that have not historically emphasized human capital in their business plans feel compelled to further leverage their people to drive success. Those looking for a short-term fix are more likely to implement one-off initiatives around engagement, skill building, recognition, etc.

There is a paradox in these one-off initiatives. By attempting to put a spotlight on employee engagement by doing a survey, leaders actually marginalize the effort before it gets started. Managers view the survey and the inevitable action planning that follows as "one more thing to do" and not as an opportunity to build their business. The cynicism that can develop makes doing these surveys worse than doing nothing at all. Companies focusing on engagement solely to become an "employer of choice" or because it is the right thing to do typically face a similar fate.

However, integrating engagement effectively into HR and business strategy is just the price of admission. The critical importance of execution gets lost in this discussion. Even when engagement is positioned effectively in the context of broader strategies, business value and impact are far from guaranteed. Improving engagement presents a unique challenge for managers. Managers are rewarded for taking on a problem, developing and implementing a solution and moving on to the next problem. With engagement, they are expected to personally alter and sustain their behavior over time in the hope that engage-

> Making surveys strategic requires focused thinking. It is custom. It is uniquely solved for each organization.

ment will improve their team's impact at an undetermined point in the future. In short, you can't put a "check mark" next to engagement.

Is this a call for organizations to focus less on engagement? Absolutely not. If it were easy to leverage human capital to competitive advantage, everyone would do it. Organizations that view engagement as an end in itself typically invest more resources in the survey process than in the ongoing communication, training, modeling and reward systems needed to achieve true impact. Organizations with commitment to the "long haul" know that ongoing reinforcement of behaviors associated with engagement eventually become a seamless and powerful part of how business is done.

In conclusion, engagement by itself may be like motivation without ability. But the same can be said for engagement linked to business strategy without effective, sustained execution.

Dave Binder is the vice president of talent and organizational capability at Pfizer Inc., supporting the specialty care and oncology business units. In this role, he advises senior executives on a range of human capital and organizational issues. Binder has significant experience in the financial services, insurance and advertising industries.

The Best Strategy Is Only as Good as Its Implementation

By Eivind Slaaen

Scott Brooks and Jeff Saltzman are indeed onto something here. Engagement is celebrated as the key focus for the HR work of organizations. By focusing on engagement as a standalone topic without embedding it into the business context, HR reinforces the picture of itself as being out of touch with the need of the business.

The best strategy is only as good as its implementation. One of the biggest challenges leaders have is to align an organization behind a common direction. In most cases, to achieve the goals, it requires team members to get out of their comfort zone, their circle of habits, to do things differently in the future. The question is, therefore, how good leaders can translate the company's strategy to something that provides meaning for people at the different levels in the organization and get them to act on this strategy. Peter Gruber discussed the power of compelling stories in "Telling Purposeful Stories: An Organization's most Under-Utilized Competency" in an earlier version of this journal. People want to do worthwhile work, to be part of something that is bigger than them. This holds true for all generations and is on the top of the list of the millennium generation. Purpose, values and vision of a company can provide this meaning. The strategy enables people to envision how to get there.

The next question is, then, if people are capable of executing the strategy. Do they have the competence and means to get the work done? We all need confidence to push ourselves beyond our current ability and comfort, and we need to know that we are allowed to take calculated risks and learn from mistakes. Without that, people and organizations will not be able to perform to their potential. Confidence builds when our actions are in harmony with our values and we have a high emotional identification and connection with the purpose and vision. Having confidence—both individually and collectively—together with ambitious targets generates energy. A good strategy with clear and aligned priorities creates the focus needed to successfully implement the strategy. Organizations can then accomplish things that once seemed impossible. And how would we judge such an organization? An organization with high engagement! As Brooks and Saltzman describe, engagement is the result, not the means to get there. The means are alignment and capability.

The implications for HR and employee surveys are twofold. First, the core of the survey should address alignment and capability of the strategy of the organization. This will catch management attention and provide insights to management on what to address to improve business results. Second, the results of the employee survey must be discussed in a business context, as part of the standard business agenda and not addressed as a people/HR topic standing alone. By doing so, leaders and HR signals that the topic is not only relevant, but it drives the business results. People do business, and it is our task to ensure they are aligned, capable and engaged.

Eivind Slaaen is the senior vice president of human resources and the head of people and culture development at Hilti Corporation. Slaaen has more than 10 years of executive-level human resources and organizational development experience.

Change the Conversation

By Matt Valenti

The muddling of engagement and strategy that Scott Brooks and Jeff Saltzman describe does not happen by accident. The disconnect is highly susceptible when there is an inordinate focus on response rates, "best-in-class" benchmarks and "prove it" linkage analysis, all of which, at their worst,

misdirect goals, stifle uniqueness and do little to drive action.

Response rates are often touted as a success metric of an employee survey program. When this happens, it com-

> In reality, the surest way to drive up a response rate is to treat the survey as a tool to execute the strategy, not an end to itself ... that is, actually using the data and showing employees their voice was heard.

municates "the work is done" when, in reality, the end of an administration cycle is the true beginning of the program. The trap has sprung when dialogue and energy are expended in the name of "getting everyone to participate." In reality, the surest way to drive up a response rate is to treat the survey as a tool to execute the strategy, not an end to itself—that is, actually using the data and showing employees their voice was heard.

Best-in-class scores are often derived from a top quartile calculation. Although intended to offer an aspirational point of comparison, it is at odds with the emotion that managers attach to their scores. The trap is sprung when the report card mentality creates a rearview mirror fixation with the score instead of looking forward to drive improvement. Putting the survey results within the context of the organization's strategy will motivate improvement to create a competitive edge, not because I want a better grade.

It is a common plight of HR to feel the need to prove itself. When linkage analysis overly focuses on "proving" the relationship between engagement and business outcomes ("See! The relationship exists!"), HR becomes susceptible to the panacea predicament that Brooks and Saltzman describe. When HR over-relies on the demonstration of a linkage, other functions hear that engagement is the answer

to every problem and may tune out HR's voice. If those same functions are prone to turning those results into a causal versus correlational debate, HR's seat at the strategic table can diminish.

It is my experience, having sat within two functions (HR and marketing), that the most successful linkage conversations about engagement are not framed around "Is there a relationship?" but instead around "What is the nature of the relationship?"

One way Starwood Hotels & Resorts has been successful in this regard is by aligning its metrics (e.g., employee survey, customer survey, mystery inspections, social media, etc.). Contextualizing performance is done by defining and reporting scores across metrics in relation to their impact to one another and, ultimately, business performance. By integrating the strengths of the methodologies and designs of each tool, engagement data

> Engagement scores are no longer relegated to the annual event of when reports are distributed ... Action plans have become more holistic with data informing the how, not defining the what. The conversation has changed.

is reviewed and discussed in the same breath as other metrics. Consequently, engagement scores are no longer relegated to the annual event of when reports are distributed and action plans have moved away from "improve engagement scores." Action plans have become more holistic with the data informing the how, not defining the what. The conversation has changed.

Matt Valenti is the director of global market research at Starwood Hotels & Resorts Global. He is a business partner with a reputation for turning data into credible, confident actions. ▪▪

LEARNING GUIDE

Point Counterpoint II: 1.4

The Role of Strategy and Employee Engagement

DISCOVERY QUESTIONS

- What are you dealing with in your organization today that relates to this content area?
- How does your organization use employee engagement surveys? Is there a better way?
- To what degree is your HR department involved in setting organizational strategy?
- What suggestions might you have for the redesign of your engagement survey?

SELECTED FACTS

- What new facts that were presented got your attention?
- Employee engagement requires the ability to show results beyond increased motivation.
  › Purpose, values, and mission help organizations create meaning and motivation.
  › The best strategy is only as good as its implementation.
  › Confidence plus ambitious targets generate positive energy.
  › Aligning with business strategy and a focus on implementation drive results.

KEY DISCUSSION POINTS

- What were the key points being made in this presentation?
- What are the three characteristics of strategy?
- Is employee engagement a logical strategy?
- How can employee surveys be made more strategic?
- What is the difference between measuring "How I feel inside" vs. "What I see outside"?
- How does Binder describe the key role of effective, sustained execution?
- How might engagement be the result of performance, rather that the reason for it?
- According to Slaaen, what are two implications for HR and engagement survey design?
- How did Starwood Hotels and Resorts incorporate their engagement results with the business?
- How is the conversation about employee engagement changing?

REVIEW OF SOLUTIONS

- Identify two to three big Ideas worthy of exploring in your organization.
- Could your organization use the Starwood approach to integrating engagement and business results?

IDENTIFYING THE PARADOX

- How is it that a solution appropriate for yesterday's organization is no longer valid?
- Consider how very different perspectives might be correct given different situations.
- What are the potential downsides of putting a major focus on engagement surveys?

LEARNING OUTCOMES

- What one new piece of information did you learn that will be important to you in the future?
- Identify one thing that you will do differently based on what you learned.

PART 2:
LEADERSHIP AND
TALENT DEVELOPMENT

Developing the Right Leadership Skills

By Marc Sokol

The more our world continues to change, the more we should expect new skills to emerge in response. Some of these skills will surely provide new sources of competitive advantage to companies. Leaders who display these skills or martial them amongst their teams will achieve success, especially in contrast to those who fail to adapt and change.

What if you could predict which skills will emerge and make the greatest difference?

What if you could create an environment where such skills would emerge?

In our lead Perspective, **Bob Johansen** and **Alessandro Voto**, from the Institute for the Future, invite us to think about the consequences of a future that will be increasingly volatile, uncertain, complex and ambiguous (VUCA). They describe five skills that will emerge and significantly reset the playing field. Those who overlook these opportunities may find themselves hopelessly behind.

Four commentaries build on Johansen and Voto's ideas. Three are from Senior Human Resources executives, each of whom work at the front lines our changing world. A fourth commentary is from a college president who describes an environment where leaders of the future can develop the potential to see and respond to the trends emerging around us.

Bob Morrissey of Campbell Soup Company reminds us that disruptive forces also emerge from within organizations, often by design. Agility and innovation in human resources services are but two of the hallmarks of an integrated response by senior executives.

Alison Horner of Tesco shares her observation that effective response to a VUCA world will come from coalitions, both inside and outside orga-

nizations. These coalitions won't just wait for problems to appear; rather the members of these coalitions will collaborate to articulate and shape the challenges they face, and then compete through the combination of skills, technology, and new organizational capabilities.

Mary Tilley of W.L. Gore expands on the Lead Perspective, noting that it is not just the emergence of skills upon which we should be focus; it is the melding of people with different skills that drives competitive advantage. The true power of diversity is realized by leveraging combinations of people and teams to ensure they contain the skills required for success.

David Anderson, president of St. Olaf College, provides our final commentary. As we contemplate the potential of a VUCA world and the emergence of new skills, Anderson reminds us that college settings in present day can already foster development of and practice using the very skills we expect

to make a difference in the future.

If you think the future of your organization requires new skills, new ways of working, and novel solutions, then this issue of Perspectives is for you.

Marc Sokol is Perspectives editor.

Leadership Skills to Thrive in the Future

By Bob Johansen and Alessandro Voto

Traditional leadership skills are not sufficient to weather an increasingly volatile, uncertain, complex, and ambiguous (VUCA)[1] world. Human resource professionals will need to consider the external future forces that will disrupt their organization and identify new capabilities that will enable success in the VUCA World.

Leaders Make the Future introduces 10 future leadership skills that build the resilience necessary to engage with the VUCA World. The use of these skills has implications for how organizations more successfully compete in the context of a hyperconnected and values-based world.

HR leaders have a chance to get ahead of the talent curve by anticipating future skills—not just evaluating people by traditional measures. For example, a large manufacturing corporation led by engineers is now recruiting bio-engineers based on their understanding of the importance of bio-empathy (see graphic below). Similarly, enlightened HR organizations realize that social networking skills in online worlds will be just as important for leaders as their in-person skills.

Five Skills that Provide Competitive Advantage in a VUCA World

To stimulate this conversation in Perspectives, we highlight five of these skills. The most basic of the leadership skills is the **Maker Instinct,** the inner urge that we all have to build or grow things. What's new is not the urge to make. What's new is the ability to create communities of makers for much larger impacts. Maker instinct can empower leaders to rethink current ways of doing

business and seed new innovations. Human resources professionals can encourage this type of creativity by providing spaces or groups where new approaches to business problems can be brought to life in interesting ways, without the pressures of top-down approval.

Clarity is the ability to see through messes and contradictions to a future that others cannot yet see. It is about effectively communicating goals, but being very flexible in the approach used to achieve those goals. The military, police, and fire services refer to clarity as "commander's intent." What wins in the VUCA world is to be very clear where you are going (that's clarity or commander's intent), but very flexible about how you get there.

Often, the challenges of the VUCA World will not have a clear solution, requiring another skill called **Dilemma Flipping.** Such wicked problems cannot be solved, but can be flipped into interesting ways forward.

Foresight helps leaders see the options. One such dilemma is the explosion of services that allow work to be broken down into smaller microtasks. Microtasking presents new opportunities for flexible work, while threatening to undermine traditional concepts of long-term work and consistent employment. Human resources leaders will have to flip this dilemma to find the best middle ground between job stability and adap-

tive teams, depending upon the values of the company and the tasks at hand. Looking 10 years ahead, the bad news is that there will be fewer traditional jobs and lower job security. The good news is that workers will have more flexibility and more ways to make a living.

To make the most out of micro-

> By aligning human resources with the coming waves of change, and by developing new leadership skills to engage with this change, organizations will be in a better position to envision a future worth making.

tasking and collective work in general, human resource professionals will have to develop a skill called **Smart Mob Organizing.** Originally coined by Howard Rheingold, "smart mobs" refer to groups of people brought together for a business or social change purpose, making savvy use of available media. By channeling the energy of many into a productive goal, empowered and am-

10 FUTURE LEADERSHIP SKILLS

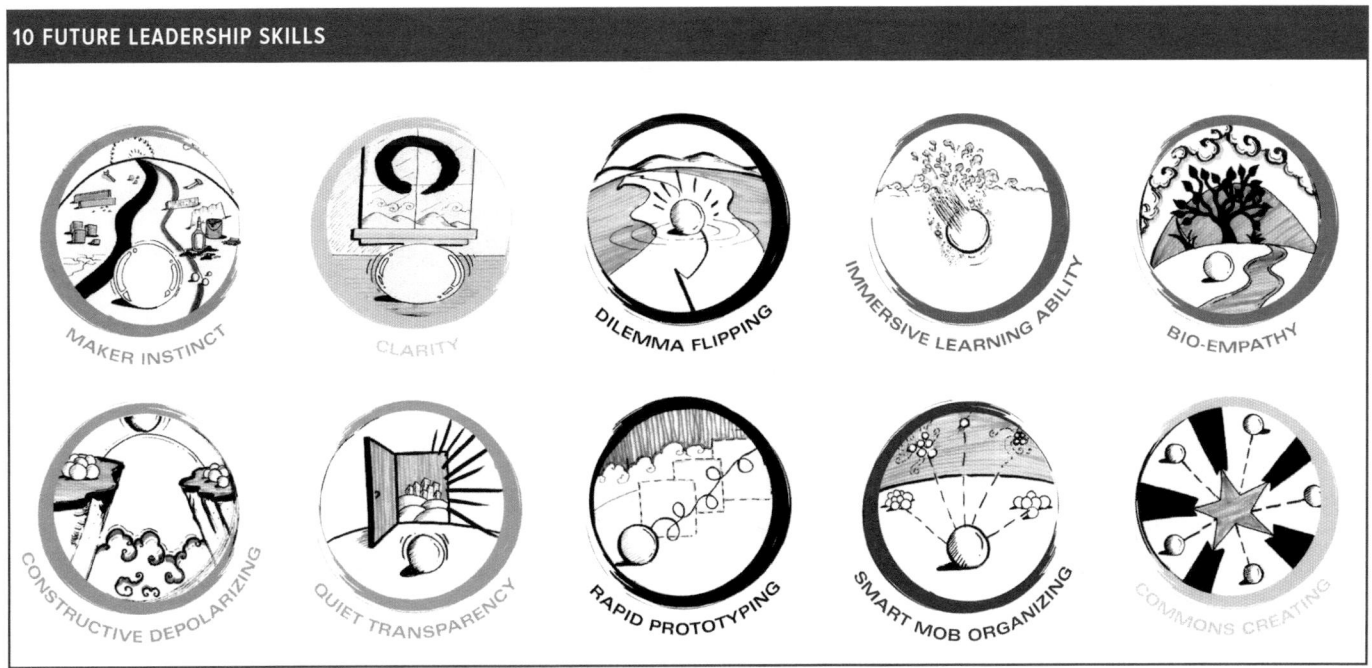

MAKER INSTINCT
CLARITY
DILEMMA FLIPPING
IMMERSIVE LEARNING ABILITY
BIO-EMPATHY
CONSTRUCTIVE DEPOLARIZING
QUIET TRANSPARENCY
RAPID PROTOTYPING
SMART MOB ORGANIZING
COMMONS CREATING

plified by media platforms, the human resources function can help foster organizational capacity to solve pressing business and societal issues in an adaptive way, while still using minimal resources.

Bio-empathy refers to the ability for leaders to sympathize with the principles of nature, and to take the interconnected, systematic metaphor presented by natural systems to reorganize and guide effective teams. These teams can

> We also must be prepared to lead when volatility, uncertainty, complexity and ambiguity arise from within the organization itself.

build upon one another in a symbiotic way, even reaching outside of the organization for support. Often this will take pooled resources available to many, rather than a hording approach that shuts off other interdependent parts of the system that can support new partnerships and businesses.

To create these pooled resources, leaders need to develop the most complex and challenging leadership skill, **Commons Creating.** Commons creating is the ability to make common cause with others for mutual benefit through sharing of assets. Human resource leaders can think about new ways to connect human consciousness, data, and physical resources to enable success at the individual and collective level.

The present can be paralyzing without a long-view perspective on the future. By aligning human resources with the coming waves of change, and by developing new leadership skills necessary to engage with this change, organizations will be in a better position to envision a future worth making. The Human Resources field has a wonderful name that has often been referred to as only "HR," a term that doesn't always command great respect. You should proudly announce that you are from "human...resources," with a pause for emphasis. Human resources

will be profoundly important in the VUCA World of the future.

Reference

[1]Johansen R. (2012). Leaders Make the Future: *Ten New Leadership Skills for an Uncertain World*, San Francisco: Berrett-Koehler Publishers.

Bob Johansen is a Distinguished Fellow at the Institute for the Future, and author of *Leaders Make the Future: Ten New Leadership Skills for an Uncertain Age.*

Alessandro Voto is a research assistant at the Institute for the Future.

Leading Culture through Times of Organizational Change

By Bob Morrissey

As important as it is for leaders to guide their organizations through disruptive external forces, we also must be prepared to lead when volatility, uncertainty, complexity and ambiguity arise from within the organization

> Our cultural evolution... has required agility, innovation, and creativity.

itself. Leadership changes, business performance, reorganizations, divestitures and acquisitions can stress an organization's culture. But with a clear strategy and a strong human resources partnership, we can adapt to changing times and cultivate the talent our organizations need to deliver positive business outcomes.

In 2011, Denise Morrison became CEO of Campbell Soup Company and implemented a new strategic framework called Focus Forward—a plan designed to deliver sustainable growth. To deliver on that strategy,

we needed to create a culture of high performance; so we've engaged our leaders and developed a systematic approach across the organization, driving cultural alignment by pulling four strategic "levers": company strategy; leaders and organization; symbols and rituals; and people processes.

Creating clarity around our Company Strategy was the first step toward engaging employees in the evolution of our high-performance culture. We articulated our desired outcome—"to drive sustainable, profitable net sales growth"—and what we needed to do to get there: strengthen our core business and expand into higher-growth spaces.

We also needed to have the right people in the right roles, not only to deliver results, but to lead others. Strengthening our marketing function by hiring our first chief marketing officer in 2012 is just one of the changes we've made to Campbell's leaders and organization, and it directly supports one of the focal points of our strategy: putting our consumer first in everything we do.

The "consumer first" mindset was brought to the center of a revised Campbell Leadership Model, which was also updated to support decision making and owning results. The evolution of our Symbols and Rituals—key cultural elements that act as behavioral anchors at Campbell—also included adding "courage" as a core company value.

Finally, we've changed important people processes to emphasize our employees' focus on our business success. One such change is a new performance management approach, designed to give employees a framework and the motivation to set ambitious objectives and deliver more meaningful outcomes.

Our cultural evolution at Campbell has required agility, innovation, and creativity by rethinking the way we deliver human resources services. We still have much more work to do, but I'm encouraged by our progress.

Bob Morrissey is senior vice president and chief human resources officer of Campbell Soup Company.

The Role of Leadership in a VUCA World

By Alison Horner

It is obvious to see but harder to copy how winning organizations—soccer teams, gangs, or global corporations—end to have at least one thing in common. For me this is the overlap between the goals and values of the organization, those of its members and often other stakeholders too. Sometimes the team comes together by bringing in new players, but more often it is the result of leading existing players better.

For a business like Tesco, with 525,000 colleagues across 12 countries connecting with millions of customers every day, shared advocacy of our brand is our biggest prize. As personnel director, my purpose is to help 5,000 leaders improve the business for customers, live the values, and take people with them. We've seen rapid growth of some organizations to become giants in their sectors like Tesco, IBM, Apple, and Microsoft, because everyone marches to the same tune to get results, and everyone is pointing in the same direction.

At the same time, at Tesco we recognize ourselves to be in a time of elevated risk as we navigate from bricks and mortar to multichannel retailing. This awareness has led to the introduction of Blinkbox, our digital media business, and of Hudl, through which we share scale and knowhow with partners (sometimes ours and sometimes theirs) as in China with CRE, or in coffee with Harris and Hoole. Ongoing innovation such as this requires widespread leadership to ensure execution.

In a VUCA world we need leaders who not only share the "commander's intent," but can also make sense of it in the context of their changing environment. For Tesco, this means leaders who have their eyes wide open—not waiting to be told what to do. This is a big cultural change for traditional management hierarchies like ours. It will take years, not months, and starts with us as leaders. To help we've introduced five new leadership skills—collaboration, empathy, responsiveness, resilience and innovation. Rather than "teach" in the normal way, we've asked leaders to make sense of these skills for themselves. They also need to leverage social and digital communication for connecting and sharing what they learn.

Increasingly, success will be more about teams and leaders coming together as coalitions outside traditional hierarchies, either within organizations, outside them, or across their boundaries. They need to find common problems and co-create solutions. The big successful businesses of tomorrow will have to find the time and space to seed new businesses from within and equip their leaders to do it

Alison Horner is group head, human resources for Tesco.

Can Anyone Really Have All The Leadership Skills Needed?

By Mary Tilley

Leadership skills have been debated and discussed for decades. What's really changing in this increasingly VUCA world and how will we deal with it?

It is difficult to find and develop leaders with all the skills we need today. This will be even more difficult in the future as skills need to sharpen and new skills need to be developed. We will less and less be able to rely on an individual to have all the skills we

> The more effective recipe is to create leadership teams that are made up of very talented people with very different skills.

need. I believe leadership teams are the answer. In my team-based organization, we rarely rely on a single leader, but build complimentary leadership teams throughout our organization, even at the highest levels. Throughout time, the best leaders have surrounded themselves with advisors and often this is invisible to the organization. By making it visible and expected, we can be more deliberate in ensuring the right combination is in place.

In our current paradigm of the single leader, we are so often trying to develop a skill that is not there or just accepting that it's not there and living with the consequences. Some of the most visionary leaders have no visible interest or capability to connect and empathize. If we keep expecting them to develop that skill, then we will be waiting forever, or we will shortchange the organization. These incredibly

talented individuals see the complex issues, analyze them, and imagine and see where things can go. However, when they cannot connect with people, either directly or through inspiring messages, they can be disastrous to the organization and important goals are never achieved. Some of the most empathetic and connected leaders are great translators, but they can't see the future as clearly or sort through the external factors as effectively. If we keep expecting them to develop that, we'll get the same result—waiting or shortchanging.

The more effective recipe is to create leadership teams that are made up of very talented people with very different skills. This does require a shift in paradigm—a successful climb to the top may not be a peak but a plateau that is shared.

Mary Tilley is human resources leader at W.L. Gore and Associates.

Where the Future Is Familiar

By David R. Anderson

What struck me most about the kind of workplace Johansen and Voto imagine in "Leadership Skills to Thrive in the Future" is its resemblance to the learning environment experienced by students today at good liberal arts colleges. Johansen and Voto forecast a world where leaders create "communities of makers"; where maximum flexibility reigns in pursuit of goals; where "smart mobs" form, dissolve, and re-form in response to particular needs; and where teams build on one another and share assets to achieve their goals.

Colleges are messy places, and—especially if you are a college president—that can be vexing some days. But it's mostly a good thing, especially if we want colleges to be preparing leaders who can thrive in the VUCA environment. "Messy" here means unscripted, adaptive, collaborative, informal, anti-hierarchical, and speculative.

The days of the "sage on a stage"

lecturing to students who then go to the library and study in solitude are mostly over. Learning has become a collaborative activity. Both in-class activities and out-of-class assignments

> The days of the "sage on a stage" lecturing to students who then go to the library and study in solitude are mostly over. Learning has become a collaborative activity.

tend to favor group work, and technology is key to enabling this learning environment, especially social media, which has accustomed students to a constant flow of inputs and the ability to engage with them 24/7.

Interviewers looking to identify those college graduates equipped with the tools to flourish in a VUCA environment should focus in an interview on prompts like, "Talk to me about a time you helped a group get past a roadblock in its thinking and what happened as a result." "Tell me about your experience in reaching outside your group to gather the resources you needed to meet your goal." "Tell me about a time when you had a clear vision of what needed to be accomplished but it took inputs from others to figure out the best way to get there."

Of course, not every idea is a good one, and not every thought needs or deserves to be expressed. Not all mobs are smart. At the end of the day, discipline and rigor will always be pre-requisites of effective leadership. But leaders looking to align human resources with what the authors predict to be "the coming waves of change," will be able to tap into the competencies, habits, and styles of well-prepared college graduates for whom a flexible, collaborative, less hierarchical, innovative workplace feels like home. ▪

David R. Anderson, Ph.D., is president of St. Olaf College.

LEARNING GUIDE

Point Counterpoint II: 2.1

Developing the Right Leadership Skills

DISCOVERY QUESTIONS

- What are you dealing with in your organization today that relates to this content area?
- How are organizations becoming more VUCA?
- Which of the skills described seem most familiar to you?
- Which of the skills described were most surprising to read about?
- Why might these skills be critical to employee success in the future?
- How might the skills described make for a more effective leader?
- How are HR leaders applying the VUCA concept in their own organizations?
- How do leadership, courage, and the consumer-first concepts fit together as described in the Campbell Soup commentary?

SELECTED FACTS

What new facts that were presented got your attention?

- VUCA stands for volatile, uncertain, complex, and ambiguous.
- The Maker Instinct is the urge to build or grow things.
- Clarity is the ability to see through messes and contradictions to see a future that other cannot yet see.
- Dilemma Flipping is the ability to see a problem from a different perspective.
- Smart Mob Organizing refers to groups of people brought together for a business or social change purpose, making use of social media and spontaneity.
- Bio-empathy is the ability of leaders to sympathize with the principles of nature, taking the interconnected systems metaphor of natural systems to reorganize and guide teams.
- Commons Creating is the ability to share assets and in the process create mutual benefit.

KEY DISCUSSION POINTS

- What were the key points being made in this presentation?
- What implications does a VUCA world have for Human Resources practices?
- What are the implications of a VUCA world for the autonomy and decision-making authority of front-line managers and employees?
- In what ways do you see classrooms and colleges as training grounds for the skills of the future?
- How might leadership teams be essential to the future?
- How might microtasking change the focus of human resources professionals?
- Why might the rise of microtasking require new skills to manage the workforce?
- If you were in charge of hiring, how would you assess capability and readiness to perform for these new skills?
- How would you score your team or company leadership against these new skills?
- What might be the risk to a company if leaders lack these skills in the future?
- How might you develop some of these skills on the job?
- Which of the skills for the future seem most important to the workplace today?
- Which skills for the future seem most different from the workplace today?
- One of the commentary authors makes the observation regarding smart mobs that not all mobs are smart. What does he mean by that?

REVIEW OF SOLUTIONS

Identify two to three "big ideas" worthy of exploring in your organization.

- What are the key skills you believe leaders need to develop for the future?
- Which of the skills described by the authors seem most important to you?
- Which skills seem easiest to develop?

- Which of the skills are you better off to hire for because they are harder to develop?
- What do trial and error, experimentation, and failure have to do with developing skills like the ones described?

IDENTIFYING THE PARADOX

- How is it that a solution appropriate for yesterday's organization is no longer valid?
- Consider how very different perspectives might be correct given different situations.
- How might the skills for the future seem inconsistent with today's world of work?
- Why might colleges, as training grounds for the future of work, provide opportunities to develop skills that are harder to develop in organizations?
- Mary Tilley, HR Leader of Gore Associates, argues that no leader can do it all, and they need to be part of leadership teams. What might be the contradiction of leaders looking to a team of leaders? How might this make any one leader even more effective?
- How can college environments be both "messy places" and places that foster development of leadership skills?

LEARNING OUTCOMES

- What one new piece of information did you learn that will be important to you in the future?
- Identify one thing that you will do differently based on what you learned.
- Which of these new skills do you already possess, and how have you used them to be effective in the past?
- Which of these new skills do you most want to develop and how might you do that?
- How can college experience help prepare people for less hierarchical and more innovative workplaces?

Leaders Building Leaders

By Marc Sokol

One of the greatest tests of executive leadership is how a person manages competing values. Good leaders recognize the reality of competing values; great leaders guide their company and culture to embrace competing values in a productive manner.

In our lead Perspective, **Tan Chong Meng**, Group CEO of PSA, headquartered in Singapore, describes the yin and yang of nurturing talent to help guide a multinational enterprise. He writes of context and process and complementary approaches to talent management, and the role senior leadership plays in setting the tone for both.

In the commentaries that follow, four senior executives share their own stories in response to Chong Meng's perspective.

David Small of McDonald's describes how values, even in a successful global firm, can become unbalanced. He then shares leadership's efforts to restore the dynamic tension that allows the enterprise to thrive.

Mike Henry of BHP Billiton points out that as we seek to balance process and context, we must remember that even context is context dependent. Each company must decipher the unique context that contributes to the competing values they need to embrace and manage.

Ritchie Bent of Jardine Matheson puts the yin and yang of nurturing talent into practice as he describes the history of leadership development initiatives across his firm. As their executives develop, they discover first-hand the yin and yang of their own experience as executives in development.

In our final commentary, **Varun Bhati**, former CHRO of Levi Strauss & Company, expands the discussion, encouraging us to see that the yin and

yang of nurturing talent requires we attend to the paradox of present capabilities and future talent, as well as the paradox of being broad and specific in our focus.

If you believe the best executive leaders nurture talent, and that doing so is a skilled balancing act of competing organizational values, then this installment of *Perspectives* is for you.

Marc Sokol, Ph.D., is Perspectives editor.

POINT

The Yin and Yang of Nurturing Talent

By Tan Chong Meng

While it is widely acknowledged that talent is key to the success of an enterprise, there is divergence on how talent is best nurtured. Some companies even

create a sense of chaos when they focus on talent development, only to abruptly shift focus to achieving performance and business results, as they reset to success of the enterprise. Let's take a look at the interplay between the nuturing of talent and the success of the enterprise.

I believe that two forces need to be in balance, which I will refer to as yin and yang, borrowing from the Chinese philosophy of life forces which complement each other for harmony. Indeed the belief is that the forces give rise to each other as they interrelate to one another. It is impossible to talk about one force without reference to the other, and when one force reaches its peak, it will naturally transform into the other. An example of this in nature is how plants achieve full bloom in summer ("yang"), produce seeds, and die back in winter ("yin"), while retaining the essence of life for the next cycle.

Yin, for this column, is about *setting the context*, while yang refers to *the process for nurturing talent.* The objective of good yin is to inspire, and the objective of sound yang is to liberate and transform.

Setting the context (yin) involves people having clarity to questions such as, "What is the company's purpose and values?" and "Is there a strong, widely shared vision?" Having the right yin is important for aligning direction and enabling appropriate autonomy. As management consultant and author Stephen Bungay aptly writes in his book, *The Art of Action*, "what we need is not more details but more clarity; not tighter control but better direction … giving people freedom of action within defined boundaries."

A process for nurturing talent (yang) is required to complement yin, and involves addressing questions such as, "Are performance expectations clear and properly managed?" "Is the organization designed to enable individual and team excellence?" "Do leaders prioritize personal and professional growth?" There are many good examples of yang in companies, often shared and adopted because the processes are attractive and seemingly effective.

At PSA, we strive to achieve a yin-yang balance. Our most recent employee opinion poll shows very encouraging results from a 90 percent participation base. "confidence in the leadership" and "satisfaction with the company" were each a full step higher, with significant improvements in "clarity in the organization's direction" and "clarity of individual's role in PSA's mission."

These results reflect our actions over the last two years to lift yin and yang simultaneously. We did this by reshaping our group vision and strategy, a process that was led by a team from two levels of leadership, thus ensuring alignment while executive knowledge and creativity were being tapped. This then cascaded through multiple engagement forums, providing interplay of leadership summits, townhalls and global webcasts, and covering cross-sections of the organization, emphasizing our purpose and direction. At these engagements, a discussion on talent development is in-

variably included, and our group HR leader speaks to the group strategy on talent matters.

Another example of yin-yang in balance occurs at the PSA leadership level, and can be seen in how we deliberately include selected senior vice presidents (SVPs) in our Senior Management Council (SMC) meetings. The SMC is the highest execu-

> At many companies, this top table is the preserve of the management club, but at PSA, we capitalize on it as an engagement and personal development opportunity.

tive decision-making body in PSA. At many companies, this top table is the preserve of the management club, but at PSA, we capitalize on it as an engagement and personal development opportunity. This provides for better formulation and traction with top-table decisions, while enabling personal and professional growth of the SVPs. In 2012, we had SVPs in global commercial and global strategy join the top table meetings, and in 2013, SVPs from global HR and global strategy were on board.

When people are comfortable with both the yin and the yang of the enterprise, it means there is clarity on where they are going as an enterprise, and by association, their own career destiny. They feel supported by talent processes that are in alignment with the business. And when people embrace such clarity, and feel supported and valued in the process, it never fails to inspire, liberate, and transform their spirit. Success of the enterprise cannot be far behind.

The right choice of yin and yang depends on the company's situation, but what is always important is that it attracts serious attention and commitment at the executive level. Too often

we fall into the trap of leaving yin, yang, or the balance or yin and yang to sub-teams that must operate outside of the mainstream of enterprise priorities. Maintaining the balance of yin-yang forces requires time and deliberate effort on the part of senior management.

Many companies are already excellent in yin or yang, but it is the ones who have learned to harmonize the two that will triumph in the long run. Perhaps it is time to give heed to the wisdom of the ancient, and bring order to the chaos of nurturing talent.

Tan Chong Meng is Group CEO of PSA, a multinational company headquartered in Singapore.

When Competing Values Are Out of Balance: The True Test of Leadership

By David Small

Tan Chong Meng's discussion of yin and yang implies a thoughtful balance of competing forces, something seasoned leaders aspire to achieve. But what happens when unanticipated business conditions significantly change this precarious balance?

Seismic shifts in technology, consumer tastes, competition, and other macroeconomic trends are having a significant impact on the balance of key priorities at McDonald's. If attention is not continually paid to the balance of these dynamics, results can suffer and employee engagement can be challenged. During such times, senior leadership teams have to not only reexamine the business strategy, but also be ready to evolve the organizational culture to rebalance the focus on all key values.

Too Much of a "Good" Thing

At McDonald's, "operational excellence" has been at the heart of our culture and success, resulting in high quality standards and consistency of restaurant operations across the globe. The ability to scale the business in a way that assures efficient and consistent restaurant operations has been a hallmark of our success for almost 60 years.

Given that our business has been predisposed to growing leadership talent from within, it is no surprise that many business leaders came up through the operations side of the business and naturally view the busi-

At McDonald's, "operational excellence" has been at the heart of our culture and success, resulting in high quality standards and consistency of restaurant operations across the globe.

ness through that lens.

We have also seen that when the business becomes too enamored with operations and an operations culture begins to permeate the business, a focus on the customer and consumer preferences becomes secondary. When

the precarious balance between a maniacal focus on the customer and operations excellence tips towards operations, we inevitably see a decline in business results.

Restoring the Right Balance

To re-establish balance we are seizing upon opportunities to identify, select, and develop leaders who have demonstrated the ability to lead a customer-driven culture while balancing the need for driving operations excellence.

For internal leaders, we focus on providing more cross-functional development experiences in marketing, consumer and business insights, and finance, along with significant "outside-in" exposure and experiences. Our strategy is also to bring in more key leaders from outside of McDonald's who have effectively led customer-driven businesses and have demonstrated the knowledge and ability to balance a fanatical focus on the customer with high levels of execution and operations excellence.

Our goal is to bring the dynamic tension between operations and customer-focus back into balance: operational excellence needs to be an enabler of a customer-driven culture and not the driver itself. The true test of leadership will be the way we monitor and embrace competing values and guide the enterprise to keep them in balance even as the world changes around us.

David Small is vice president, global talent and leadership development, McDonald's Corporation.

Even Context is Context Dependent

By Mike Henry

Tan Chong Meng's message resonates

with me as it speaks to the journey that my company has been on for the past decade.

BHP Billiton is the world's largest diversified resources company, with a market capitalization of $180 billion and 110,000 employees and contractors in approximately 60 operations across 14 countries. A number of years ago, we embarked on an ambitious effort to transform the company, including our structures, systems, processes, and leadership. We needed an operating model that would help us better meet the challenges of scale, growth, and market volatility, and would support our ability to achieve consistently high levels of operational and financial performance.

We restructured, streamlining accountabilities and standardizing structures and roles. We distilled our centrally determined controls to focus on those that are truly critical, and in doing so devolved decision making as close as possible to where the work was occurring. We redefined the way people work, deploying a standard suite of imperative work processes. We implemented a company-wide, end-to-end, standard enterprise resource planning system, which would both lock-in these processes as well as provide us with performance transparency, enabling the identification and replication of best practices across the group.

Context Is Unique to Each Organization and Its People

Having established this platform—seeing our people contributing to their maximum potential and having them come together in a powerful way—we recognized that it was important that we provide them with context, and the more personally relevant we could make that context the more positively they would be engaged and the more effective they could be. This started with recognizing that the setting of context is in itself context dependent. The context that engages different individuals in the organization will vary depending on their roles, their personal drivers, and their environment, which is in many instances dynamic.

We have increased the direct engagement of our senior leaders, from the CEO on down. We have invested effort in reshaping the central narrative in a way intended to make it more relevant, understandable, and uplifting for those in the field. We are also investing in the leadership development required to ensure that our field leaders are able to effectively engage their direct teams with directly relevant context.

A key element in our approach is to undertake objective surveys that assess our employee engagement. Correlation of survey outcomes with operational and financial performance

> Seeing our people contributing to their maximum potential and having them come together in a powerful way, we recognized that it was important that we provide them with context, and the more personally relevant we could make that context the more positively they would be engaged and the more effective they could be.

helps us to identify where context is being set and helps ensure that our employees are engaged in a way that unlocks their potential and improves performance.

The early signs of our efforts are positive. Our trends are moving in the right direction, and we are seeing concurrent improvement in our operational and financial performance as well. To quote Tan Chong Meng, "When people embrace such clarity, feeling supported and valued in the process, it never fails to inspire, liberate, and transform their spirit. Success of the enterprise cannot be far behind."

Mike Henry is president HSE, marketing, and technology for BHP Billiton.

Balancing Yin and Yang in Executive Development

By Ritchie Bent

The 1997 Asian Economic Crisis came as rude awakening for many businesses in the region. Up until that point, most companies had experienced several years of uninterrupted growth. The crisis changed all that. Many companies were at a complete loss as to what to do.

My own company, Jardines, was no exception. The crisis became the catalyst for an initiative that was to significantly change our approach to executive development. Tan Chong Meng's "yin" (context) and "yang" (process) balance proved to be a critical factor in that change.

Until then, executive development had rarely extended beyond the VP level. The core development model of "diagnose–develop–apply" had survived the test of time, and was into its tenth year. Development centers, executive education, and managed projects comprised the model's core components.

Embedding Yin and Yang within Executive Development

The challenge facing the group was how to get complacent boards to think beyond basic cost rationalization. The answer lay in "live" case studies, designed to open the mind and engender a can-do attitude. Birth of the Director Development Initiative (DDI) was the outcome. The DDI is now in its 14th year, with more than 160 managing and senior directors having visited more than 200 CEOs across the world.

Tan Chong Meng's context operates at two levels: Firstly, identifying the specific needs of each participant's business, underpinned by the individual's personal needs to achieve these outcomes. Identification of needs and alignment of goals are achieved through structured interviews, with both the participants and their bosses. The findings then form the DDI's focus (the theme and nature of companies to visit), strategic business change projects, and individual coaching agendas.

Having gained agreement from companies for a visit (typically up to 20 in two different countries), the process then consists of three stages: a one-day

> In the new world of the cloudsourcing and crowdsourcing, the talent pool has expanded dramatically.

"tune-in"session, in which up to a maximum of 10 participants are given two companies to analyze. Next, two-week overseas visits to targeted companies with review and tune-in sessions at the end of each day.

Accountability for Learning and Progress

Three months later, participants report back to the Holding Company Board, in the form of a CEO Forum. This is where the rubber meets the road: Participants are required to show what their projects have achieved so far and intend to achieve in the next three months.

Today, Jardines is a $61 billion Fortune 500 company, with more than 400,000 employees. A cursory look at the Group's performance shows that significant growth in profitability and share price began in 2000. Many think the DDI has played a role in that.

Through DDI, participants discover the yin and yang of development: how to keep learning both personal and group oriented; how to link insight to action; how to identify strategic business needs that set the context for external benchmarking; and how to embed the temporary experience of a development program into the longer-term mindset of an executive.

Ritchie Bent is group head of human resources at Jardine Matheson Limited.

Should We Nurture Talent or Capability?

By Varun Bhatia

The age-old issue of focus on what matters most haunts us more than ever before. We have more information and more challenges and opportunities presented to us on an almost daily basis. With this daily assault, the here and now is as important as the long term. We must also remember that the long term is not that long off, as anyone who is trying to plan beyond three years is wasting precious "today" resources for a very uncertain tomorrow. We live in a constantly and rapidly changing business, social, and economic climate. The big question is, "How do you prepare for the unknown and clearly address the rapidly moving target of nurturing talent?"

The way established blue-chip companies manage talent needs to change. We can't just think of the context of the company and put people processes in place in line to nurture and grow talent. Rather, we need to take a look at the broader context of the external environment; we need to think of talent much more broadly, while at the same time being much narrower in our focus on what specifically we need to address for immediate and mid-term business and capability needs. When it comes to talent, we need to see the yin and yang of present and future, just as we need to see the yin and yang of being broad and focused.

Ensuring Talent in a Transformed World

In the new world of cloudsourcing and crowdsourcing, the talent pool has expanded dramatically. Along with that, our choices have also exploded exponentially. In this broader context, we need to be nurturing not talent, but capability. We need to think of the core competency that we need to *have* and not necessarily the one we need to grow. Companies cannot afford to

sacrifice present performance to nurture talent for the future, nor can they afford to sacrifice the future while meeting current demands.

To enable future talent and current capability in this transformed world of ours, we need to have a core of high-potential leaders who are targeted for enterprise-wide crucible roles that have high business impact and high complexity. We have to make disproportionate levels of investments in their development and involve them in pivotal issues and projects as part of ongoing growth.

> We live in a constantly and rapidly changing business, social, and economic climate. The big question is, "How do you prepare for the unknown and clearly address the rapidly moving target of nurturing talent?"

We should also supplement organizations with a strong entry-level talent program so there is a core pipeline of talent that will bring with it the new external reality and be willing to challenge the status quo.

For the middle of the organization, we have to consider external crowdsourcing capabilities supplemented with a few critical number of middle managers. In light of that, nurturing talent takes on a totally different meaning, as the focus is now on building capabilities with rapid return and not just for the far-off future.

The yin and yang of talent becomes the inherent contradiction of going very broad with securing capabilities using crowdsourcing to focusing acutely on building talent in enterprise-wide crucible roles and having a robust entry-level talent pipeline. ▪

Varun Bhatia is former CHRO, Levi Strauss Company.

LEARNING GUIDE

Point Counterpoint II 2.2

Leaders Building Leaders

DISCOVERY QUESTIONS

- What are you dealing with in your organization today that relates to this content area?
- How well does your organization do in setting both the yin and the yang? Examples?
- In your organization, how much focus is on Business Operations vs. on the Customer?
- Would a program such as Jardine's DDI be effective in your organization? Why?
- How well does your organization balance current capability and future talent? Examples?

SELECTED FACTS

- What new facts that were presented got your attention?
- Yin is about setting the context, and yang is about the process for nurturing talent.
- The objective of good Yin is to inspire; and of Yang is to liberate and transform.
- McDonald's has been focused of "operational excellence" for over 60 years.
- BHP Billiton is the world's largest diversified resources company with 110,000 employees.
- Jardine's is a $61 billion company with more than 400,000 employees.

KEY DISCUSSION POINTS

- What were the key points being made in this presentation?
- What behaviors should leaders show in order to properly set the yin?
- What behaviors should leaders show in order to properly set the yang?
- How does PSA use their Senior Management Council meetings?
- Why would McDonald's have such a strong focus on "operational excellence"?
- At BHP Billiton, what does it mean to "provide context" and that it is "context dependent"?
- How would you describe Jardine's model of "diagnose—develop—apply"?
- What are examples of yin and yang within Jardine's DDI program?
- What does Levi's refer to when talking about the yin and yang of present and future?
- How does Levi's approach talent at the top, middle, and bottom of the organization?

REVIEW OF SOLUTIONS

- Identify two to three "big ideas" worthy of exploring in your organization.
- What are some of the things that PSA did to raise both yin and yang?
- What is the balance that McDonald's is now trying to achieve?
- What are the key elements of Jardine's Director Development Initiative?
- What has Levi's done to stay "in balance"?

IDENTIFYING THE PARADOX

- How is it that a solution appropriate for yesterday's organization is no longer valid?
- Consider how very different perspectives might be correct given different situations.
- Are there some situations where it is advisable to focus more on either yin or yang?

LEARNING OUTCOMES

- What one new piece of information did you learn that will be important to you in the future?
- Identify one thing that you will do differently based on what you learned.
- How does the yin and yang concept affect you personally?

Debunking Talent Strategy Myths

By Marc Sokol

What if the strategies used by your company to develop global leaders turned out to be simply based on outdated myths? What if there was a better way, not necessarily one that was easier, but one that really made a difference in developing global leadership?

And what if competitive advantage of the firms in your industry ultimately came down to who does a better job developing global leaders?

Ángel Cabrera and **Gregory Unruh**, in our lead Perspective, examine three myths surrounding global leadership development and reveal the reality of each myth. Read carefully; in time their views will become the "new normal" of how we think about developing global leaders.

What do global leaders from around the world have to add to this lead Perspective? The commentaries that follow describe both personal and organizational lessons of experience in fostering global leadership.

> There is no global leadership without engaged global followership.

Leslie Joyce shares insights from 20 years at the front lines of leadership development. She has seen what works and what happens when companies try to get by without doing what is really required to develop global leaders.

Our second commentary comes from Istanbul, Turkey. In case you did not know, the Bosporus River runs through and divides this great city: on one side Istanbul is part of Europe, while the other side is part of Asia. **Alper Utku**, from the Management Centre Turkey,

describes the mindset one develops from working at the crossroads of two continents.

In our third commentary, **Michael Hardwick** and **Naomi Harrison** share stories of Australia's Cotton On Group; they have discovered ways to maintain the deep emotional connections of a family business, even as Cotton On has developed into a thriving global enterprise.

Yolanda Conyers provides the final commentary, writing about Lenovo, a Chinese firm intentionally fostering a global mindset. Yolanda reminds us that there is no global leadership without engaged global followership. Read on to see how leaders can embrace the diversity that surrounds us, while also forging common ground and alignment.

If you want to know what it looks like to execute against the goal of fostering global leadership, this issue of Perspectives is for you.

Marc Sokol is Perspectives editor.

Think Global, Act Local? Think Again

By Ángel Cabrera and Gregory Unruh

While globalization has brought the world to every manager's office door, persistent myths about how to prepare leaders for this reality are hindering executive development and ultimately organizational success. The fact is that leading successfully in the 21st century requires reaching across cultural divides, connecting with individuals who don't share our frames of reference, bringing together talent from disparate backgrounds, forging shared goals, and ultimately finding solutions that contribute to the well-being of diverse groups. Successful 21st century leaders think, act and lead globally; they are required to "be global."

Few managers educated in existing training institutes have the requisite skills for this complex challenge. And their organizations, by clinging to outdated beliefs, inhibit global leadership development. The statistics are discouraging. The United Nations Global Compact found that 76 percent of interviewed executives ranked global leadership development as critical for future success. But a separate study by the American Management (AMA) found only a third of companies have programs in place. While the reasons for this discrepancy are multifold, our work with executives indicates three outdated beliefs hinder organizational and individual thinking.

Myth 1: You Can Have a Successful Career without Being Global

Becoming global is hard work. It requires a commitment to challenging our long-held beliefs and exposing ourselves to very different worldviews over an extended period of time. It is understandable that established leaders hesitate in making such a commitment. Persistent myths enable managerial procrastination, especially the belief that you can still be a successful leader without developing global skills.

Global leadership is not just a necessity for internationally focused organizations; it also has become a requirement for domestic organizations for two reasons: diversity and social pressure.

First, domestic markets and work forces are becoming increasingly diverse. Today's leaders source components from overseas manufacturers in multiple locations, they take products to new markets with distinct cultural identities, they serve overseas customers, they participate in globally distributed design teams, they negotiate contracts, and they make deals with investors, partners and consumers around the world.

The second reason is that social pressures are demanding that organizations partner across sectors. Whether it is government sourcing services from the private sector or businesses partnering with NGOs to respond

to a complex social issue, leaders are increasingly finding themselves in situations that require reaching across sector-related cultural divides that can at times dwarf national boundaries. Interestingly, many of the same skills that foster cross-cultural leadership play out in cross-sector situations.

The reality is that managerial success or failure increasingly depends on understanding and managing the global forces and opportunities of today's worldwide marketplace. There is no "local" place to hide anymore.

Myth 2: Developing Cross Cultural Awareness is Global Leadership

We've all seen the typical foreign assignment preparation regimen. Take a Berlitz language class after work to learn how to say "Hello" and ask for directions to the taxi stand. Squeeze in a half-day seminar on if and when to offer a handshake to a foreign counterpart, and whether or not to cross your legs when sitting, and you're ready to go. These quaint remnants from the age of "cross-cultural awareness" and "international business" were only marginally successful in their time, but completely obsolete today.

Long gone are the days where it sufficed to train a few expatriates in the idiosyncrasies of a new overseas location. Cultural etiquette is simply not enough to prepare today's managers to navigate a multitude of contexts, not only abroad, but even at home. Becoming global is less about the surface behaviors and more about the way leaders think about themselves and "others." While information about other cultures can be acquired from books and training, the cognitive skills required to connect and collaborate globally most often come from transformational real-life experiences in global settings.

Developing global leadership skills requires approaches that may not fit well within traditional executive development models but may require a broader perspective. Investing in helping leaders develop global experiences in lower risk settings where they can build confidence and skill is not something most organizations consid-

er, let alone provide. Instead, becoming global is a "do-it-yourself" endeavor pursued by self-motivated employees, a situation guaranteed to ensure an ongoing dearth of global leaders.

Myth 3: You Can Think Globally, But Act Locally

The old mantra "think global, act local" is the most persistent myth of all. It is at a minimum an inadequate and, more realistically, a misleading description of today's leadership challenges. There is no local anymore. Local events have global repercussions. Global events, local repercussions: This is the definition of a global world.

These myths inhibit the ability of leadership programs to develop the set of competencies that our research

> Global leadership is not just a necessity for internationally focused organizations. It has become a requirement for domestic organizations as well.

revealed as core successful global leadership. In short, global leaders *connect, create* and *contribute* across boundaries. They connect with diverse individuals and organizations by showing cognitive flexibility, by continuously learning facts about multiple environments, and by building trusting relationships based on mutual respect, honesty and service. They create value sometimes by leveraging commonalities across contexts. Some examples include: 1) through market expansion; 2) by leveraging divergence across contexts; 3) through supply chain partnerships; and 4) by constructing value-adding networks—think Wikipedia. Finally, they create long-lasting solutions by finding ways to contribute to the needs of the multiple constituencies they interact with.

Fostering these global competencies among manawgers will demand new approaches to leadership development. They will need to become increasingly experiential and long term in focus. This will also make them more costly and complex. But successful global organizations will need their leaders to become global, so the pressure on development teams will only grow.

Ángel Cabrera, Ph.D., is president of George Mason University former president of the Thunderbird School of Global Management and Dean of IE Business School.

Gregory Unruh, Ph.D., is the Arison Group professor of Doing Good Values at George Mason University. They are the authors of *Being Global: How to Think, Act and Lead in a Transformed World.*

Global Leadership Development Requires Investment and Pervasiveness

By Leslie W. Joyce

After reading the Lead Perspective, my initial reaction was "what's new here, aren't we all doing this?" I then realized that my definition of "we" was restricted to successful global companies having faced the shortage of global leaders for at least two decades. My journey began in 1993 when I joined a multinational pharmaceutical company. Our business was entering countries where we had no leadership capability. During the last 20 years, we focused on building global leaders and learning hard lessons. Here are two that stand the test of time.

Lesson One: Developing successful global leaders takes time and money
In 1996, I learned the term "Factor 8." Anyone who wanted to run a global section of our business must have served in at least two functions, in at least two regions, and for at least two years. Factor 8 was the multiplier of 2 x 2 x 2 to achieve the minimum level of global

acumen we needed in our leaders. Only through such diversity and immersion could they truly learn to lead across boundaries and cultures. The essence of Factor 8 is that global leadership skills are best built and maintained by

> Everyone must understand the global business picture and be able to connect their local actions to that picture; they need to act "glocally," with local action that supports the global agenda.

ongoing leadership experiences in new situations.

As budgets tightened, leadership development was cut, expensive international assignments ended and we started looking for cheaper alternatives. We told ourselves that comprehensive leadership programs could be a cost-effective substitute for life experience. The fact that global leadership has remained a top concern of chief executive officers (CEOs) for the last eight to10 years is evidence that these programs are not.

Novelis, with $11 billion in annual revenue and 12,500 employees in 11 countries, is the world's leading producer of aluminum rolled products and the world leader in aluminum recycling. At Novelis, we are committed to developing truly global leaders. International assignments are core to that commitment. It is not an "either/or" tradeoff; it's a "both/and" strategy. To be successful, you need both experiences and education—assignments and programs—not one or the other.

Lesson Two: Think globally, act "glocally"
Globally integrated companies can achieve cost efficiencies not found in decentralized ones. In 2009, we launched "One Novelis," joining other global companies that realized "one-ness" can add competitive advantage. We knew the key was establishing "global mind-

set" for every employee, where everyone must be clear about his or her part of the global strategy. We started with the global/glocal distinction, and then quickly learned it was insufficient. We've settled on the notion of global/glocal: Everyone must understand the global business picture and be able to connect their local actions to that picture; they need to act "glocally," with local action that supports the global agenda.

In global leadership, as in life, the easy answer may be to see the world in terms of either/or tradeoffs, but the real opportunity is to persevere and discover the potential of both/and set of actions.

Leslie W. Joyce, Ph.D., is senior vice president and chief people officer for Novelis, Inc.

Global Leadership Calls for Collaboration as Opposed to Competition

By Alper Utku

Turkey stands as a cultural bridge between the Middle East and Europe, where it shares certain characteristics from each region.

I have worked as a leader, first in Turkey, and then across Europe, the Middle East and North Africa, primarily in the organizational development and consulting field. From a leadership perspective, I have observed Turkish managers focus more on relationships while European managers focus more on outcomes. In other words, in Turkey, your connections and networks matter the most. You are inseparable from your relationships. On the other hand, in Europe, outcome is critical so your track record matters more than whom you know. For many leaders, these assumptions are ingrained; they never consider that there could be a different reality for others.

Focus on developing and continuing relationships with many people requires extra work, but it also builds valuable re-

...in Turkey, your connections and networks matter the most. You are inseparable from your relationships.

lational capital for creating new possibilities over time. To illustrate this point, I would like to share some examples from my professional history. After 20 years, I still work with my first client in Turkey but in a different capacity. Not only do I still maintain contact with the alumni of my former business programs, we continue working together in different capacities as our careers and situations have evolved over time. The Lead Perspective position that global leaders must connect, create and contribute is deeply rooted within Turkish culture and our management approach, particularly in how we foster relationships.

Our faith in relationships takes us even further and allows us to cooperate with potential competitors. For example, our firm has been organizing a Human Resources Summit for the past 18 years; it has been open to our competitors from Turkey, Europe, the Middle East and North Africa with the clear intention of developing the once immature HR services market in Turkey. Today, the summit includes more than 100 of our competitors as exhibitors or sponsors who see the summit as a business development platform. Over time this has not only helped develop the HR services market in Turkey, but it has also become a forum for developing partnerships across our diverse backgrounds.

The summit has in fact become a global leadership development experience, a forum where providers and consumers from many cultures find common ground, even as they seek to showcase services and solutions that foster more effective organizations.

Alper Utku is the founding partner for Management Centre Türkiye (MCT). He has coauthored two books on organizational development and advises MCT clients on leadership development and organizational change.

Developing the Emotional Side of Global Leadership

By Michael Hardwick and Naomi Harrison

The Cotton On group is a global retailer established in 1991 as a small Australian family-run business. We've done some serious work during the past 20 years, expanding across the globe, now with a portfolio of 10 brands, more than 1,000 stores in 14 countries, and a workforce in excess

> From induction to executive level, our leadership programs require the partnership of a mentor to help each person make sense of a culturally different function or location.

of 17,000. We have no intention of slowing down. Our constant frame of thinking is how do we grow our global presence and also capture the Australian spirit, which is an essential part of our branding.

We agree with the Lead Perspective: To connect and collaborate globally often comes from transformational life experience in global settings, and although we did this unconsciously, it has become a significant part of our strategy, our storytelling and our ongoing development.

Very strong in the Cotton On culture is the emotional connection we feel toward our brands and our people. We invest significant time on the ground with our suppliers around the world. We like to have an innate understanding of their culture, systems and processes, and our mutual expectations of each other.

We also believe we have a duty to those less fortunate, which is why we created the Cotton On Foundation to empower youth in various sustainable projects around the world. One of those projects is the rebuilding of Mannya village in Uganda, which had been decimated by HIV/AIDS and had little hope for the future. However, after six years and with more than 500 visits from our worldwide team, the village is now filled with hope and opportunities.

When we send our team to Uganda, we don't prescribe what they should do, but rather allow them to live with the locals and experience life in the villages. Our global leaders, as cultural ambassadors, range from early career stage to senior executives. The projects they pursue develop flexibility, resourcefulness and an ability to adapt to any situation. We ask them to represent our foundation and then return, sharing their experiences of people and culture with others around them.

Similarly, Cotton On University emphasizes cultural sensitivity and curiosity for others. Our recent launch of a Cotton On University Asian hub led each person currently enrolled in the Australia program to send a postcard to an individual in Asia and become learning partners across culture, distance and geography.

From induction to executive level, our leadership programs require the partnership of a mentor to help each person make sense of a culturally different function or location. We believe that the more conversations people have, the more they understand and connect with one another.

For us, global leadership requires deep emotional connection. We are a large family company, and we want people world over to feel they are truly part of the Cotton On family.

Michael Hardwick is the chief financial officer of the Cotton On Group. He is also responsible for People and Culture and the Cotton On Foundation.

Naomi Harrison is a psychologist and executive coach from **Psych Insight** working within Cotton On for the past two years.

Great Global Leaders Foster Global Followership

By Yolanda Conyers

In 2007, I joined Lenovo, a Chinese-heritage technology company that had just acquired IBM's PC division. Little did I realize that despite 25 years of leadership experience, the journey I was about to begin would open a whole new world in what it means to be a truly global—not just international—leader. The past years at Lenovo have taught me that global leaders can accomplish great things when they cultivate global followership.

Lesson One: Global leaders leverage the best ideas, wherever they exist

Keenly aware of global influences that impact their business, global leaders translate their insights into plans for the present and the future. They offer a compelling vision, one that captures others' hearts and minds and inspires outstanding achievement. Too often that vision, and how to achieve it, is simply a translation of headquarters' views: Other regions are expected to "adapt" to the thinking and culture of the parent company. In contrast, at Lenovo we have grown in multiple regions at once, so we drew from the best ideas across our global footprint and used these to create a single culture. This alternative model is better aligned with current business realities, as the world becomes flatter and the playing field becomes more level.

Lesson Two: Global leaders embrace diversity while fostering common ground

Working with people around the world is challenging; differences in time zones and language are just two of the obvious difficulties. Successful global leaders leverage cultural differences among their teams, while building trust in diversity. My observation of great global leaders has been that they "flex" their style when working with

Keenly aware of global influences that impact their business, global leaders translate their insights into plans for the present and the future.

diverse team members depending on the individual, the team and situation. They recognize similarities and differences among people and cultures, highlighting what contribute to team effectiveness.

Just as important, global leaders embrace diversity while creating common ground. We designed East meets West Training for teams to talk about cultural differences in the ways they approach their work, and then we establish rules of engagement "where appropriate" to align and move forward. It is never easy at the beginning, but once the team understands the cultural differences, the why behind their differences, and the team's commitments, it is then that we begin to see committed followership.

Leading in a global organization is a test of one's ability to optimize the diversity of ideas, talent and experience. When you think about it, global leadership is really about fostering global followership. So ask yourself: What are your leaders doing to build the level of global followership your company needs to succeed around the world? ▪

Yolanda Conyers is vice president of HR Operations and chief diversity officer at Lenovo.

LEARNING GUIDE

Point Counterpoint II: 2.3

Debunking Talent Strategy Myths

DISCOVERY QUESTIONS

- What are you dealing with in your organization today that relates to this content area?
- What does the phrase, "Think global, act local" imply?
- What type of HR practices might fit with the idea of local adaptation?
- Describe an example of a common leadership expectation that might work well in the United States, but not in Asia.
- What exposure do you expect most managers have to global diversity, even without leaving home?
- What does cross-cultural awareness have to do with becoming an effective leader?
- What is the potential risk to a company that tries to export its home country, headquarters culture to every country in which they do business?
- Why might empathy and emotional intelligence help managers better appreciate cross-cultural differences?
- Why are global and cross-cultural awareness important for companies that are not multinational?

SELECTED FACTS

What new facts that were presented got your attention?

- The United Nations Global Compact found that 76 percent of interviewed executives ranked global leadership development as critical for future success.
- Studies by the American Management Association found that only one-third of companies have global leadership development programs in place.
- Domestic markets and workforces are becoming more diverse.
- Global leadership has remained a top concern of CEOs for the last eight to 10 years.
- Turkey is the geographical bridge, straddling Europe and the Middle East.
- The term "glocal" refers to understanding the global business picture and connecting local actions to that picture.
- Cotton On, a global retailer with 1,000 stores in 14 countries and 17,000 employees, builds opportunities for cross-cultural learning into its leadership development approach.

KEY DISCUSSION POINTS

- What were the key points being made in this presentation?
- How does being a global leader differ today from 20 or 30 years ago?
- Is cross-cultural awareness essential for leadership development?
- Why is cross-cultural awareness even more important now than in the past?
- Why do U.S.-only companies also need their leaders to develop cross-cultural awareness?
- How can globally sensitive leaders be more effective in helping to foster common ground?
- Why do you think global leadership development requires both education and experience, as does Novelis?
- How might you determine cross-cultural leadership needs in your company?
- If you were interviewing leadership candidates and wanted to assess their cross-cultural leadership skills, what questions might you ask? How else might you assess these skills?
- Consider Cotton On's approach to putting leaders in new settings without clear instructions. What difficulties do you think they might encounter? What do you think they might learn?
- What do you think curiosity, empathy, and emotional intelligence have to do with becoming an effective global leader?

Point Counterpoint II: 2.3

Debunking Talent Strategy Myths

REVIEW OF SOLUTIONS

- Identify two to three "big ideas" worthy of exploring in your organization.
- What is the potential value of a development program that sends employees into a foreign culture without clear directions, as Cotton On does?
- How might you adapt Cotton On's approach to developing empathy in your own class, university, company, or city?
- What would be potential measures of an effective global leadership program?
- How might global leaders leverage cultural differences to build stronger teams?
- How would you embed global and cross-cultural awareness into onboarding efforts at your company?

IDENTIFYING THE PARADOX

- How is it that a solution appropriate for yesterday's organization is no longer valid?
- Consider how very different perspectives might be correct given different situations.
- What is the inherent paradox of thinking global and acting local?
- What could be the paradox of thinking global and then acting the same way locally?
- International assignments are expensive and may deprive locals from leadership opportunities in their home countries. How might a company address that paradox?
- What is the paradox of inviting competitors to present or be a sponsor at your conference, as did the Human Resources Summit in Turkey?
- How can leaders create common ground through the diversity in their teams?

LEARNING OUTCOMES

- What one new piece of information did you learn that will be important to you in the future?
- Identify one thing that you will do differently based on what you learned.
- How could you start to increase your cross-cultural leadership sensitivity right now?
- How might you combine education and experience, or programs and assignments, into a global leadership program?
- What is the potential competitive advantage of having a more globally sensitive and capable workforce?
- How can companies with limited budgets continue to develop global leaders?

PART 3:
PERFORMACE AND POTENTIAL MANAGEMENT

Riding the Performance Management Rollercoaster

One topic that consistently draws strong interest among conference participants is best practices and innovation in performance management (PM). At the HR People + Strategy annual conference in April, Perspectives Editor Anna Tavis hosted a keynote panel on the main stage, leading a vibrant, thought-provoking discussion of how this area is evolving and what factors are driving significant change.

With this installment of Perspectives, we bring to you a slice of that energy and experience, with the lead perspective laying out the ways performance management is being reinvented. Panelists each share a synopsis of their own experience and how their companies are experimenting and adapting the process.

The panel members, which included **Deborah Becker** of Eli Lilly, **Jennifer Beihl** of GE, and **Jeffrey Orlando** of Deloitte, each share their company experiences as well as viewpoints on the subject. Contributions from **Julie Gravallese, Priscila Metzgar,** and **Dan Ward** of MITRE and **Holly Engler, Joe Kutter,** and **Don Moretti** of Sears Holdings round out these perspectives.

If you believe performance management should be improved or even entirely overhauled at your company, or you just want to learn more about what other companies are pioneering at theirs, then this Perspectives is for you. After reading the lead Perspectives and commentaries that follow, you can contact the authors to ask a question or share how you are approaching this issue in your company. Or, contact Anna to find out more about what factors are shaping the future of PM and what other changes we can expect to see in the near future.

POINT

When the Performance Management Bubble Burst

By Anna A. Tavis

When the full story of the ongoing performance management transformation is finally told, the years 2014 and 2015 will go down in history as the time when the annual performance appraisal bubble finally burst. After decades of increasingly loud signals of discontent and mounting evidence that the legacy process was not delivering on its intended value, a few pioneering companies broke out of the mold and were able to face the urgency for change. Adobe, Medtronic, Juniper Networks, and Kelly Services, to name just the first few, made news with their radical departure from the heavily administrative annual employee performance evaluation exercise. The traditional annual performance review finally met its end.

Dropping performance ratings and replacing the once-per-year appraisal process with regular "check-ins" became business's battle cry for change. The first "rateless" performance management cases unsettled the behemoth of HR bureaucracy, built on top of a single rating. From then on, the monolith process that used to be known as performance management split into multiple manager–employee conversations, often blending informal touch points with "shadow" ratings and talent calibrations on the backend.

Every one of these pioneering companies would admit that it was not about the ratings for them to begin with. Every part of the legacy performance system had to undergo a review. With the rateless idea being novel and benchmarking scarce, the original science was called upon to help review the underlying assumptions about employee motivation, engagement, and overall work experience.

The new language of progress, mastery, and purpose emerged to replace appraisal reports. "Check-ins" and "pay for contribution" became the preferred vocabulary of the day, leading the reevaluation of the entire performance system to start with purpose and goals and to back into the larger systems for talent and rewards. As the new growth mindset toward managing and assessing performance began to gradually replace the ratings fetish, ditching ratings became the trigger event that got everyone's attention.

The Media Factor

The change might have taken its measured evolutionary course, were it not for the media. The performance management revolution owes its meteoric ascendance to gaining status as the hottest business news item partly due to the enormous amount of media attention it received.

Take Adobe's story that set pace for the trend worldwide. It all started with the *Economic Times of India* getting an interview with Donna Morris, then Adobe's chief people and places officer, who admitted that "the performance review was an antiquated, painful, and unproductive HR process that had outlived its time." Her revelation made the front pages in India, with the headline, "Adobe Set to Scrap Performance Review." Furthermore, the news got worldwide coverage before it was vetted with Adobe's CEO, and Donna's peers. Luckily, the organization was ready for the change and got behind the new performance management agenda. Hundreds more interviews and thousands more citations followed, marking the end of the "quiet" phase in the performance revolution.

Media for Months to Come

From there, performance management became the hot topic to capture the headlines of every important business publication in the United States and beyond. *Harvard Business Review* covered "the performance revolution" extensively with Deloitte's milestone story, "Reinventing Performance Management," co-authored by Ashley Goodall and Marcus

Buckingham. *Strategy+Business* featured David Rock's eye-catching feature, "Kill Your Performance Ratings." *The New York Times* followed suit with the headlines such as, "10 Reasons Performance Reviews Do Not Work," and *Forbes* joined in with its own, "Let's Kill Performance Reviews." In 2015, the *Washington Post*, called PM the "corporate Kabuki" and *Vanity Fair* went as far as to blame Microsoft's PM for the company's sliding market performance.

What the Media Got Wrong

The media helped bring attention to the issue, but it did not always ask the right questions and did not have the answers to bring to the table to help get the right decisions made. If you were wondering why the complex issues of measuring, incentivizing, and rewarding employee performance came down to the simple question of ratings, and ratings only, it has to do with the choices that the media made for us.

Performance appraisals have always been everyone's dreaded workplace experience, which is why the headlines got public attention in the first place. We brought the story of "ratings" back from the media. Some lessons need to be learned here. The power of (social) media needs to be faced up to even if lived behind the tallest corporate firewalls. Now is the time for HR to reclaim performance back again from the legacy of the past and from the media hype of the present. The actual story of performance management transformation still needs to be told in full, as we are settling in with a distinctive new pattern for managing performance in the 21st century.

The Next Practice and the Best Practice

As HR professionals, we have learned a great deal from walking the path of performance management transformation in just these last few years. There seem to be two distinct directions to take when joining the performance transformation movement:

- The innovator path has opened up to many more companies than ever before. These bold companies broke away from the past early and set themselves up to discover solutions aligned with their own unique pur-

pose (Adobe, Juniper, Gap, and the companies represented in the Perspectives that follow: GE, Deloitte, Eli Lilly, Sears, and MITRE). Facing the unknown, the innovators turned to science, analytics, and technology to look for guidance in designing their singular future.
- The second cohort of companies has been more circumspect. These companies have been looking for more evidence and more compelling practices around them before starting on their own change journey.

Both approaches are legitimate, both ultimately lead to desired change. The difference has been in the role that the HR function has played. The innovators boldly took on strategic leadership roles in their businesses. In the second scenario, the HR function gained more internal confidence but remained to be the "partner" to the business it has been up until then.

Looking ahead, it has become even clearer that the future of HR will be more with the innovators and pathfinders among us. Reinventing performance management is the first step in giving HR its strategic mission it is beginning to embrace. It will most likely take a few more rounds of these types of "revolutions" to move the function solidly to the new role of organizational innovators and talent leaders in their own businesses.

Where Do We Go From Here?

By mid–2016, the new practice has matured enough to be learned from and applied in organizations looking for more guidance. The new norms have been settling in, presenting an achievable standard for those catching up on the trend.

Despite the attention it initially has gotten, the "ratingless" process now is one of the options to follow, but definitely is not the universal rule on how to do performance management going forward.

With or without ratings, most companies already now follow much shorter evaluation cycles, decentralize goal setting, and determine quantitative and qualitative measurement of "contribution," "impact," and "value." Managers are expected to play the coaching role and own key decisions on employee performance standing, rewards, and development needs.

The performance management revolution started as a trend launched around 2011 by a few bold detractors. It reached its peak in 2014 and 2015, and now it is a global phenomenon, ushering in a massive shift in organizational cultures and challenging HR functions to step up to innovator roles in moving their business forward through people.

As the cases of GE, Deloitte, Eli Lilly. MITRE, and Sears Holdings presented here show, each company's innovation scenario is a solution that could be learned from and inspired by, but it could not be imitated.

Anna A. Tavis, Ph.D., is Perspectives editor and a faculty member at New York University and Columbia University.

GE: Staying True to Its DNA

By Jennifer Beihl, Janice Semper, and Valerie Van den Keybus

At GE, evolution and change have been part of our DNA for 130 years. Today, GE's transforming itself as the leading digital industrial company. By pairing digital technology with deep expertise in building powerful machines—from jet engines to gas turbines to health care imaging equipment—GE is transforming industry with software-defined machines and solutions that are connected, responsive, and predictive.

As part of this transformation, we recognized the need to infuse new ways of working in a company that had developed an intrinsic bias toward complexity and process perfection, when in fact the world and our employees were expecting us to act more simply and nimbly. We responded in three ways:
- We introduced FastWorks, our version of a stronger and more entrepreneurial focus on our customers and competency in experimentation

working with Eric Ries of *Lean Start-up* and other Silicon Valley advisors, married with the work of thought leaders in the company.
- We took a strong position that the go-forward leadership and performance expectations are very different from our long-held and often-tweaked values and introduced a new set of aspirational GE Beliefs to guide us.
- We then reexamined at our performance management approach, which did not support or help build these new behaviors described by GE Beliefs and FastWorks.

The New Approach

In 2014, we introduced performance development, a more personalized, real-time, and flexible approach to performance and development. It emphasizes coaching and continuous dialogue (touch points) between manager and employee, instead of heavy, once-a-year evaluations. "The world isn't really on an annual cycle anymore for anything," said Susan Peters, GE's senior vice president of human resources.

The approach reflects the mindset and behaviors that are driving GE's culture forward:
- Strengthening our muscle in sharing real-time, contextual feedback with both our manager and colleagues to increase self-awareness about behaviors that support our effectiveness and impact and that minimize the same
- Becoming much more connected and dialoging early and often with our customers to understand what work we need to prioritize to get to outcomes important to them
- Completing a simple annual summary narrative about the employee's impact and behaviors which is co-created by the manager and employee together

Replacing a backward-looking yearly assessment on a long form, performance development focuses on real-time conversations—facilitated and supported by a simple, digital app that functions as a notebook to capture key comments, serves as an aid to alignment and memory, and simplifies the year-end process.

Finally, we are testing a no ratings approach to find alternative ways to motivate and build performance, as a subset pilot of the overall performance development approach.

Performance development focuses on real-time conversations— facilitated and supported by a simple, digital app.

Where Are We?

We are about two years into the performance development journey. Through a phased approach of testing and learning (FastWorks), we started by intensively dialoguing with our customer groups (employees, managers and senior leaders) to understand their most important needs, then testing components of the approach with several dozen employees to validate (or invalidate) our assumptions. We transitioned around 6,000 employees to a "wing to wing" approach developed based on those learnings. Since the beginning of 2015, we have continued to scale and increase adoption amongst larger populations. We have tested, learned about the impact, and iterated along the way to increase that impact. We will continue to do so.

We have learned that when employees and managers actively engage in performance development behaviors, it has significant positive impact on the outcomes that are important to them individually and us collectively as an evolving organization. And we know from the data we have collected that there are some who are still trying to make sense of it. It is where we are now focusing our efforts and testing new ways to accelerate adoption that will in turn accelerate our ability to deliver on the future for GE—the digital industrial.

Advice
- Validate assumptions early with small tests. If something does not work for 10 customers, it won't work for 200,000.
- Calibrate for a marathon. Changing mindset and behavior to evolve a

company culture does not happen overnight. But it is very possible. And absolutely amazing to see when the "spark" ignites.

Jennifer Beihl, Janice Semper, and **Valerie Van den Keybus** are members of the GE team leading the company's culture change efforts, with performance development as a key aspect of that initiative.

It All Adds Up to Change at Deloitte

By Jeff Orlando

We have been able to motivate change on performance management at Deloitte due to two primary factors. First, based on a 2013 study we conducted, we discovered that we spent close to two million hours on performance management just in the United States. We determined this investment not in line with the value the process created. We knew we could do better.

The second is what we learned about ourselves. Starting with Gallup's seminal research on engagement and performance, we identified 60 Deloitte teams that our most senior leaders said they'd like to have more of (nearly 1,300 employees). We asked them six survey questions. We contrasted their survey responses with the organization's average of a control group of nearly 2,000 individuals. Our study showed the same results as Gallup's: When people believe they are playing to their strengths, performance soars. These factors—getting more yield from our time investment and finding ways to bring out our people's strengths to drive greater organizational performance—were the foundation of our change.

Piloting Our Way to Rollout

The entirety of Deloitte's U.S. practice is now "live" in our new model. We have had a deliberate build-up where we have learned a lot along the way, and incorporated design changes—keeping what worked and altering what aspects needed to be revised. Our process has three goals: fuel, see, and recognize performance.

To fuel performance, we relied on our own research and designed the "check-in," a future-focused conversation about work. Here, team members and leaders meet one on one to discuss real-time feedback and future expectations. It is how they align on priorities for what's coming next, and they do that with a strengths lens. They discuss how the individual will deliver on these priorities given their unique skills and strengths. These happen, on average, every other week. In busy periods, they may occur more often. This lets us match the activities of PM to the cadence of the business.

The performance snapshot is the primary tool that lets us "see performance" via four quick questions. It is a vehicle for the team leader to capture his or her assessment about each team member's performance. Snapshots are completed at the end of a project, phase, or at least quarterly. By the end of the year, there are numerous snapshots completed for each person. The design of these questions is research based and intentional. We've built

> Every people decision that our system leads to is data-informed, but not data-driven.

questions that ask evaluators to predict their own intended future actions vs. attempting to rate a skill and bringing in concerns about rater bias.

To recognize performance, we combine the quantitative inputs from performance snapshots with the input and decisions of our leaders. The quantitative inputs are the "starting position" for our recognition processes—be they promotions, merit increases, or managing low performance. The key is they are the start. Every people decision that our system leads to is data-informed, but not data-driven—not data driven. Our leaders carefully make decisions, not a computer model or algorithm.

Advice

PM is one of any organization's clearest and loudest communications channels—it articulates what is valued and what is not, what it means to succeed, and what it means to fail. And at a base level, it puts employees' concerns on stability and career front and center, which it is why it is hard work. Three pieces of advice:

- The business and HR/talent teams need to carry this together. As your project expands its population, expand HR and line representation to support the weight of the change.
- Every process decision should be informed (but not driven) by data. This gets us out of the opinion business and into sound decision-making processes.
- Create initial goodwill with employees by removing burdensome process elements and replacing them with positive ones that serve both their and the organization's interests.

Final Thought

I've come to realize that one of the big advantages of our model is it is nimble. It doesn't lock into a stale organizational hierarchy. It follows the teams and the work they lead—process and rigidity do not. This helps with speed and flexibility—something that every organization today is working to embed in their operations and culture.

Jeff Orlando is chief learning officer, leader development and performance, at Deloitte.

How Eli Lilly Fixed a Broken Performance Management System

By Deborah Becker

Many companies talk about how employees dread the performance management process, but many are nervous about changing both the processes and behaviors necessary to create a different environment. Eli Lilly and Company decided to listen and make a global change in a very short period of time.

Both supervisors and employees at Lilly expressed dissatisfaction with the current performance management process. Supervisors felt the company's guidance on meeting a performance distribution did not enable them to accurately assess their employees. Employees focused more on the label associated with the rating and less on the conversation and feedback for improvement. Negative impact on employee engagement was actually demonstrated through our employee survey data. After ratings and year-end compensation decisions were delivered, employee engagement stayed the same for the highest rated employees, and went down for all other individuals. It took three months for engagement levels to recover.

With data in hand, the CEO and his executive team were highly supportive of making a significant change and commissioned a team to quickly deliver a new solution. The team was led by a highly experienced senior director accustomed to global roll-outs, a director skilled in change management, and several consultants, both in and outside the United States. All project members devoted themselves full time to making the changes. This helped with overall design and change management required to ensure all business areas and geographies could adjust their approach. Once the design was determined, it enabled a quick implementation timeline, and all changes were globally effected within eight months. In addition to the core team, extended members were added as necessary. One of the key areas of focus was compensation. The compensation programs were modified to align to the elimination of ratings, allowing supervisors more discretion to make the best decisions.

Lilly's intent in making such a big shift in the performance management approach was to align employees' work more closely with organizational goals, to improve the quality of coaching and feedback discussions between supervisors and employees, and to foster continuous improvement.

You can't just change a process without also changing behaviors and expect a difference. Therefore, Lilly developed

mandatory performance management (myPM), compensation, and coaching training for employees and supervisors—even the CEO participated. Coaching at Lilly is defined as a "trusting, collaborative relationship that helps an individual improve performance at work and achieve his/her full potential." Coaching should be a two-way conversation that includes active participation between employee and supervisor. Coaching aims to help employees develop insights, achieve work goals, and perform at their best.

After completing two cycles, both employees and supervisors agree performance management is no longer an event. It has shifted to ongoing conversations throughout the year, with a focus on learning and growth. The goal is to help all employees increase their performance and achieve their goals. At the end of the year, supervisors assess each employee as to whether or not they sufficiently met expectations.

In January, supervisors make compensation decisions based on an employee's performance and contributions, both for the year and over time, and they no longer focus on specific labels for an individual.

Advice

Companies thinking about making a change should have strong CEO and senior leadership support for the program and be able to leverage them as message leaders. This sets the tone for the organization and helps with organizational change management. Consider which is better for your organization: a wholesale change versus a pilot program. For Lilly, a highly complex, matrixed environment, implementing globally allowed all supervisors and employees to operate in a similar manner. In addition, the compensation changes necessary to align with the new approach can occur across the organization versus keeping two systems running.

Deborah Becker, SPHR, GRP, is senior director, global compensation at Eli Lilly and Company.

MITRE: Rethinking Performance Management

By Julie Gravallese, Priscila Metzgar, and Dan Ward

Over the years, MITRE managers and employees expressed frustration with the company's performance management system. MITRE surveys showed employees wanted more involvement from people who knew their work best; they wanted to better understand what was expected of them; and they wanted more meaningful feedback with increased focus on professional development. MITRE leadership knew it was important to address those concerns and, at the same time, strengthen our culture of collaboration and teamwork.

What MITRE Changed

We migrated from a traditional performance management approach to a process of providing continual feedback, with a focus on developmental coaching. We eliminated the traditional performance management ranking/rating processes. We designed a process that went from "pay for performance" to a "pay for value" that compares each individual against a market value of their work, not against colleagues. We identified three factors—roles, results, and behaviors—that we feel provide consistent feedback (across the enterprise) matched to year-end compensation.

Introducing MITRE CLEAR Conversations

Combining employee feedback with industry best practices, MITRE introduced its new approach, CLEAR Conversations, which replaced a performance and development (P&D) management system that primarily focused on weighty year-end documentation followed by a ranking process.

CLEAR is an acronym for the employee experience: communicate, learn, evolve, achieve, and results. It reflects state-of-the-art thinking on how to provide feedback and coaching between managers and employees. It also emphasizes individual growth and development.

CLEAR Conversations has three components: expectations, feedback, and development:

- **Expectations** is employees setting expectations and aligning them with both their direct supervisor and work leader/s to ensure clarity around roles, results, behaviors.
- **Feedback** stresses the importance of continuous feedback and conversations throughout the year. It includes both the review and compensation conversations. It also shows the connection between continuous feedback and the year-end review.

- **Development** looks for opportunities to enhance employees' current roles as well as their career aspirations and helps them grow.

These components are linked by conversations throughout the year that reflect on performance, offer more transparency through continuous feedback, and support development opportunities.

Key MITRE Differentiator

To emphasize the growth and development aspect of CLEAR Conversations, MITRE also introduced Careers in Motion, to illustrate that people can move in various directions to achieve their career aspirations.

Careers are personal and dynamic. One person's career path is not necessarily another's. Employees are coached to look for opportunities that excite them. It is up to each employee to take charge of his or her career and pursue the journey that is right for him or her. MITRE's culture, flexible workforce, and highly matrixed environment encourages people to seek out these roles and managers to support employees as they pursue their interests.

CLEAR Conversations Implementation and Rollout to All Employees

A team that included business managers and directors across MITRE, as well as HR specialists and business partners, designed and implemented this new process. Though HR assumed the "project management" role, it was frequently emphasized that this is a business process, not an HR program. We used a cascading communications approach to ensure managers owned the process. This further emphasized the new approach was done as a corporation and was not just yet another process imposed by HR.

Educational materials, change management, and communication collateral were put in place. The HR business partners and generalists were available to provide guidance, and this strengthened the partnership between business and HR. During the first year, focus groups and pilot groups provided input to provide feedback on how the

process is working. The process was recently tweaked for a more user friendly experience and encourage employee buy-in.

For those embarking on a new performance management process, it's critical to research best practices that align with your organization's unique organizational characteristics and goals. MITRE spent months looking at organizations working in this direction and started to benchmark them. We learned what was working—and what wasn't.

Moving Forward

More time must pass to understand full results of this process, but the team, leaders and employees all agree that changes in performance management were necessary and that CLEAR Conversations is on the right path to addressing those issues that specifically affect MITRE.

Julie Gravallese is chief human resource officer at MITRE. **Priscila Metzgar** is manager of performance management at MITRE. **Dan Ward** is chief workplace economist at MITRE.

Sears Holdings Datafies and Democratizes Ratingless Performance Management

By Holly Engler, Joe Kutter, and Don Moretti

Triggers for Change

Faced with financial performance challenges and a rapidly changing retail environment, the leadership team at Sears Holdings decided it was time to make a cultural shift. With the introduction of a new set of cultural beliefs and mission statement, we knew that we needed to, at a minimum, change the words in our performance process to align appropriately with the behaviors we were expecting from individuals. Additional research in neuroscience quickly became the catalyst for realizing the change that needed to happen in order to fulfill our mission and drive greater performance and accountability of our associates.

> This frequent and individual goal-setting technique allows associates agility in the organization and progress of their work throughout the year as business needs change.

Introducing Performance Enablement

Prior to August 2014, Sears Holdings conducted a traditional performance management (PM) process; an annual and mid-year review, complete with manager-generated performance ratings, and annual goal setting. In the new Performance Enablement approach, salaried associates kick off each new fiscal year by writing Individual Priorities. These priorities represent an associate's broader key initiatives for the year, and are directly aligned to transparent business unit and company priorities. Individual associates then utilize the objectives and key results (OKRs) methodology, a thought framework used by Intel, IBM, Google, and other organizations, to set individual objectives on a quarterly cadence.

This frequent and individual goal-setting technique allows associates agility in the organization and progress of their work throughout the year as business needs change. Throughout the year, associates are enabled with a home grown feedback tool called SoundBoard, which allows individuals to give and source feedback at any time from their manager or leadership, peers, internal customers, colleagues, and partners. Feedback is aggregated in easy to use dashboards for individuals and managers to identify real-time trends in *how* they are achieving their objectives.

At the start of each quarter, associates and managers conduct a check-in. The check-in is an associate-driven conversation that facilitates quality discussions around what the associate was working on, how it went, and what is next with regards to quarterly objectives, growth, and career development. Together, these tools and their frequency allow for stronger alignment of individual objectives, more frequent conversations rooted in a growth mindset, and a more robust perspective of associate behaviors and opportunities for adding more value.

Creating 10 Times the Data

The Sears Holdings talent management team designed these tools and processes with both our associates—and data—in mind. We consciously constructed OKRs, SoundBoard, and check-ins in a way that at least 10 times the data (compared to a single annual performance rating) could be extracted in an effort to know our talent as well as we know our customer base. We now house over 100,000 pieces of individual feedback that provide us with insight into how well our teams embrace feedback, the strength of their networks internally, and individual/team strengths and opportunities as relates to our leadership capability model.

The data have shown that associates who use these tools regularly, compared to those who don't or who use them inconsistently, are 10.5 to 21 percent more likely to improve their performance or potential to move up in the organization. We have also found that those who use the tools are less likely to turn over. This is meaningful data for understanding our talent needs in the organization.

Advice to Those Embarking on the Journey

- **You can't over communicate.** A move away from the traditional PM process is far more than a simple process change. It is a change in the way we think about our own work, a change in the way managers address performance with their associates/teams, and a new mindset and culture for the organization. Communicate early and often to ensure that your teams understand the reason for the change and how to effectively manage the new process. Videos, infographics, and other bite-sized learning can be effective in communicating your message.
- **There is no "one-size-fits-all" solution.** Many organizations have now implemented a ratingless PM platform. There are some common themes among all of their approaches, including feedback in some form (some use a digital platform, others facilitate via verbal communication), more frequent conversations, and stronger goal alignment. No two organizations have facilitated this change in the same way. It is important that the approach you are implementing is conducive to your culture and your environment. In fact, some organizations aren't ready for a change of this magnitude quite yet. However, more frequent conversations can be layered on to a traditional PM approach to begin shifting to a growth mindset and illustrating more frequency in the PM process. Some organizations have facilitated OKRs using excel spreadsheets to allow their associates the opportunity to think about their goals in a more agile way. You can start small and build to the mindset needed to make the shift.
- **Don't underestimate the change management required.** It took us a full 12 months of undivided effort to launch our new approach. You will likely face challenges with your own HR and legal teams early on. Moving to a ratingless PM platform requires consistent change management, even after deployment including continuous education of individuals and managers on how to manage in the new world, consistent training on how to properly facilitate feedback and agile goal setting, and frequent communication illustrating the advantages of the new approach. ▪▪

Holly Engler is director of strategic talent at Sears. **Joe Kutter** is manager of talent analytics at Sears. **Don Moretti** is director of selection at Sears.

LEARNING GUIDE

Point Counterpoint II: 3.1

Riding the Performance Management Rollercoaster

DISCOVERY QUESTIONS

- What are you dealing with in your organization today that relates to this content area?
- The trend has continued to evolve in the last few years. How do you assess the achievements of the last few years of experimenting with new forms of performance management?
- Explain how the media has been influencing the course of PM transformation and how it changed the course of the trend.
- What were the two main trends in companies' response to the PM challenge?
- How is HR's role changing as a result of the performance management revolution?
- Of the cases presented here, identify the:
  a) most innovative
  b) new science-based
  c) best executed
  d) most radical

  Explain why you chose each.

SELECTED FACTS

- What new facts that were presented got your attention?
- What facts support the statement that media was responsible for the acceleration of performance transformation process overall.
- Why was GE's move to performance development evolution, not revolution in their culture?
- What was "nimble" about Deloitte's approach to their performance management?
- What was the cornerstone of Eli Lilly's overhaul of their PM system?
- What was the focus of CLEAR Conversations at MITRE? How did they work?
- How was Sears able to create 10 times the data after they abolished performance ratings?

KEY DISCUSSION POINTS

- What were the key points being made in this presentation?
- Identify the role of change management in ensuring the right outcomes.
- What skills are important for HR teams to successfully drive the transformation needed?
- What breakthrough innovations have emerged in organizational practice as a result of undergoing performance management transformation?

REVIEW OF SOLUTIONS

- Identify two to three "big ideas" worthy of exploring in your organization.
- Name two distinct directions companies have taken in reinventing their performance management process.
- Review the advice successful companies are giving to those who follow. Pick one or two each but cover them all as a team: GE, Eli Lilly, Deloitte, Return Path, Statsoil, Mitre, and Sears.

IDENTIFYING THE PARADOX

- How is it that a solution appropriate for yesterday's organization is no longer valid?
- Consider how very different perspectives might be correct given different situations.
- Explain the new law of performance management in your own terms: "Simple, clear purpose and principles give rise to complex, intelligent behavior. Complex rules and regulations give rise to simple, stupid behavior." (Dee Hock, former CEO of Visa)

LEARNING OUTCOMES

- What one new piece of information did you learn that will be important to you in the future?
- Identify one thing that you will do differently based on what you learned.

Reimagining Performance Management

By Marc Sokol

More common than the presence of performance management systems is the dislike employees and managers have for the systems with which they seem to be stuck. In many companies, the expectation is to follow a required evaluation process, to get reviews completed on time and then to get back to "real business." Many companies try to enlist managers to use performance management for development and coaching, and to make it an ongoing process, but too many managers and employees just see it as a broken process, far too time-consuming relative to the impact it has on individual and organizational effectiveness.

What if there was a better way?

Smaller firms can be trendsetters, and in the lead Perspectives article we read of one company that is engaging all 375 employees as owners of the performance management process. **Angela Baldonero** and **Matthew Hoffman**, both of Return Path, and **Marc Maltz** of TRIAD Consulting Group, LLC, describe Return Path's multi-year effort evolving performance management processes to drive the business forward *and* engage the employees of the firm. If you ever dreamed of a day when employees would truly step up to full accountability for their own performance, this Perspective is for you.

The commentaries that follow each expand on the lead Perspective, with input from a large company, from two researchers steeped in organizational learning, and two seasoned consultants who have seen the future of performance management. At least for some organizations, that future of a better approach to performance management has already arrived.

Bjarte Bogsnes from Norway

In many companies, the expectation is to follow a required evaluation process, to get reviews completed on time and then to get back to "real business."

reports on Statoil's efforts to reform performance management to be multi-faceted and drive more intelligent behavior across the firm.

Gyan Nagpal, from Singapore, tells us we need to "reboot" the performance management operating system if we are to indeed drive different behavior. He draws upon his research across developed and developing nations.

Valerie Sessa and **Jennifer Bragger**, both from Montclair State University, challenge us to look at Performance Management through the lens of a committed gardener: We don't just need to adjust the organization; as HR professionals we need to adjust our own attitudes regarding the care

and ongoing nurturance of performance management systems.

Nancy Tippins, from CEB Valtera/ SHL, offers a final commentary, writing about different futures we can expect to see, and why our approaches to performance management must continue to evolve.

How has your company wrestled with the challenge and opportunity of performance management? What successes have you had and what have you learned along the way? Read the Perspectives in this issue and challenge your own company to take a bold step forward.

Marc Sokol, Ph.D., is Perspectives editor.

A New Perspective on Managing Performance

By Angela Baldonero, Matthew Hoffman, and Marc Maltz

Traditional performance management systems are out-of-sync with the needs of the modern workforce. Employees and managers loathe the use of these systems and HR departments do not derive much actionable information from the reams of data collected along the way. One of the most valuable assets in today's workplace is specific, in-the-moment feedback, an asset that is buried and often lost in today's ineffective performance management systems.

What if there was a better way? In examining high-performing organizations, we concluded that self-correcting systems have far greater promise. We are evolving the management of performance from a 360° performance management system, through "live 360s," and now moving responsibility for managing performance into the team, utilizing the work as the criteria for evaluation.

At Return Path, we have worked to evolve how we measure and improve role and work performance, provide actionable feedback, separate evaluative from developmental conversations, and advance the overall "operating system" of the company. We began this journey 10 years ago, first developing a custom 360-degree performance system, then migrating to a standard commercial system as the company grew. This process began to take an enormous amount of time, especially for those who had to provide feedback on a number of people. We began to conduct facilitated "live 360s" for managers in which we would bring together a 360-degree view of a person's key stakeholders for 45 minutes, resulting in a detailed report that highlighted important developmental opportunities. Yet, as we drove efficiencies into the organization, we wondered how to bring the conversation closer to impacting the work while simultaneously developing a culture of accountability and continuous feedback.

Return Path is the worldwide leader in email intelligence. We analyze more email data than anyone else in the world, using that data to power products so that only email people want and expect reach their inbox. As a values-based organization, we offer a casual work environment, where dreaming up new ideas is more important than following old formulas. Here, employees enjoy being part of a thriving company of smart, hard-working, innovative and passionate people who are committed to individual growth.

Return Path wants all employees to be engaged and satisfied—offering an array of programs to empower employees to acquire new skills, develop as leaders and chart an enviable career. We focus on trusting employees and design all processes to increase freedom wherever possible; we don't have one-size-fits-all solutions. The impact is that Return Path has been ranked No. 11 in the United States as a Great Place to Work by *Fortune Magazine*, recognized by Crain's in New York City, and ranked by *Colorado Business Magazine* as one of the top three employers in Colorado.

As part of our journey, we spent time in numerous organizations exploring what ideas drive excellence[1]. We learned that teams fully authorized for managing and measuring their work performed the best. In fact, our own technical departments who had adopted an agile/lean approach stood out as great examples of higher functioning teams. We are in the process of changing how we operate to put the team in the driver seat by:

1. Asking every team and team member to identify what they are respon-

---

[1] We have been to Morningstar, Nucor, WL Gore, Amazon, Zappos, Google, Netflix and numerous other well-known organizations. Our attention was drawn to self-motivating, self-managed systems, which seemed to exhibit higher performance coincident with higher motivation and satisfaction.

---

sible for delivering and to whom in the organization. Once established, team members/teams meet with their stakeholders to negotiate deliverable(s) and determine how performance will be measured.
2. Establishing personal/team charters in which people/teams commit to delivery within the measures established. These charters will be published openly, amended and commented on by any person who has input or is impacted by the outcome.
3. Identifying personal and team development needs that will improve performance. Once established, these individual/team documents are published as a development plan.
4. Measuring performance and publishing these data on company-wide dashboards.
5. Providing facilitated (teams will ultimately be trained to self-facilitate) feedback sessions to review individual/team performance in short cycles (weekly, biweekly, monthly, etc.) much like the lean "sprint."
6. Ensuring individual development conversations are continuous among all teammates and, at a minimum, conducted every 60 days.

Neither management nor our "People Team" will intervene unless requested. The manager becomes a facilitator, focusing on team performance, coaching teams and individuals, and refining the operating system for which they are responsible. Managers will also receive feedback from their teams and their peers in the same way as described above.

While currently the intent is to allow managers to use this "crowd sourced" feedback as key decision data when evaluating performance and compensation, our hope is to bring the organization to a place where the entire process is transparent and performance, performance development and compensation decisions are solely owned by the team.

We are giving the responsibility for managing performance to where it has the most impact, to the 375 people across our company. We will monitor progress as we evolve our way of operating, allowing Return Path to internalize this new way of working. Our hope is to dramatically improve performance, eliminate less efficient practices, and move review processes to those who deliver, measure, develop and manage the work of our business.

Angela Baldonero is senior vice president of people and client success at Return Path.

Matthew Hoffman is the senior director, people at Return Path, based in New York. He has an extensive background supporting both Fortune 500 companies and start-ups in organization and talent development, change management and communications.

Marc Maltz, MBA, RODP, is a partner at TRIAD Consulting Group LLC, an executive and organizational development consultancy based in New York City, and a principal of the Boswell Group, a consortium of psychoanalytically informed organizational practitioners. He has worked with Return Path for more than 10 years.

COUNTERPOINT

Can Performance Management Foster Intelligent Behavior?

By Bjarte Bogsnes

The world has changed, not just in increasingly fast-changing and unpredictable ways, but also the competence and expectations of people in our organizations. Unfortunately, too few seem to understand or accept that these developments call for radically new and different ways of leading and managing. Traditional management practices do not make us the agile organizations we need to be.

The problem starts with the label, "Performance Management" implying, "If I don't manage you, there will be no performance." We need a new mindset, one that is less about managing performance and more about creating conditions for great performance to occur. We need self-regulating models, requiring less management, but more leadership from everyone.

Think about traffic, where we want good performance and a safe good flow. Traffic authorities have different ways of making this happen. The traffic light is a popular choice, but those managing the process (programmers) are not in the situation; information used in their process is not fresh, which is clear as you wait in front of that red light.

The roundabout is a very different alternative. Those managing are the drivers themselves. The information used is real-time, coming from own observations. While that information is also available in front of the traffic light, drivers do not have the authority to act on it. By the way, the "zipper" or "every second car through" is not a rule, but a guiding principle.

The roundabout normally is more efficient than the traffic light, because of two significant differences in the decision-making process, information and authority. A third element is also required for the roundabout to be more efficient: while the traffic light is a simple-rules based system, the roundabout is values-based. A value-set based on, "Me first, I don't care about the rest," is not a big a problem in front of the red light, but is a serious problem in a roundabout. Here, a positive common purpose of wanting a safe and good flow is critical. Drivers must be more considerate, open about own intentions while trying to understand the intentions of peers. Instead of managing performance, traffic authorities have created conditions for self-managed performance to occur.

What would the implications be for the loathed performance review? The principles and practices described at Return Path are sensible and interesting. I like the concept of horizontal commitments toward peers, instead of vertical commitments to higher management. At the same time, we need to broaden our definition of performance. In traditional performance, a commitment is too often about "hitting the number." This is too narrow. We need to ask questions such as, how are we doing compared to peers? How are we using KPIs to reflect on performance, or using hindsight and management assessment to verify results? Did we really move

> The world has changed, not just in increasingly fast-changing and unpredictable ways, but also the competence and expectations of people in our organizations.

toward our longer-term ambitions? How sustainable are the results? Last but not least, there has to be room for values if performance systems are to foster intelligent behavior; we need to ask, how where those results achieved?

At Statoil our integrated performance management approach links ambitions to actions. Our targets reflect a broad set of ambitions, including people, health, safety, environment, operations and financial performance. Read more about our management model and how we apply a holistic and values-based approach to this broader performance agenda.

The words of Dee Hock, former CEO of Visa, should guide the design of our management processes, including our performance reviews:

> "Simple, clear purpose and principles give rise to complex, intelligent behavior. Complex rules and regulations give rise to simple, stupid behavior."

Bjarte Bogsnes has an international career in finance and HR. He is currently heading Beyond Budgeting implementation at Statoil, Scandinavia's largest company with operations in 36 countries. He is chairman of Beyond Budgeting Round Table Europe, and winner of Harvard Business Review/McKinsey's 2012 award for Management Innovation. He is the author of *"Implementing Beyond Budgeting—Unlocking the Performance Potential."*

Rebooting the Performance Management Conversation

By Gyan Nagpal

While researching my book, *Talent Economics*, I interviewed employees about what really motivates today's workforce. I discovered a disconnect between the performance support my interviewees wanted versus how managers recounted their contribution to these conversations.

Over the last 20 years, the employee mindset has evolved faster than has the art and science of management. Nowhere is this starker than in the area of performance management practices, particularly the annual review. In both the developed and developing world, employees report that this end-of-year activity breeds stress, anxiety and mistrust. How ironic that a process aimed at improving organizational performance, is itself underperforming!

It's time to "reboot" our performance management operating system, installing two specific system updates:

1. **The "democracy" update.** As much as we try to make the performance appraisal a two-way dialogue, we cannot run away from the fact that at its core, the conversation today is often a top-down review. My research shows that many 21st century employees are rejecting conversations that are one-way: in hot job markets today, managers must realize "who is appraising whom." With other offers readily available, many employees enter a performance dialogue privately considering if their manager is worth another year of their career. The performance management conversation now reflects a company's Employee Value Proposition, much as we learn in the lead Perspective.

The democracy update means that managers only gain the right to give feedback when they first genuinely seek the same on their own performance as leaders. Not just through 360-degree reviews, but also through authentic conversations asking, *"How am I performing as your manager?"* and *"How can I help you succeed?"* Only then can the conversation shift to, *"How you can improve?"* and *"This is what you should focus on."*

2. **The success module.** Greater employee autonomy and empowerment also changes the meaning of management. We have gone from a "supervisor of task and outcomes" to an "enabler of performance, innovative thinking and collective success." To make this shift, we must give up the judge's robes for the coach's uniform. If employees don't succeed, managers are on the hook, too.

This is particularly relevant when coaching a team to success. People bring different skills to a team and how well they work together really matters. If team reviews work better to achieve a goal, so be it. The Return Path story illustrates how review processes can be designed and executed around what matters most, and where everyone dons the uniforms of player and coach.

What if, instead of making the heart of a performance conversation the evaluation, it became a vehicle to improve success of the individual, the team and the business? What if performance feedback was paired with dialogue about transforming the business, the product or customer experience? This genuinely reboots and upgrades performance management to focus on individual *and* organizational success.

It is indeed time to upgrade performance management practices: we can no longer manage a 21st century employee using 20th century mindsets.

Gyan Nagpal is the author of *"Talent Economics: The fine line between winning and losing the global war for talent"*, in which he draws upon 35 case studies to describe how global landscape for talent may look in 2020 and beyond.

Can Performance Management Systems Grow Like a Spring Garden?

By Valerie I. Sessa and Jennifer D. Bragger

The garden outside looks grey, twiggy, and dead in late winter, waiting for the arrival of spring and a new season. As we look outside, we see how the basics of gardening mirror the process of performance management: managers, HR and executives need to plant the "seeds" of performance management. They provide creative design and regular upkeep, gaining the satisfaction of seeing a garden bloom. Just as gardeners pour over seed catalogues that arrive in January, months before the planting season, organizations need to anticipate the seeds of performance well ahead of time to assess performance.

Gardeners know that if they try to grow acid-loving plants in alkaline soil, the plants won't grow. Similarly, performance management systems fail when they are out of sync with their organizations. Return Path describes their environment as team-based, learning focused, and not having one-size-fits-all human resource solutions. They know that only certain seeds will grow here. Return Path explored and learned about other performance management gardens, but designed something for their unique plot of land. They focused on such ideas as teams, face-to-face, and frequent feedback. Other organizations can learn from Return Path's process and draw from their ideas, but must still design their own system around the competencies, needs, and characteristics of their own jobs, organization, and industry.

Like gardens, performance management systems are complex systems, requiring constant monitoring to ensure that they remain healthy. Gardeners water, fertilize, repel pests, and weed, often daily. Many gardeners love this nurturance, finding it calming, while making the garden resilient. Too many organizations unfortunately forget this. Return Path, however, has continued to nurture its performance management garden, and regularly as the organization has changed—custom 360s, commercial 360s, and now "live 360s." They continue to monitor, intervene and transform, and will likely continue to do so over time. Can you sense the pride they must feel as they look out upon their garden of performance management?

The initial seeds, environmental analyses, and design work that Return Path undertook increases their chances of success. Over time, however, their current approach may allow for weeds of bias and reduced consistency, or the pests of loss of validity and perceived unfairness to creep in. It is important to allow employees input and control, yet if monitoring does not occur, seemingly benign aspects of an organization's culture may unintentionally render the system ineffective and even demotivating. Return Path's leadership needs to monitor this garden, even as it continues to bloom and grow.

> Like a committed gardener, Return Path nurtures its environment, finding new ways to help its people and teams to blossom. Can you say the same about your own firm?

The gardener enjoys the design, the process, and the outcome. Yes, performance management systems and their upkeep can be construed as an unpleasant chore. Rather than loathing the process, perhaps it is our perceptions that need to change. Like a committed gardener, Return Path nurtures its environment, finding new ways to help its people and teams to blossom. Can you say the same about your own firm?

Look at the performance management system in your company and ask

yourself, *"What might grow and blossom if we were to really cultivate this garden?"*

Valerie Sessa and **Jennifer Bragger** are associate professors in industrial and organizational psychology at Montclair State University, Montclair, N.J. Sessa's interests include learning at individual, group and organizational levels. Bragger's interests include the job interview, bias in personnel processes, work/family conflict and downsizing. Combining these interests has led them to a number of research projects on learning and performance management.

Why Performance Management Systems Must Continue to Evolve

By Nancy T. Tippins

Baldonero, Hoffman, and Maltz highlight the challenges of performance management in the new work environment of many organizations and emphasize the importance of establishing an individual's responsibilities and measuring team members against those duties. Importantly, they tie performance measurement to development opportunities and encourage continuous efforts to improve. The Return Path performance management system provides an example of how the changing nature of work and workers necessitates many commensurate changes in performance management practices.

When constructing performance management systems, many organizations must take into account the fact that some teams are geographically dispersed and some supervisors do not work side by side with their direct reports. Many workers have flexible work schedules and may not work the same hours as their supervisors, even when colocated. Large spans of control or influence in downsized organizations may limit the opportunities supervisors have to observe their employees directly as well as to provide feedback and coach in face-to-face settings. Matrix

management structures can create confusion about who is responsible for managing performance. Consequently, the source of performance data in new performance management programs must come from other people or systems. In addition, traditional performance management systems must find ways other than face-to-face conversations between supervisor and employee to communicate effectively with a diverse group of employees to provide feedback and shape and motivate future performance.

Similarly, the concept of a job with a set of specific responsibilities may be replaced with the idea that a person has set of duties that may change frequently. Global organizations may have similar jobs around the world that have different responsibilities and different standards for performance. Cultural differences among team members may limit the willingness or ability of team members to communicate appropriately, requiring special educational efforts regarding the importance of performance feedback. Thus, the performance management system must be as dynamic as the work itself.

In addition to changes in the workplace, attitudes and expectations of workers are also changing. Many workers expect opportunities for continued personal growth and development as well as rapid career progression. The importance of rewards and recognition remain important, as does the desire for work-family balance. To the extent that organizations want to attract and retain highly qualified workers and minimize turnover, performance management programs must incorporate strong development components and appropriate reward structures.

A performance management system can be a valuable tool; however, it must continuously adapt to changes in the work environment and the workers themselves. ▪▪

Nancy T. Tippins is senior vice president at CEB Valtera/SHL and past president of the Society of Industrial Organizational Psychology. She is the lead author of a chapter on "Performance Management of the Future," in the book, *Performance Management: Putting Research into Action*.

LEARNING GUIDE

Point Counterpoint II: 3.2

Reimagining Performance Management

DISCOVERY QUESTIONS

- What are you dealing with in your organization today that relates to this content area?
- What is the consistent business case in all represented companies for transforming performance management?
- Explain what really drives the performance based on the applied research and new practices at Return Path and Statsoil.
- If ratings are removed, what needs to be installed to ensure sustained continuity in individual and team performance?
- Does transparency in these revised performance systems matter?
- Do these Perspectives make a case for the change in performance management systems overall or to take the "secure" path of staying with the true and tried?

SELECTED FACTS

- What new facts that were presented got your attention?
- How has the 360 assessment process evolved at Return Path?
- How has the use of feedback evolved in the new performance management system?
- Find proof of the changing manager role across all company cases
- Explain what is meant by "horizontal commitment" vis- à-vis "vertical commitment."
- What are the two main facets of the "reboot" of the old performance system?

KEY DISCUSSION POINTS

- What key points being made in this Perspectives?
- Discuss the connection between motivation, behavior, and outcomes in performance management systems. (Compare and contrast "before" and "after" examples given.)
- What is the role of senior management in organizational change toward new processes?
- Explain how employees' expectations are changing and what emerging needs are driving transformation in the performance management system.
- What is the role of HR in this transformation?

REVIEW OF SOLUTIONS

- Identify two to three "big ideas" worthy of exploring in your organization.
- Is the "democratization" of the workplace is inevitable?
- Return Path is a technology start-up. Can their experience translate and scale to the bigger, more traditional companies?

IDENTIFYING THE PARADOX

- How is it that established PM systems in most organizations are no longer valid in the 21 century?
- Consider how different solutions (redesigns) might be applied in different business situations.
- Explain how to apply to performance management what Dee Hock, former CEO of Visa, meant when he said, "*Simple, clear purpose and principles give rise to complex, intelligent behavior. Complex rules and regulations give rise to simple, stupid behavior.*"

LEARNING OUTCOMES

- What one new piece of information did you learn that will be important to you in the future?
- Identify one thing that you will do differently based on what you have learned.
- What skills do you personally need to acquire to drive PM transformation in your organization?

Balancing the Critical Factors of CEO Succession

By Marc Sokol

I remember a college professor who enthusiastically reviewed the benefits and techniques of logical analysis, only to conclude with a warning, "Wonderful as this is, don't think you can use it for life's really important decisions, like choosing your spouse!" Perhaps it's the same for CEO succession: We aspire to have a logical toolset guiding us through the process with certainty, only to find ourselves or the board of directors begin to rely on intuition and emotion because so much is at stake. There is an art to balancing logic and emotion, as well as evidence and intuition, and many companies struggle to engage all facets within their succession process.

If anyone has figured how to balance the critical factors for CEO succession, it is surely **Noel Tichy.** For decades Professor Tichy has been at the forefront of leadership development, both as a thought leader and a practitioner. His publications and clients are each

> There is an art to balancing logic and emotion, as well as evidence and intuition,

numerous. In our lead Perspective, Noel outlines the case for a radical transformation of what we must focus upon to ensure better succession.

Expanding on the lead perspective, we have invited four other leaders, each steeped in succession practice, to share their own reflections:

As the executive director for a consortium of HR executives, **Patty Woolcock** is well positioned to provide advice for CHROs, particularly as they strive to align the focus of the CEO

and the board around the succession process.

Kathleen Ligocki knows firsthand the role of a CEO with regard to succession and how to best leverage your board of directions. If you want to increase the chances of getting succession right, help your board ask and have answers to the essential questions posed in this commentary.

J. Lynne Cannon brings the dual vantage point of having been a CHRO and a board member to provide a third commentary with three challenges for the CHRO. Among her observations: Don't let smaller company size keep you from creating a robust succession process.

In our final commentary, **Jane Marvin**, who leads people and culture for Peet's Coffee & Tea, challenges all of us to rethink succession for a constantly changing world, where it's not just about the CEO, but also the surrounding team.

If you believe senior level succession

practices are essential for the long-term competitiveness of your firm, then this installment of Perspectives is for you.

Marc Sokol, Ph.D., is Perspectives editor.

POINT

Succession: The Need for Radical Transformation

By Noel Tichy

CEO Transitions Gone Wrong

One of the critical jobs of any CEO is to add value to the assets they are handed and leave them to a successor who continues the process of simultaneously adding value while building a pipeline of leaders so that the next successor is developed.

Eighty percent of companies get it wrong as measured by shareholder value over time when the new CEO takes over. For example, Steve Ballmer took over for Bill Gates at Microsoft; by the time Ballmer retired in 2014, market capitalization of Microsoft went from $600 billion to $270 billion, while Google went from $111 billion to $363 billion in same time period. Could you easily share that statistic with your board if you were the CHRO at Microsoft?

Going outside to find your next CEO isn't the solution either; it means that your leadership pipeline has failed. Hewlett–Packard (HP) is the poster child for this, appointing four external CEO's in a row in a decade. Carly Fiorina was fired; Mark Hurd was fired; Léo Apotheker was fired; Meg Whitman, the current CEO, was also recruited from outside HP. When Carly Fiorina started her tenure in 1999, the market cap was at $114 billion; when she was fired in February 2005, it had dropped as low as $61 billion. Meg Whitman is now in the shaky situation of needing to improve upon her successors' failures and create value in this high-tech world.

Four decades of research and practice has convinced me that there is a better way to structure, manage, and maintain succession, but we need to radically change what occurs in many companies. I've also seen, all too often, the signs that a succession approach is missing the mark.

Seven Indicators That Your Succession Approach Is Failing

Is your well-intentioned succession plan missing the mark? Ask yourself if your firm is suspect of any of the following seven failure factors:

Failure Factor No. 1: SPOTS. Succession Plans on Top Shelves, which are where they stay, unused, and simply become a paper exercise.

Failure Factor No. 2: The Beer Truck Test. The CEO dies or is fired suddenly, like Carly Fiorina, Mark Hurd, Léo Apotheker, all at HP, and when you ask who is ready to step in, there is no one from inside. HP kept failing the "beer truck test," and is

now trying to get it right with Meg Whitman, their fourth outsider in a row.

Failure Factor No. 3: The Domineering CEO Who Won't Let Go. Microsoft's Steve Ballmer was pushed out as CEO, but with no successor ready.

Failure Factor No. 4: The Superstar Outside Bias. This happens when the board scouts high-profile external

> ## Effective succession practices involve the CHRO, the incumbent CEO, the board, and the candidates themselves.

candidates rather than building a solid internal bench. HP's Carly Fiorina was cover news story material at the time of her hire and a total failure over time.

Failure Factor No. 5: The Halo Effect. Similar to No. 4, this is when a board looks to a high-flying company to source a CEO. Unfortunately Carly Fiorina is also poster child for this failure factor.

Failure Factor No. 6: Assessing CEO Candidates on Traits as Opposed to Experience. Aptitude is a wonderful thing, but by the time someone is a CEO candidate, they should have years of substantive experience to complement the right traits.

Failure Factor No. 7: Winner-Takes-All CEO Succession. Or, those who lose need to leave; contenders, who are in a "horse race" to the finish line, become convinced they cannot work for each other. This is a totally unnatural act among leaders who really have the right stuff and fosters a political dynamic that undermines teamwork across the executive level.

A Better Approach

Effective succession practices involve the CHRO, the incumbent CEO, the board, and the candidates themselves. It's a partnership between all parties, but the CHRO is the one best positioned to be an honest broker of the process. It is a complex process,

a mixture of technical, political, and cultural forces at play.

I use a metaphor of a rope woven from three separate strands—technical, political, and cultural—to illustrate the three subsystems found in all organizations:

Technical system. The rational scientific management precepts of strategic planning, organization design, and human resources.

Political system. Who influences strategy—managing political coalitions, allocating power in the organization structure—as well as the human resource political issues of who gets ahead, and how much money they make.

Cultural system. Accepted norms and values, how the human resource systems screens for, develops, and rewards for norms and values.

Most succession processes fail, not because of the technical component, but rather due to failure of the parties to manage the political and cultural elements.

Playing Their Part

The **incumbent CEO** builds the leadership pipeline and ensures talent development at all levels. This person has the obligation to create a collaborative environment with the CHRO and the board to continue the leadership pipeline and succession process both during and after his or her tenure. The incumbent CEO must take the initiative to discover new talent to present to the CHRO and board while stepping back and not allowing personal biases to rule the process.

The **CHRO** ensures preparation of a pipeline of candidates. At the best companies, this is at least a decade long process. Just as finance carefully manages a review of the numbers, HR collects and organizes information on talent related to succession. They facilitate involvement of other stakeholders, ensuring continual review and updating over time.

Board members look at who can make the transition leading the enterprise, while also being suited to partner with the board. The board is responsible for making succession a top priority and tackling not just the technical but also the political and cultural issues head-on. Its other responsibilities include assisting in developing the leadership pipeline at all levels, benchmarking internal versus external candidates, and ensuring fair and equal exposure for all candidates to the board, among others. At the end of the day, the ultimate responsibility of hiring and firing CEOs lies with the board.

Candidates also have a role: to recognize that they will win by performing and lose by becoming political.

If I had only one lesson to leave you with, it would be this: CEO succession and executive transition is not, should not, and never will be only about selecting the best CEO from a pool of likely candidates. It must always be about building a continuously transforming succession pipeline carefully constructed and designed to grow truly transformative leaders on the inside. That is the challenge to present and future organizations as we move forward into and increasingly complex and diverse world.

Noel M. Tichy is a professor of management and organizations at the Ross School of Business at the University of Michigan and a senior partner in Action Learning Associates. Author of numerous books and articles, Noel's most recent book is *Succession: Mastering the Make or Break Process of Leadership Transition.*

Not Just Names on a List

By Patty Woolcock

Too often we hear about succession planning as an annual process of creating organization charts with names below each incumbent leader, a check-the-box exercise, after which the CHRO, CEO, and board move on to seemingly more important things. Why is this not taken more seriously? Why is more effort *not* put into doing it right?

From my experience, there are a few barriers that get in the way of doing the deep, robust work required to have a strong succession plan in place.

Expectations of the Board and CEO Are Not Aligned

Too often the CHRO bases his or her activities on the expectations of the board and CEO. The board many times is happy that the CHRO and CEO are thinking about succession, but their demands do not go deeper than that. Many times the CEO does not think this is part of his or her own job, and it is difficult for the CHRO to get much airtime to discuss succession, let alone have a robust process in place.

Tenure and Long-Term Succession Planning

This is a long process, taking up to 10 years to fill the leadership pipeline when done right. It works best with the same CEO and CHRO working together to create the systems and processes to fill the pipeline. Unfortunately, when someone is only with a company a few years, whether it be the CEO or CHRO, their greatest priorities are the short-term ones right in front of them.

What Can a CHRO Do?

The CHRO can look at the leadership development and talent management as one system, and focus attention on the following questions:

- If you overlay the expectations of a good succession plan over that system, what do you see? What processes are dead ends? What yields results?
- How can you set the expectation that the entire C-suite is jointly responsible for developing future leaders? How can you create customized development opportunities for leaders a few levels down in the organization?
- What can you do to get the CEO and the board familiar with talent two and three levels lower in the organization?

The answers to these questions are not easy, but they can be the most important contribution any CHRO can make.

Patty Woolcock is executive director of CSHRP, the California Strategic Human Resource Partnership, a nonprofit consortium of 45 San Francisco Bay area CHROs. She is also the owner of Woolcock Consulting, and most recently was interim director of global leadership and talent development at NetApp.

Upping the Odds of Success

By Kathleen Ligocki

Great leadership succession is tough. Despite the board of directors' best intentions and vast sums spent on leadership development and CEO recruitment, success is far from guaranteed.

> Seldom are external candidates presented by a sitting CEO, particularly someone who might be ready... tomorrow.

Emergency Transition Often Trumps Ongoing Development

Too many CEO succession processes lack the robustness to withstand an emergency transition (due to a firing, an unanticipated retirement, or a death) and, what should be an ongoing thoughtful development process, collapses into a chaotic scramble that, not surprisingly, yields suboptimal results.

Exiting Gracefully

To make matters more complicated, many CEOs won't willingly "write their obituary." Think of the leadership analogies that reinforce this CEO behavior: "One quarterback on the field;" "one pilot at the helm;" "one seat in the chair;" "one king of the realm." Sure, sophisticated CEOs conduct the annual talent assessments identifying one or two potential internal successors who might be ready in a three-to-five year window. Other CEOs want to anoint their successor, preferably some type of "mini-me," which may

> Other CEOs want to anoint their successor, preferably some type of "mini-me," which may or may not be the best leadership profile for the company's future.

or may not be the best leadership profile for the company's future. Seldom are external candidates presented by a sitting CEO, particularly someone who might be ready...tomorrow.

Five Succession Questions for the Board

Inevitably, CEO tenure is finite, and the board must own and provide oversight to the succession process. The best processes are open, dynamic, and ongoing. Although good boards spend at least one meeting annually on talent development, poring over binders of profiles, the real test is how well they can address the following five questions:

- **Passing the Beer-Truck Test.** In an emergency, who steps in? An internal executive? A board member? As an interim or a permanent replacement? If you can't answer the first question in five seconds, you fail the beer-truck test!
- **Developing internal candidates.** Of the top internal heirs apparent, what are the crucial "move-the-needle" development assignments or experiences they should each take on in the next year to better prepare them to be CEO? Even if uncomfortable, assure these happen.
- **Monitoring external candidates.** Of the top external CEO candidates, do board members know them personally? Why wait until a vacancy looms to develop an external slate? Board members should actively develop a list of talented external candidates who might be a cultural or political fit for the company.
- **Looking beyond competence.** When CEOs fail, it is more often an issue of character or chemistry than competence. Are integrity, mental agility, empathy, and political savvy adequately weighed in your development and selection process?

- **Ensuring a robust leadership pipeline.** How deep is your pipeline? The best litmus test of CEO succession depth is an evaluation of bench strength one to two levels deeper in the company. True transformation comes at the heart of an organization. Even if the next CEO comes from the outside, the new leader will inherit a much stronger, more talented team if rigorous leadership development has been woven into the fiber of the company.

If your board cannot answer the above questions quickly and with consensus, your succession process isn't really ready.

Kathleen Ligocki is CEO of Harvest Power, a venture-backed organic and renewable energy company. After three decades in global senior leadership roles at General Motors, United Technologies, and Ford Motor Company, she became a serial CEO, leading a Fortune 1000 global auto supplier, a private Mexican auto retailer, and a venture early-stage auto company.

Three Key Challenges for the CHRO

By J. Lynne Cannon

As someone who looks at CEO succession from the vantage point of having been a former senior global head of HR in pharmaceuticals *and* a chairman of the board of trustees for RWJ Hamilton Health Care, *and* consultant to a range of biotechnology companies at all stages of growth, I see three key challenges for CHROs:

The Challenge of Board Accountability

Noel Tichy in his book, *Succession: Mastering the Make or Break Process of Leadership Transition*, raises the board's role. As I have observed firsthand, board culture and dynamics are critical. Even a very well-intentioned board with passionately committed members can develop groupthink and succumb

to wishful thinking such as, "if we just turn the corner." The outcome of such behavior is retention of a CEO or other key executives far beyond what is best for the enterprise. A board's executive committee must shoulder the accountability to confront itself and bring in independent external challengers. One way for the CHRO to drive this is to set up regular outside reviews and evaluations to engage the executive committee.

The Challenge of Company Size

Does size of the company or organization matter in succession? A big challenge for companies such as biotechs is to build bench strength and talent from within. Building from within must and can happen in any company at any size. The myth often perpetuated is, "we are too small to have a potential CEO talent or other top talent." This simply is not true! Even for startups, it is essential and possible to hire the best and most experienced talent. The key is to avoid the mindset of hiring "for today only," or "for what we need now." If startups are to succeed, they have to project strategic talent needs for the future and acquire talent for both the short and long term. This includes hiring a strong CHRO on the business team and not under-hiring or allowing the CFO to run HR.

The cool thing about smaller companies, is that the CHRO truly inspires the C-suite to attract talented leaders with entrepreneurial mentality at every level, and then gives them the exposure and accountability to foster their rapid development.

The Challenge of Making It More Than Just an Exercise

The big bold opportunity for the CHRO is to engage the leadership at all levels in dynamic and rigorous dialogues. Discussions about talent must be designed into cross-functional and special peer review sessions, which is common among more successful research and development organizations. A robust exchange facilitated by the CHRO models the way and challenges the process to avoid superficial or routinized agendas. The objective is to keep it real, confront the overstatements, and surface the talent, while dealing with a business unit's or manager's tendency to hold onto talent. As Tichy cautions, the CHRO makes sure that the company's cultural and political dynamics do not distort the process.

J. Lynne Cannon is CEO of Princeton Management Development Institute, a firm serving biotechnology and pharmaceutical businesses. Lynne is also chair of the Robert Wood Johnson Health Care Board at Hamilton, and a member of the American Hospital Association Board Governance Committee. Previously, Lynne was global senior vice president of human resources for the Novartis Institutes for Biomedical Research, and global vice president, human resources for Bristol Myers-Squibb Pharmaceuticals.

When Past No Longer Predicts Future

By Jane Marvin

With the astounding speed, complexity, and transformative nature of business today, is it really any surprise that so many senior leaders fail? Organizations are dynamic, complex, and erratic, with new technologies, competitors, and capabilities fundamentally changing the rules of the game at speeds never before contemplated. How does a taxicab company respond to the arrival of Uber, or the music industry to Pandora? Should they have anticipated and prepared for these arrivals, or are they destined to react as best they can when new conditions and requirements present themselves?

As the World Changes, So Must Succession Practices

Just as past operational success is no longer always a great predictor of future performance, perhaps past leadership behavior isn't necessarily a great predictor of future performance either. What it takes to succeed in one stage of an organization's evolution is often completely different from the skills, attributes, and experience necessary to lead that organization through the next phase of its development. So, while a thoughtful, deliberate decade-long approach to succession may be appropriate in a more stable environment, all too often discontinuities and unexpected changes mean this simply cannot be.

Succession planning in today's environment is no longer a top-down, autocratic process of kingmaking. It is neither orderly nor deliberate. Rather, it is fluid, opportunistic, and often reactionary—demanding agile, quick responses to discontinuities and changing sets of circumstances. As Tichy points out, it is about building truly transformative leaders for a variety of scenarios. It cannot be a simple evaluation of candidates in isolation, but must be paired with ongoing organizational assessment of future changes and requirements, with a series of back-up scenarios and contingencies.

Succession Is Really About the Larger Team

Consideration must be given to building complementary teams of interdependent leaders, such that one set of experiences can act as a balance to the others. Did Microsoft truly make the wrong decision in selecting Steven Ballmer as their leader? Should the board and prior leadership better anticipated the criticality of ongoing technical innovation, vision, and continuous reinvention and selected a more appropriate candidate? Perhaps so, or perhaps they should have surrounded him with a complementary team of technologists, futurists, and developers as a counterbalance to his operational prowess, and then monitored the ongoing effectiveness of the team overall.

It is no longer realistic to expect that one leader can do it all. The wiser course is to continuously strive to build diverse, broad, complementary teams, and to develop shared leadership and accountability for results—both from the executive team and the board of directors. Succession planning thus shifts from an attempt to orchestrate a leadership transition (an activity that all too often is a zero-sum game) to efforts to ensure leadership sharing and continuous learning.

No longer win or lose, the emphasis shifts to capitalizing on different experiences and perspectives, balancing wisdom and experience with innovative ideas and fresh perspectives. Under this scenario, board members act as sounding boards and executive coaches, and the job of HR is to continuously create opportunities for interaction, introspection, learning, and executive growth. ⊞

Jane Marvin is senior vice president of people and culture at Peet's Coffee & Tea, and has also held CHRO roles at Solazyme, Ross Stores, and AT&T Wireless.

> Succession planning in today's environment is no longer a top-down, autocratic process of kingmaking.

LEARNING GUIDE

Point Counterpoint II: 3.3

Balancing the Critical Factors of CEO Succession

DISCOVERY QUESTIONS

- What are you dealing with in your organization today that relates to this content area?
- What surprises you most as you read this set of perspectives on succession?
- How varied is the role of human resources in company succession?
- What are the risks of not having a robust succession plan?
- What is the board's role in succession planning?
- Why might the CEO, CHRO, and board *not have a strong partnership around* succession?
- How can the CHRO work closely with the board to ensure strong succession practices?

SELECTED FACTS

What new facts that were presented got your attention?

- Eighty percent of companies get succession wrong when measured by change in shareholder value.
- Effective succession practices involve the CHRO, the incumbent CEO, the board, and the candidates themselves.
- Three subsystems of organizations that are part of succession planning are the technical system, the political system and the cultural system.
- HP appointed four external CEOs within a decade.
- After CEO Steve Ballmer retired from Microsoft in 2014, market capitalization dropped from $600 billion to $270 billion, but in the same time frame Google increased from $111 billion to $363 billion.
- Good boards spend at least one meeting annually on talent development and succession planning

KEY DISCUSSION POINTS

- What were the key points being made in this presentation?
- Why is a pipeline of candidates more important than just having a designated successor?
- Which of Noel Tichy's seven indicators of failed succession practices do you think is most prevalent and why?
- Why might succession planning be emotionally difficult for some CEOs?
- Why might an outside CEO or senior executive be highly successful in one company but not as the CEO successor in another company?
- What is the risk of creating or allowing a 'horse race' among internal leaders who are succession candidates?
- Even though the commentary authors all agree with the lead perspective in principle, how do these different authors differ in their approach to succession?
- How transparent should companies be around succession processes and candidates?

REVIEW OF SOLUTIONS

- Identify two to three "big ideas" worthy of exploring in your organization.
- What traits might you look for in a CEO successor candidate?
- What experiences might you also look for to complement the right traits?
- How do you see the board, the CHRO, and CEO working together to ensure CEO succession that works?

IDENTIFYING THE PARADOX

- How it that a solution appropriate for yesterday's organization is no longer valid?
- Consider how very different perspectives might be correct given different situations.
- How can CEO succession be both a logical and an emotional process?
- Why might a CEO, who presumably benefits from the continuity of a company after they leave, undermine efforts to find a successor?
- Why is it both important and risky to have multiple succession candidates inside the company?
- How can the board and CHRO work closely with a CEO on succession planning and set limits to the CEO's involvement?
- How might emergency succession planning conflict with ongoing development of succession candidates?

LEARNING OUTCOMES

- What one new piece of information did you learn that will be important to you in the future?
- Identify one thing that you will do differently based on what you learned.
- What would be your "elevator speech" to the board about the importance of their involvement in succession planning?
- Why does CEO succession require attention to the technical system, the political system, and the cultural system?
- Why docs the board need to be exposed to succession candidates two and three levels below the CEO?

PART 4: ORGANIZATIONAL DESIGN

Matrix Management

By Anna Tavis

This Perspectives panel has been convened on the occasion of the publication of Kevan Hall's new book: *Making the Matrix Work, How Matrix Managers Engage People and Cut Through Complexity* (Nicholas Brealey Publishing, 2013). Kevan Hall's premise is based on the assumption that matrix organizational structures are unavoidable in the complex cross-border business economy. To resolve arising managerial challenges in the matrix, Hall argues, we need to assume a pragmatic stance. Anyone involved in the matrix management has to ultimately recognize that the power has been gradually shifting from structure to skills.

Indeed, Nicolay Worren of Norway, one of the panel contributors, reminds us here of Peter Singe's earlier remark "If the ship is already at sea, the best we can do is to train the crew to cope with the way the ship has been designed." But, when possible, we should begin before that. In other words, we should develop better tools and methods and help leaders to become better organizational designers.

Hall's overall approach is ultimately the following: The matrix conversation now is about its management. A new mindset and skill set and leadership is required to be successful much more than the focus on well-designed structured organizations. The matrix requires a different navigation skill set than the traditional hierarchical structures. I see Hall's approach as ultimately empowering to matrix participants. After all, new management skills could be trained and matrix leadership learned while structures ultimately require a different kind of engineering. In fact, the last chapter of Hall's book clearly calls for a proactive learning approach: "Be a matrix manager, not a victim."

Our distinguished panel represents "a global who is who" of organizational design experts. Individually they've each said a lot on the subject of org. design in their respective books, articles and blogs. Together, this panel brings a wealth of experience and helps us navigate the complexity of organizational challenges.

The discussion that follows illustrates the broad range of perspectives on the topic of matrix management. It is enough to say that Jay Galbraith, one of the most distinguished names in the org. design movement, agrees with Hall's conclusion that there is a clear shift to skill that is occurring in the approach to the matrix. Another distinguished veteran of the field, Ken Shepherd, and his no less distinguished colleagues from the Global Organization Design Society Editorial Board do not go along with Hall's assertions.

No one could argue that it is the leaders' responsibility to perfect their personal org. design skills while cultivating new behaviors and ways of operating in the majority of their matrix subordinates. It is people in the middle and below them who still have to cope with ambiguities, confusion and complexity of those structures on their own.

Andrew Campbell of Ashridge Consulting in the United Kingdom, Amy Kates and Greg Kesler of Kates Kesler Organization Consulting (New York/Connecticut) along with Stephen T. Clement of Organizational Design Inc. (Canada), and Ken Shepard of the Global Organization Design Society (Canada) represent the global authority on how to explain and help navigate the matrix for both the leaders who design organizations and for matrix managers who are called upon to deliver within the matrix structures.

The conversation in these pages is about the practice of matrix management. Kevan Hall, the founder and CEO of the consulting firm Global

Integration, knows how to navigate his way through the complexity of the matrix as well as respond to the diversity of opinions on the effectiveness of the matrix. After you read the pros and cons of the discussion that follows, we recommend that you pick up Kevan Hall's practical management guide and equip yourself with a toolkit that is designed for practice, not theory.

Anna Tavis, Ph.D., is Perspectives editor.

POINT

Revisiting Matrix Management

By Kevan Hall

Traditional organizations were structured "vertically" with functions within a country. In recent decades, work has become increasingly "horizontal" crossing the traditional vertical organisational silos. This new type of work is powered by business complexity and globalization and is enabled by information technology.

Supply chains cut across the world, global customers insist on a single point of contact and business functions become more integrated to share expertise and costs and to provide a better service to their businesses. Teams increasingly need to operate across barriers of distance, cultures (national, cultural and organizational), time zones, technology and business complexity.

A matrix organization structure with multiple reporting lines is now becoming the organizational structure of choice for large complex organizations. Even those organizations who resist a matrix structure are finding that the matrix way of working is inevitable; the old-fashioned silos just can't cope.

But this more matrixed way of working, with multiple reporting lines, competing goals and higher levels of ambiguity is a significant step up in complexity in the way people work together.

In 1990, Christopher A. Bartlett and Sumantra Ghoshal, writing on matrix management in the *Harvard Business Review*, quoted a line manager saying "The challenge is not so much to build a matrix structure as it is to create a matrix in the minds of our managers."

Our work with hundreds of clients around the world confirms that the structure itself solves nothing, it just provides a framework in which we can start to develop new ways of working.

Here are some of the critical people management challenges that we have observed in companies that operate the matrix.

1. Being connected, and effective

One of the top reasons that companies introduce a matrix structure is to increase cooperation and coordination across the traditional vertical silos. But be careful what you wish for!

> The secret in matrix management is to enable individuals to clarify their own goals and role.

If you are a HR manager in a vertical organization, you report upward to the HR director. You are included in their team meetings, calls and email distribution lists. You are already busy.

Then we add a matrix, in addition to your vertical line to the function you now have a horizontal line to a business unit head. You may also support more than one client group and be part of a number of virtual teams. All of these teams and reporting lines have a call on your time. They copy you on their emails and invite you to their meetings. If we are not careful, the matrix can double the amount of communication and connection.

People in matrix and virtual teams tell us they spend two days a week in meetings and only 50 percent of the content is relevant to them or their jobs. This represents a potential waste of one day a week, every week, for expensive professional and managerial staff — 20 percent of your headcount.

So in a matrix, at the same time as we become more connected, we also need to be more selective about where we cooperate. Teamwork becomes more expensive and complex as we work with colleagues in different locations and functions, so we have to do use it more sparingly. A powerful concept in matrix working is to understand where you don't need to be a team, otherwise the risk is that everyone becomes involved in everything, decision rights become unclear and we descend to consensus in areas where it adds no value.

2. The balance of control and trust

In complex structures like the matrix there are more opportunities for misunderstandings and conflicts. Communicating through technology, cultural differences in communication and competing goals can all lead to misunderstandings that can undermine our trust and confidence in our colleagues.

When trust is undermined, managers tend to increase control. In the early days of a matrix implementation, we often see an increase in control mechanisms such as meetings, reporting, approvals levels, etc. Inappropriate control causes delay, additional cost and dissatisfaction. It also further undermines trust that can lead to a vicious circle of reducing trust and increasing control.

In the past, trust building was a free by-product of proximity; we got to know our colleagues over coffee and lunch and often became friends. In matrix teams, particularly when they are international, we have limited opportunities to get face-to-face. We need to provide explicit opportunities and to structure the way we work to accelerate the building of trust.

Managers don't delegate to people they don't trust and decentralized decision making and empowerment is critical to the success of a matrix. In the absence of decentralization, expect to see high levels of escalation and delay.

3. Clarity and alignment

People new to a matrix often complain that their goals and role are not clear and are not aligned within the organization. In a matrix, there will be higher levels of uncertainty. If we could decide on a single stream of goals and clear roles, then we probably would not need a matrix; we could just decide centrally and cascade the answers. The matrix is a recognition that we are trying to manage complex dilemmas and trade-offs. We need to be successful with both the global and local, the function and geography, the business unit and the region.

The secret in matrix management is to enable individuals to clarify their own goals and role. If you have two bosses, you may be the only person who actually has a full understanding of your own role. You should certainly be the person with the highest level of motivation to achieve clarity then to be successful. If you rely on a boss who may have only half the picture and a quarter of the motivation to do it for you, you are likely to be disappointed.

Kevan Hall is the chief executive officer of Global Integration. He founded Global Integration in 1994, and developed the world's first virtual teams and matrix management training programs. Today, he runs his own global organization as well as training and consulting in matrix, virtual and global working – and has to practice what he preaches. He is an accomplished author, blogger and consultant.

Matrix Management: Structure is the Easy Part

By Jay R. Galbraith

I find that I am very much in agreement with Hall. I too, have experienced the shift in thinking about matrix organizations. About 10 or 12 years ago, managers viewed matrix as toxic. It was to be avoided at all costs. Today, the thinking is that matrix is impossible to avoid. We have to learn how to make them work effectively. Not all structures follow the strict definition of matrix, where people report to two bosses. But almost all organizations—large and small—are multidimensional. That is, the heads of functions, countries and business units all report to the leadership team.

I also agree with Hall on the importance of structure. Most leaders get strategy and structure right. The design difficulty is in getting all of the other organizational factors aligned with the structure to make the matrix work. These other factors are the roles and responsibilities, the communication patterns, the acceptance of escalation and conflict resolution practices, the incentives, the collaborative behaviors and key interfaces, and most importantly, the business and management

> I believe that the more complex the structure is, the more important the processes are ... the star of the show is the resource allocation process.

processes. As a generalization, I believe that the more complex the structure is, the more important the processes are. In a matrix, the star of the show is the resource allocation process.

As a matter of fact, a lot of organizational innovation today is in the management processes. Companies are using Decision Accelerators or large-scale meetings to align the plans and budgets of countries or regions with the business units. Instead of conflicting country and business plans, a reconciliation process is needed to produce a single company plan for growth and profit goals. Other technologies for involving large numbers of people are also being used. IBM's online "Jams," internal crowd sourcing and social media discussions allow people at all the interfaces of the matrix to enter the discussions.

The final factor is that we need to get the right people into the key matrix positions. Not everybody is cut out to perform in a matrix. People who want control, autonomy, and the freedom to do their own thing will not perform well. While we may like these attributes in entrepreneurs, they will create misfits

in a matrix. The most successful practitioners of matrix also use rotational assignments. People behave better in a matrix when they have had responsibility on both sides of the structure.

One of the reasons that matrix is difficult, is that we need to get all of these other factors aligned. The good news is that the best aligned organizations will be the best performing organizations.

Jay Galbraith is president of Galbraith Management Consultants, professor emeritus at IMD, and author of *Designing Matrix Organizations that Actually Work: How IBM, Procter & Gamble, and Others Design For Success.*

Activate the Matrix for Integration

By Amy Kates and Greg Kesler

Matrix is a mechanism to support integration across an organization structure. Paradoxically, however, if the matrix is not well designed or if it is not deliberately activated, the matrix can actually become a barrier to collaboration and integration.

While we agree with Hall that the right mindset and skill set is essential, we have found that this is too limited a view of what is needed for effective matrix enablement. Mindsets and skill sets are necessary, but not sufficient.

Our research and experience over the past 10 years, building on the work of Jay Galbraith, has found four factors that are required to bring the matrix to life.

1. Structure

The matrix allows a company to do more than one thing well: drive functional excellence, build global brands, organize by customer segment, and be locally relevant. The managers that report into multiple dimensions link the organization together. In too many companies, however, time is wasted on debates over "straight line" and "dotted line" reporting. Start with the premise that both reporting lines are equally important. Then, get granular and focus on key decisions.

The matrix can also become a barrier to speed when there are too many layers of matrix. A common symptom is matrixed team members (peers who report to multiple bosses) cannot make deci-

> Leaders in the matrix must learn to lead a diverse, sometimes dissonant orchestra. Alignment among the leadership team is critical.

sions together without checking above. The effect of this confluence of vertical and horizontal power confusion creates a slow, grinding cadence. Remember, not everyone needs to be in a matrixed reporting relationship to have a matrix mindset.

2. The right operating mechanisms

Committees don't make decisions in fast companies. One player across the matrix must be able to make the call on a given issue when agreement cannot be reached. Picture a 51 percent /49 percent partnership, where the golden vote depends on the subject matter. One voice in the matrix gets a stronger vote on brand decisions, while another owns the tipping point on channel management, and yet another on product design.

Profit and loss metrics create accountability. Robust planning and business review processes and rhythms bring the players in the matrix together to manage joint target settings, resourcing and results tracking in a collaborative manner. The goal is to create as much clarity as possible, not to anticipate every scenario, but to create the frameworks in which managers can make good judgment calls.

3. Networks and social capital

Organizational clarity must be complemented by close, effective working relationships. IBM utilizes technology extensively to enable cross-border working groups to sort through business pri-

orities. But leaders in IBM are brought together face-to-face on a regular basis to build human connections, widely regarded as the glue that ties its many diverse units together. At P&G and Coca-Cola, leaders build deep social capital by moving across functions and businesses in diverse assignments around the world, guided by well-established talent networks.

4. Boundary-spanning leadership

Leaders in the matrix must learn to lead a diverse, sometimes dissonant, orchestra. Alignment among the leadership team is critical. They have to be seen as sharing values and working together. Core skill sets include building the right relationships, influencing through compelling, data-based ideas and comfort with delegation and conflict. In addition, we have found the courage and organizational curiosity characterize those that thrive in a matrix.

Greg Kesler and **Amy Kates** are the authors of *Leading Organization Design: How to Make Organization Design Decisions to Drive the Results You Need.* Kates has also co-authored two books with Jay Galbraith. The authors consult with global companies to help clients maximize value-delivery through organization design and making complex organizations effective.

How to Get the Gain with Less Pain

By Andrew Campbell

Kevan Hall elegantly exposes some of the dilemmas and challenges in matrix structures. The pain a matrix creates for those with two bosses, and the control dilemma it creates for those with two thirds of a subordinate are real. Moreover, the confusion that results can be costly to organizational effectiveness. So don't create a matrix unless the gain you are aiming for is large enough to make the pain worthwhile.

Often there is a better way: It is possible to get most of the gain without

most of the pain. For example, take the typical product/geography matrix. The country manager for product A in Spain has two bosses. She reports to a global product boss, the head of division A, and a geographic boss, the head of Spain. Not infrequently the two bosses disagreed, and she has to pick up the pieces.

There are many alternatives to the matrix. One solution is to set up the global product division as a central policy unit responsible for worldwide product consistency, marketing message and other global policy areas. The product manager in Spain, then only has one boss, the head of Spain; but she has to work within policy constraints.

Another solution is to set up the country manager as a coordinator and champion for the country. His job is to encourage product managers in the country to work together to save costs and build a strong country presence. In this case, the product manager in Spain only has one boss, the head of her product division.

Another example where matrix management is common is in global functions, like HR or finance. Typically, the business partner for HR will have a solid line to group HR and a heavy dotted line to a business. The gain comes from reducing the number of HR staff and ensuring closer adherence to HR policy.

But both objectives can be achieved without the full matrix solution. Tough targets for HR costs in the budget process can bring business units to the table with regard to sharing HR costs. Clear HR policies and a supportive CEO can deliver the standardization of behavior that is needed. With these solutions, HR business partners can continue to report to the head of a business, rather than being matrixed between a business and Group HR.

So how do managers decide when to create a matrix and/or how to get the gain with less pain? The tool I have found most useful, when dealing with matrix-type issues, is the decision grid. Along the top of the grid, list the people concerned. Down the side, list the decisions or responsibilities or dilemmas that are causing you to consider a matrix structure. In the boxes, record the role you would like each individual to play in each contentious area. My preference is to use the Bain & Co tool, RAPID—Recommend, Agree, Perform, Input, and Decide. Often it is best to create your own words to suit the problem you are addressing.

Using this tool, I find that nine times out of ten a matrix, in the sense of an individual having two bosses, is not necessary. It is possible to solve the problem by giving some extra authority on some selected issues to one party or another. Of course, to some degree, dotted lines are created whenever you interfere with the power of a boss. But by using decision grids as the way to identify where power should be shared and where it does not need to be shared, and by having a language of relationships that is richer than "line" and "dotted line," it is possible to create a laser-like focus on the areas of gain and, at the same time, greatly reduce the pain.

Andrew Campbell is director of the Ashridge Strategic Management Centre. He is the co-author of *Strategies & Styles, A Sense of Mission, Corporate-Level Strategy, Synergy, Designing Effective Organisations, The Growth Gamble and Think Again: Why Good Leaders Make Bad Decisions.*

Simplify Complexity

By Nicolay Worren

The main point that Kevan makes—that internal complexity is increasing—has been confirmed in several surveys, including one conducted by the Economist Intelligence Unit in 2011. The potential consequences for managers and employees are unclear accountability, information overload, and increasing meeting activity. The kinds of interventions that Kevan and his colleagues offer can help increase the ability of people to cope with these kinds of challenges.

At the same time, we should also do what we can to improve the structural design of the organization. Peter Senge remarked, "the neglected leadership role is the designer of the ship." If the ship is already at sea, the best we can

do is to train the crew to cope with the way the ship has been designed. But when possible, we should begin before that. In other words, we should develop better tools and methods, and help leaders to become better organizational designers.

In my view, the choice is not between a "silo" and a matrix. There are many types of multidimensional organizations, and not all are equally complex to manage. It is stated that the matrix is becoming the organizational structure of choice. I think it is more appropriate to say that organizations are becoming *multidimensional*, in the sense that they increasingly combine

> In my view, the choice is not between a "silo" and a matrix. There are many types of multidimensional organizations, and not all are equally complex to manage.

geographical, product, and internal service provider units at the same hierarchical level, instead of a having a unidimensional structure (e.g., either a product or market-based structure). Studies also show that organizations today rely more on horizontal business processes and temporary projects, compared to organizations 30, 40 or 50 years ago. But only a subset of large companies have a matrix structure (i.e., one where employees formally report to more than one boss).

The problem with the matrix is that it uses the formal reporting structure as a key "linkage" between units. But there are other ways to link up units. An alternative model is to establish internal customer-supplier roles. Such a model does not necessarily mean that you have fewer relationships to manage, but you can avoid many of the overlapping and conflicting goals that you would have in a matrix structure. The relationships become easier to manage.

We should not accept the complexity of the matrix as unavoidable but work continuously to improve the design of the organization to clarify and simplify roles, processes and structures.

Nicolay Worren is a consultant and author of a textbook on organization design. He is based in Oslo, Norway. He writes a blog: www.organizationdesign.net.

Matrix Organizational Work

By Stephen T. Clement

Some contemporary organizational theorists tout the matrix structure as the best alternative to the traditional managerial hierarchy. They cite the usual litany of economic challenges facing a contemporary organization, e.g., globalization, unparalleled advances in information technology, customers demanding a single point of contact, etc. To overcome such presumed challenges, they cite the advantages of the matrix structure that to them is flatter, more integrative and responsive, and utilizes people more effectively. Alternatively, a second group of theorists (inspired by the late management guru Dr. Elliott Jaques) argue vociferously against the merits of adopting a matrix structure. This group cites the lack of individual accountability that permeates matrix relationships. This lack of accountability applies to both the manager as well as the subordinate. The manager does not have clear accountability for assigning tasks to the subordinate and the subordinate is equally unclear as to which tasks he or she receives from multiple "bosses" takes priority. In the end, such a situation ends up with the subordinate deciding what work to focus on and what priorities are important.

The Jaques group would argue that matrices should be avoided at all costs. Organizations should be designed up front to ensure that every employee has one and only one manager. This is a fundamental tenet in their management repertoire. The matrix advocates take just the opposite tact. They sincerely believe that the individual is more than capable of assigning his or her own work and goals. Further, this group notes that in today's global economy working horizontally has become critical to the long-term success of most contemporary institutions. Advances in information technology now permit employees to be connected to nearly everyone. Unfortunately, this rise in connectivity has also brought with it a tremendous rise in cross-functional messaging (emails etc.). Ask managers today and they will tell you that they are inundated with data when what they really need is actionable information. How can one resolve the aforementioned dilemma? Is there a simple answer? Is it one solution or the other?

It has been my experience, that it is not always the case that organizations can avoid establishing matrix working relationships in their existing organizational structures. For example, in many engineering organizations, highly specialized engineers often have to work with multiple managers as they apply their unique technical skills. The "trick" in such situations is not to let the engineer decide what he or she will work on but rather to define the nature of these horizontal working relationships so that they are clear to all parties involved, e.g., the engineers' immediate manager, the borrowing (or assisted) manager and the engineer themselves. While establishing such clarity is a difficult endeavor, the absence of it is likely to result in managerial "chaos," with a dedicated engineer sometimes "caught in the middle" trying to satisfy two "bosses" equally, which often leads to personal frustration and "burnout." Thus, the solution to multiple reporting relationships should not be left up to the individual to resolve. Rather, complex cross-functional working relationships should be clearly defined and their underlying accountability and authority base agreed upon by all parties involved.

Similarly, not all organizations should immediately succumb to the "silo" mentality (centralizing functions, particularly support ones) to improve efficiency. More often than not, a decentralized organization with HR, finance and engineering assets reporting in to a single operating unit president is likely to be more effective (but not as efficient). The principle here is that staff support functions don't make money, operating units do. Being efficient is not necessarily being effective from a P&L perspective. Further, industries differ dramatically in their design needs. Today's organizational architects need to be able to adjust their design parameters to changing situations appropriately.

Finally, the impact of increased complexity on managerial capacity is a significant challenge by itself. Roles and organizations are steadily increasing in complexity driven by the very nature of rapidly changing technologies and marketplace demands. Companies have enough trouble today ensuring that their internal talent pool is sufficient to keep up with these demands. Adding more complexity by adapting a matrix structure with its unclear demands on worker behavior exacerbates the capacity challenge. Why pursue such a course of action when there are simple and logical alternative designs readily available?

Dr. Stephen D. Clement is the president/founder of Organizational Design, Inc. He is the coauthor of *Executive Leadership, A Practical Guide to Managing Complexity*.

Matrix Benefits without Matrix Costs
First Structure and Staffing ... Then Skills

By Ken Shepard, Paul Tremlett and Glenn Mehltretter

As organization design practitioners, our clients are general managers, chief executive officers of major global corporations down to vice presidents of business units, who are almost always supported by their chief people officers. They are primarily concerned with implementing strategies that require improving cross-functional working relationships. We use the term "cross-functional relationships" rather than "matrix" that is variously defined and often poorly implemented, frequently destroying accountability and creating unnecessary complexity and conflict.

Three Stories
One: Owen Jacobs, formerly of the U.S. Army Research Institute, describes how in the early 1980s, the U.S. Army shifted from an individual skills model of leadership to a *systems-based* approach. The U.S. Army began with extensive analysis of the level of work complexity of the general staff—one to four star generals. Following proof of concept, **projects over the next 25 years** involved large scale levels-based

> It is more appropriate to say that organizations are becoming multidimensional, in the sense that they increasingly combine geographical, product and internal service provider units at the same hierarchical level, instead of having a unidimensional structure.

reorganizations of both uniformed and civilian components including the world's largest Lean Six Sigma work process redesign projects—all including improved cross-functional relationships. Elliott Jaques's requisite organization (RO) concepts including the "one manager" concept served as foundation for most of this work.

Two: John Hofmeister, former executive vice president human resources for Royal Dutch Shell, told the story at a recent Human Resource Planning Society conference about how his company used the RO concept of levels of work complexity to set the level of president and other key roles in the 90 or so country-business units that comprised the global corporation.

Previously, the corporation's country business unit presidents were considered to have equal status in that they all needed to liaise with heads of state. However, through the use of RO's key concepts Hofmeister helped the company to articulate the actual level of work complexity in each country business unit and to staff each of the roles with someone with the appropriate level of cognitive capability.

It's better to fix the systems not the people.

For example, Royal Dutch Shell's country business unit in Bolivia that distributed fuel was found to operate at level 3 of work complexity; but the United States subsidiary, Shell America, was a large, fully integrated oil business, and needed to be run as a level 6 business. ***Learn more*** *about levels of work complexity.* Hofmeister described how these tools supported effective coordination across countries, functions, products and customer groups enabling Royal Dutch Shell to become a fully integrated global corporation for the first time in its history.

Three: A business unit senior team completed a competitive review of their industry and decided that they could gain market share by up-shifting the level of their construction projects first from level 3 (schools) to level 4 (hospitals) and subsequently to level 5 (design-build-operate mega projects). In addition to up-shifting the construction function their strategy also required up-shifting and aligning

marketing, sales, procurement, HR and matching levels in an external matrix with their clients and project partners. ***Learn more*** *about levels shifting.*

How RO-Based Organization Designers Can Help Cross-Functional Work

RO practitioners agree with W. Edwards Deming that it's better to fix the systems not the people. They believe that properly designed strategy, structure, staffing and systems will naturally elicit 75 percent of the desired behaviors without specific individual training.

They believe that applying requisite design principles increases trust and engagement throughout the organization. ***Compare the close result between the Gallup Employee Engagement chart and the PeopleFit Requisite Situation Integrity Index chart.*** The proposition: employee engagement is directly proportional to the degree the organization is requisitely structured.

They bring precise univocal definitions of a few foundational science-based concepts to diagnose and resolve the chronic problems of "matrixed" organizations.

Their concepts of level of work complexity, level of human capability and accountability lead to improvements in the vertical structure ensuring:

- that roles are established at the level required to implement the strategy. (Much cross-functional innovation work requires systems thinking and must be led at level 4. Inappropriately led at level 3, the project will necessarily fail.)
- that managerial roles are estab-

lished one per level without compression or gaps. The average organization has an average of **36** percent **of its roles inappropriately leveled.**
- that roles are staffed with individuals with the required cognitive information processing. The average organization has **48.5** percent **of its roles with inappropriate staffing.**
- Cross-over managers (managers-once-removed) are put in place to set context, establish appropriate cross-functional accountabilities and authorities, and to resolve the rare conflicts upon appeal.

The above structural improvements result in fewer delays, fewer failures, lower costs and enables agile cross-functional cooperation while retaining appropriate accountabilities and authorities. It is not unusual for companies to obtain 30 percent improvement in financial performance following this initial redesign.

We propose that HR and external consultants supporting matrix designs learn requisite organization concepts and teach them to managers so that all concerned understand the importance of structure and staffing to cross-functional success in addition to the mindset and behavior skills advocated by Kevan Hall. ▪

The **Global Organization Design Society** is a not-for-profit corporation registered in Ontario, Canada, to promote the establishment and operation of a worldwide society of business users, consultants and academics interested in science-based management to improve organizational effectiveness.

LEARNING GUIDE

Point Counterpoint II: 4.1

Matrix Management

DISCOVERY QUESTIONS

- What are you dealing with in your organization today that relates to this content area?
- Does your organization have a matrix structure? Multiple reporting lines? What issues does that bring up?
- What type of organizational structure do your global customers in other countries prefer?
- Does your organization have solid and dotted reporting relationships? Or, is there multiple solid reporting? What are the pros and cons of these alternatives?
- Does your organization use a decision-grid approach to getting clear on who has what responsibility? (See Campbell's RAPID example.)

SELECTED FACTS

What new facts that were presented got your attention?

- Traditional organizations were structured "vertically," with functions within countries.
- The most successful matrix organizations use rotational assignments to give people experience in different parts of the matrix.
- In a matrix where clear governance and decision making is essential, then "who makes the final decision" on different subjects must be specified.
- The RAPID model includes: Recommend, Agree, Perform, Input, Decide.

KEY DISCUSSION POINTS

- What were the key points being made in this presentation?
- What are some of the key people management challenges for matrix organizations?
- What are positives and negatives of dual reporting relationships (to function and business)?
- Discuss the balance between trust and control when establishing a matrix structure.
- According to Galbraith, in addition to strategy and structure, what are the other factors that make a matrix structure work?
- When should decision accelerators, "jams," and crowd sourcing be used to clarify organizational processes?
- What personality types do not operate well in a matrix organization?
- According to Kates and Kesler, what four factors are required for an effective matrix?
- What are some alternatives to a pure matrix structure that Campbell suggests?
- What are some of Worren's ideas on simplifying complexity in organizational structure?
- According to the Jaques' group, what are the significant downsides of a matrix structure?
- What are Clement's strongest arguments against the matrix structure?
- How did Shell use work complexity assessment in their structure?
- What do RO practitioners and Deming followers agree on?

REVIEW OF SOLUTIONS

- Identify two to three "big ideas" worthy of exploring in your organization.
- What actions can you take to ensure clarity and alignment of goals in a matrix structure?
- What challenges would you face in trying to implement an effective matrix organization?

IDENTIFYING THE PARADOX

- How is it that a solution appropriate for yesterday's organization is no longer valid?
- Consider how very different perspectives might be correct given different situations.
- Might a matrix be effective in some countries and not in others? Explain.

LEARNING OUTCOMES

- What one new piece of information did you learn that will be important to you in the future?
- Identify one thing that you will do differently based on what you learned.

The Science Behind Happy Spaces

By Anna Tavis

If we spend 90 percent of our time indoors, and most of our waking time working, how do we become smart about creating spaces that make us happy, enhance productivity, reduce stress, and motivate us to collaborate and innovate for the longest possible time? This Perspectives column gathers some of the world's leading architects and designers armed with new science and offering compelling evidence-based design solutions to the workplace challenges of today.

In our lead Perspectives, **Bill Browning** of Terrapin Bright Green launches this important conversation with the provocative thesis, "Biophilia, Buildings, and Your Brain." Browning cites emerging research in a variety of scientific fields to make the case for how our environment can deeply affect our well-being. Informed with the new science, Browning explains his 14 evidence-based principles of new biophilic design that make you "smarter at work."

David Briefel, Gensler's sustainability director, offers a cautious but optimistic response. In Briefel's view, "a truly biophilic approach must be holistic." He advises against the temptation designers may have to attribute the impact on health and productivity to a single factor in isolation from the workplace culture, management, personal preferences, and individual psychologies.

Ken Wilson, a principal and chief sustainability officer at Perkins+Will, points to a significant crossover between biophilic design and the current management focus on improved collaboration and productivity. Among signature design projects used as illustrations for Perkins+Will's biophilic approach is the American Society of Interior Design that is seeking both LEED-CI Platinum certification and also WELL Building Standard certification. The building is designed as a living laboratory with the elements of

Office interior of Art Aqua in Bietigheim, German.   Credit: Bill Browning

"prospect, refuge, mystery, and dynamic lighting," among many others.

Chris Trott, of Foster + Partners, provides a "back into the future" perspective to the biophilia debate. As a firm, Foster + Partners have been on this journey for more than 50 years, but recently, a more quantifiable body of evidence of the value of biophilic design has been developed with the particular interest in well-being and health. We are reinventing the past with the future in mind.

Lance Hosey, a principle at Perkins Eastman, asks the provocative question, what if beauty is not at all in the eye of the beholder, but in the beholder's genes? He cites the evidence of "neuro-aesthetics" and "bio-aesthetics" to support the fact that our perception of beauty is biologically wired and transcends individual differences as well as race and gender. In conclusion, Hosey confirms that supported by science, it is possible to design spaces that universally improve human responses to our environment.

The implications of these scientific discoveries and their adoption by the leaders in architecture and design are vast and impressive.

Anna Tavis, Ph.D., is Perspectives editor and a faculty member at New York University and Columbia University.

Biophilia, Buildings, and Your Brain

By Bill Browning

Is your workplace making you dumb? Literally, is the space where you work impairing your cognitive abilities? What if the conditions in your building actually improved your cognitive function, reduced your stress, and enhanced your creativity? Emerging science indicates that it is possible to design spaces

TABLE 1. BIOPHILIC DESIGN PATTERNS & BIOLOGICAL RESPONSES

Table 1 illustrates the functions of each of the 14 Patterns in supporting stress reduction, cognitive performance, emotion and mood enhancement and the human body. Patterns that are supported by more rigorous emphirical data are marked with up to three asterisks (***), indicating that the quantity and quality of available peer-reviewed evidence is robust and the potential for impact is great, and no asterisk indicates that there is minimal research to support the biological relationship between health and design, but the anecdotal information is compelling and adequate for hypothesizing its potential impact and importance as a unique pattern.

14 PATTERNS		*	STRESS REDUCTION	COGNITIVE PERFORMANCE	EMOTION, MOOD & PREFERENCE
NATURE IN THE SPACE	Visual Connection with Nature	* * *	Lowered blood pressure and heart rate (Brown, Barton & Gladwell, 2013; van den Berg, Hartig, & Staats, 2007; Tsunetsugu & Miyazaki, 2005)	Improved mental engagement/ attentiveness (Biederman & Vessel, 2006)	Positively impacted attitude and overall happiness (Barton & Pretty, 2010)
	Non-Visual Connection with Nature	* *	Reduced systolic blood pressure and stress hormones (Park, Tsunetsugu, Kasetani et al., 2009; Hartig, Evans, Jamner et al., 2003; Orsega-Smith, Mowen, Payne et al., 2004; Ulrich, Simons, Losito et al., 1991)	Positively impacted on cognitive performance (Mehta, Zhu & Cheema, 2012; Ljungberg, Neely, & Lundström, 2004)	Perceived improvements in mental health and tranquility (Li, Kobayashi, Inagaki et al., 2012; Jahncke, et al., 2011; Tsunetsugu, Park, & Miyazaki, 2010; Kim, Ren, & Fielding, 2007; Stigsdotter & Grahn, 2003)
	Non-Rhythmic Sensory Stimuli	*	Positively impacted on heart rate, systolic blood pressure and sympathetic nervous system activity (Li, 2009; Park et al, 2008; Kahn et al., 2008; Beauchamp, et al., 2003; Ulrich et al., 1991)	Observed and quantified behavioral measures of attention and exploration (Windhager et al., 2011)	
	Thermal & Airflow Variability	* *	Positively impacted comfort, well-being and productivity (Heerwagen, 2006; Tham & Willem, 2005; Wigö, 2005)	Positively impacted concentration (Hartig et al., 2003; Hartig et al., 1991; R. Kaplan & Kaplan, 1989)	Improved perception of temporal and spatial pleasure (alliesthesia) (Parkinson, de Dear & Candido, 2012; Zhang, Arens, Huizenga & Han, 2010; Arens, Zhang & Huizenga, 2006; Zhang, 2003; de Dear & Brager, 2002; Heschong, 1979)
	Presence of Water	* *	Reduced stress, increased feelings of tranquility, lower heart rate and blood pressure (Alvarsson, Wiens, & Nilsson, 2010; Pheasant, Fisher, Watts et al., 2010; Biederman & Vessel, 2006)	Improved concentration and memory restoration (Alvarsson et al., 2010; Biederman & Vessel, 2006) Enhanced perception and psychological responsiveness (Alvarsson et al., 2010; Hunter et al., 2010)	Observed preferences and positive emotional responses (Windhager, 2011; Barton & Pretty, 2010; White, Smith, Humphryes et al., 2010; Karmanov & Hamel, 2008; Biederman & Vessel, 2006; Heerwagen & Orians, 1993; Ruso & Atzwanger, 2003; Ulrich, 1983)
	Dynamic & Diffuse Light	* *	Positively impacted circadian system functioning (Figueiro, Brons, Plitnick et al., 2011; Beckett & Roden, 2009) Increased visual comfort (Elyezadi, 2012; Kim & Kim, 2007)		
	Connection with Natural Systems				Enhanced positive health responses; Shifted perception of environment (Kellert et al., 2008)
NATURAL ANALOGUES	Biomorphic Forms & Patterns	*			Observed view preference (Vessel, 2012; Joye, 2007)
	Material Connection with Nature			Decreased diastolic blood pressure (Tsunetsugu, Miyazaki & Sato, 2007) Improved creative performance (Lichtenfeld et al., 2012)	Improved comfort (Tsunetsugu, Miyazaki & Sato 2007)
	Complexity & Order	* *	Positively impacted perceptual and physiological stress responses (Salingaros, 2012; Joye, 2007; Taylor, 2006; S. Kaplan, 1988)		Observed view preference (Salingaros, 2012; Hägerhäll, Laike, Taylor et al., 2008; Hägerhäll, Purcella, & Taylor, 2004; Taylor, 2006)
NATURE OF THE SPACE	Prospect	* *	Reduced stress (Grahn & Stigsdotter, 2010)	Reduced boredom, irritation, fatigue (Clearwater & Coss, 1991)	Improved comfort and perceived safety (Herzog & Bryce, 2007; Wang & Taylor, 2006; Petherick, 2000)
	Refuge	* * *		Improved concentration, attention and perception of safety (Grahn & Stigsdotter, 2010; Wang & Taylor, 2006; Wang & Taylor, 2006; Petherick, 2000; Ulrich et al., 1993)	
	Mystery	* *			Induced strong pleasure response (Biederman, 2011; Salimpoor, Benovoy, Larcher et al., 2011; Ikemi, 2005; Blood & Zatorre, 2001)
	Risk/Peril	*			Resulted in strong dopamine or pleasure responses (Kohno et al., 2013; Wang & Tsien, 2011; Zald et al., 2008)

© 2014 Terrapin Bright Green / 14 Patterns of Biophilic Design that improve these responses. Recent studies in neuroscience, endocrinology, environmental psychology, and other related fields are revealing how the spaces where we work and live can deeply affect our health. Armed this new information, we can conscientiously design spaces that boost productivity and support well-being.

In a previous column for *People + Strategy* ("Healthier Workplaces, Happier Employees," Vol. 38.3), we explored the basics of biophilic design, or built environments that connect people with experiences of nature. Positive experiences of nature elicit beneficial psychological and physiological responses, such as lowered blood pressure and heart rate, reduced muscular tension, better mental focus, lowered levels of stress hormones, and enhanced creative problem-solving abilities.

After examining and collating numerous scientific studies, Terrapin Bright Green has identified 14 design elements, or spatial patterns, that support these desired outcomes. The 14 patterns of biophilic design are not new inventions, but rather codification of the science behind why we respond to certain traditional design elements. It is evidence-based design, or in other words, a scientific understanding of why we like certain places better than others.

The 14 patterns of biophilic design are clustered into three sets of experiences: **Nature in the Space,** which refers to direct experiences of nature, **Natural Analogues,** which are representations of nature, and **Nature of the Space,** which replicate preferred spatial experiences found in natural settings.

Nature in the Space
1. Visual Connection to Nature
2. Non-Visual Connection to Nature
3. Non-Rhythmic Sensory Stimuli
4. Access to Thermal and Air Flow Variability
5. Presence of Water
6. Dynamic and Diffuse Light
7. Connection to Natural Systems

Natural Analogues
1. Biomorphic Forms and Patterns
2. Material Connection to Nature
3. Complexity and Order

Nature of the Space
1. Prospect
2. Refuge
3. Mystery
4. Risk/Peril

These patterns are meant to guide designers on how to create healthful, productive spaces. Effective biophilic spaces may display several of these pat-

Conscientious and targeted implementation of the patterns in a workplace can achieve desirable health outcomes for employees, a minimal investment that results in high productivity savings.

terns in tandem. The scientific evidence indicates that some of the 14 patterns support multiple outcomes, whereas other patterns are only linked with one outcome (see the chart below listing an overview of the health outcomes of each pattern). Because each pattern has a specific health outcome, a designer for a workplace must carefully select patterns with the intended health outcomes appropriate for that space (for example, any patterns that lower stress, improve cognitive function, and improve mental focus would be appropriate for most workplaces). Below are some examples of use of the patterns for specific outcomes, and the science to support them.

Stress Reduction
A Visual Connection to Nature (pattern 1) can cause the brain to shift to a less stressful mode of processing. Attention Restoration Theory (ART) posits that when you are experiencing nature rather than navigating the built environment, the brain shifts to a different mode of processing. Some of the higher cortical functions take a break and you experience the world through a state of "soft fascination." When you return to the task at hand, you are refreshed and better able to focus. The question

for a number of years has been, how long does it take for the brain to shift into this more relaxed mode? A team at Melbourne University undertook an experiment utilizing an FMRI machine.

Participants were given a stress-inducing task and then a recovery task. They viewed one of two scenes: an urban rooftop consisting of concrete, or the same rooftop rendered as a green roof with extensive plantings. The participants who viewed the concrete roof during the recovery task did not exhibit a shift in brain processing mode. The participants who viewed the green roof shifted brain mode within 40 seconds and performed better on the recovery task.[1]

The Presence of Water (pattern 5)—in particular, the sound of water—can change the perception of noise in an office environment. The team at the Psycho-Acoustic Laboratory at the Fraunhofer Institute has experimented with a variety of sounds to find a way to reduce problems associated with noise and in an open office. The team investigated the effect of white noise, pink sound, music, active noise cancellation, nature sounds, and moving water to help lower stress levels in an open office.

The sounds of water were found to be the most effective in lowering the perceived noise level in an office, although the sound of water does not lower the actual noise level in a space but in fact increases it. However, the human brain will focus on the sound of water, and filter out other noises.[2] This is much like the way we filter out surrounding conversations when we are talking with a friend at a cocktail party.

Cognitive Function
A Visual Connection to Nature (pattern 1) can also enhance the cognitive development of school children. There is a known annual progression of cognitive development in children. A study of more than 2,500 children in the Barcelona school system investigated whether the amount of green space (defined as tree canopy) at home, on the way to school, or in the schoolyard has an impact on cognitive development. The children in the study were tested multiple times over the course of a 13-month period. The amount of tree canopy at home or on the way to school had a

negligible effect. However, independent of socioeconomic factors, the children in schools with more tree canopy on the schoolyards had significantly higher levels of cognitive development over the children with little or no trees in the schoolyard.[3]

Another recent study found that cognitive performance of workers in an office is negatively impacted by high levels of CO_2 in the air. The study was undertaken by the Harvard T. H. Chan School of Public Health, Syracuse University, and SUNY Upstate Medical University with the Syracuse Center of Excellence on Indoor Air Quality. The participants worked for several days in what looks like a normal office, but is actually a giant space for testing indoor air quality. The CO_2 level was set at 500 ppm, somewhat above outdoor average, 950 ppm, a typically recommended level for buildings, and 1,500 ppm.

As part of their time in the space, the participants undertook a series of psychological tests. As the CO_2 level increased, cognitive function was impaired. Humans evolved in an era when CO_2 levels were in the range of 180–200 ppm. Today the global average outdoor level of CO_2 is now over 380 ppm. Implementing the pattern of Thermal and Airflow Variability typically results in increased airflows and air changes in a space, drastically lowering CO_2 levels for better performance. In a world of elevated CO_2, we need the air and airflows indoors to be more like the natural settings outside.[4]

Emotion, Mood, and Preference

The introduction of an element of Risk/Peril (pattern 14) into the built environment can surprisingly elicit a strong pleasure response in the brain. In this pattern, space designers create a brief experience of implied danger with a clear safety mechanism. For instance, a short expanse of glass floor with a view to spaces far below can be thrilling and trigger a strong dopamine response in the brain.[5] The Risk/Peril pattern can create memorable experiences, but probably should be used sparingly.

Application

Biophilic design might seem fine for the office of wealthy tech companies, but is it relevant in a manufacturing setting? The answer for Clif Bar was yes. The maker of sports bars is building an industrial bakery in Twin Falls, Idaho. Clif Bar wanted a facility that reflects the company's outdoor heritage and supports the health and wellbeing of their team. Skylights, plants, animals, water features, and natural materials are all part of the culture of their office spaces.

Sanitary and safety standards, however, will not allow any of these features inside an industrial bakery. So instead, the facility will use, images of Clif Bar staff and customers eating their products out in nature projected onto the high interior walls of the main production space. Simulated views of nature will lower blood pressure and heart rate, although not as much as a real view to nature.[6] There will also be a limited number of windows with views to the surrounding landscape, although these will be less effective during the nighttime shifts when the view is not visible. And the common areas will have a number of biophilic design elements to help the manufacturing staff recharge during breaks.

Smarter, More Productive Workers through Workplace Design

The workplace experience is obviously determined by much more than the design. Management, programming and engagement are crucial for supporting employee productivity, health and wellbeing. One critic has said, that there is not enough evidence yet to claim that we have a genetic need to connect with nature, or that all of the response mechanisms are not fully understood.[7] That assertion should be a call to continue research, rather than ignore what science is out there to demonstrate the benefits of connecting people with experience of nature. The use of biophilic design should be viewed as another set of human resources tools to support positive outcomes in the workplace.

Biophilic design, especially interventions like the ones suggested above, can support places that stimulate our brain and keep us engaged. Conscientious and targeted implementation of the patterns in a workplace can achieve desirable health outcomes for employees, a minimal investment that results in high productivity savings. By leveraging these scientific findings, we can create better workplaces for healthier, happier employees. Let's be smart about this.

Bill Browning, Hon. AIA, is cofounder of Terrapin Bright Green. He has coauthored several publications, including *Green Development, The Economics of Biophilia* and *14 Patterns of Biophilic Design.*

References

[1] Lee, K.E., Williams, K.J.H., Sargent, L.D., Williams, N.S.G., Johnson, K.A., (2015). 40-second green roof views sustain attention: The role of micro-breaks in attention restoration. *Journal of Environmental Psychology*, doi: 10.1016/j.jenvp.2015.04.003.

[2] Personal communication with Andreas Liebi, Psycho-Acoustics Laboratory, Fraunhofer Institute, Stuttgart, November 2014.

[3] Dadvand P, et.al. Green spaces and cognitive development in primary schoolchildren, Proceedings of the National Academy of Sciences, June 30, 2015, vol. 112, no. 26, pp. 7937–7942.

[4] Allen, J.G., MacNaughton, P., Satish, U., Santanam, S., Vallarino, J., Spengler, J.D. (2015). Associations of Cognitive Function Scores with Carbon Dioxide, Ventilation, and Volatile Organic Compound Exposures in Office Workers: A Controlled Exposure Study of Green and Conventional Office Environments. *Environmental Health Perspectives* DOI: 10.1289/ehp.1510037

[5] Kohno, M., D.G. Ghahremani, A.M. Morales, C.L. Robertson, K. Ishibashi, A.T. Morgan, M.A. Mandelkern & E.D. London (2013). Risk-Taking Behavior: Dopamine D2/D3 Receptors, Feedback, and Frontolimbic Activity. *Cerebral Cortex*, bht218. First published online: August 21, 2013.

[6] Kahn, P., et. al. (May 2008). "A plasma display window?—The shifting baseline problem in a technologically mediated natural world." Elsivier Science Ltd., *Journal of Environmental Psychology* 28: 192–199.

[7] Begley, S. "Do We Really Need Nature?" *Mindful Magazine*, online 15 August 2015.

Biophilic Design: A Cautiously Optimistic Perspective

By David Briefel

After reading Bill Browning's article, I am left feeling a mix of optimism and caution.

As a designer devoted to making a positive impact on humans and the environment, my intuition tells me that designing our workplaces to better reflect patterns in nature will, as the sampling of research presented by Browning suggests, increase our health

> Perhaps the greatest value biophilic design has today is as a means to communicate the values of a company for the purpose of employee attraction and retention.

and productivity. A deeper, more personal hope is that biophilic design can be a regular reminder to those of us who spend the majority of our days indoors that we are innately connected to the natural environment.

To be successful, a truly biophilic approach must be holistic. As Browning acknowledges, the workplace experience is complex, determined by much more than just the design. As a designer myself, I understand this, and when speaking to clients am hesitant to attribute the impact of a single design feature on the health of employees without also discussing the variable conditions associated with operations, human engagement, personal preference, and individual psychologies.

Hesitancy aside, the science presented in Browning's article shows that we are getting closer to understanding the impact of particular elements in specific environments. As such, I believe the framework in the article will provide an invaluable means to aggregate the research and bear out those patterns most effective at improving health and productivity. While many forward-thinking companies are deliberately integrating biophilic design into their projects, ultimately, we need more projects that test these principles and track the impact on workers in a variety of settings.

Gensler is currently working with online retailer to incorporate an extensive interior greenery plan as well as three vegetated terraces, among many other biophilic design elements, in their new Brooklyn headquarters, which they plan on moving into later this year. Both Google and engineering firm Glumac have been experimenting with a variety of biophilic design features in their offices. Perhaps the most important but least discussed outcome of biophilic design today for our clients is a communication of organizational values resulting in employee attraction and retention.

At the end of the day, good design can never be formulaic, but it should be evidence-based. We must continue to develop measurement criteria and tools so that evidence-based design can become a more integral component of the design process. This will go a long way toward improved outcomes and helping us demonstrate the value of design to our clients.

David Briefel, LEED AP BD+C, ID+C, WELL AP, is the Northeast sustainable design leader at Gensler and coordinates sustainable design consulting services for the New York office and Northeast Region.

Biophilia and Human Performance

By Christopher Trott

Gaining an understanding of the fundamentals of human performance can only be a good thing when it comes to design. The areas of research around this are complex and the volume of material burgeoning, so Bill Browning and his colleagues' useful guidance and work that pulls this into focus is most welcome. His article references their book on the '14 Patterns of Biophilic Design', which according to me should be essential reading for all designers of the built environment.

A couple of personal examples come to mind. If I think back to my own childhood, I was fortunate to spend it in a house where my bedroom, in which I studied, overlooked a green valley with panoramic views over a canopy of trees. Whenever I felt the stress of homework or revision for exams, I simply pushed my chair back and looked out of the window for 10 minutes; recharging myself and far more able to carry on for those next few hours. So it's no surprise to me when Bill cites the study of 2,500 Barcelona school children and links their cognitive function during study to views of a tree canopy.

Similarly, in my spare time I sail yachts when I can. For me, very few things compare to the sheer pleasure of speeding across water with all the sights, sounds, smells and trimmings of the yacht as the wind changes continually—a visceral experience that illustrates the connection of man, technology and nature, of literally being alive! Risks and perils, cognitive function, thermal and airflow variability, visual and non-visual connection with nature (and the rest of the 14 Patterns) are "all present and correct skipper!"

It seems self-evident to me that our genetic code must have been developed over the millennia to optimize us for contact with nature. Until very recently we lived in close touch with it and we have started to detach ourselves from it only in the last 150 years or so. Luckily our DNA has yet to get the message that we should live in space-ship like boxes under conditions more suitable for the operating theatre (and even there we are increasingly trying to keep patients awake during procedures!).

So much for anecdote and life experience, but at least we have all been there and can relate to it.

Blending the ingredients that Bill has painstakingly and methodically identified and classified, has over the years moved from the implicit—ingredients that we have intuitively included in design—to the explicit, those which are based on an increasing understanding of the facts through scientific and medical research.

> We like ... transient changes in our environments, not the static lighting, thermal and noise levels often specified for our buildings and enshrined in regulations and codes.

As a practice, we have been on this journey for 50 years. Some of our earliest buildings, such as Willis Faber Headquarters in Ipswich, were early examples of an intuitively developed biomorphic form, bringing daylight deep into the building, with the visual connection to nature being made through the glimpse of sky. The views increased as one rose up within the building surrounded by internal planting, ultimately gaining longer views of the surrounding landscape across the rooftop garden. Internally, the nature of the space itself was dominated by a progression from ground floor up to roof via the escalators that slowly revealed the mysteries of the space as you passed by.

More recently, we have developed a more quantifiable understanding of biophilic aspects of design, engaging them in a holistic vision for our buildings. There has been particular interest in well-being and health, and their relationship to productivity. Research around these includes alliesthesia, which recognizes the change-seeking nature of our body's sensory and neural control systems. That essentially means we like, within reason, transient changes in our environments, not the static lighting, thermal and noise levels often specified for our buildings and enshrined in regulations and codes. A good example of engaging alliesthesia is through natural ventilation which can give a more natural and dynamic

feel to a space and arouses the senses, improving cognitive function and productivity.

Conversely, one of the challenges regularly arising in the design of office buildings is that clients are increasingly seeking deeper floorplates, given the improved organizational and networking advantages these can offer. Such developments are a challenge as people are often moved deep into the interior and away from the influence of the outdoors. So bringing nature into the building is a design challenge. We are now in the process of developing very deep plan biophilic workspaces for a number of global clients. These spaces include natural ventilation, radiant cooling systems, dynamic lighting capable of circadian programming with diffuse appearance, and ceiling systems with textured appearances, all of which mimic conditions found in nature.

It seems that the more we learn about how buildings and our brain are linked, the more "biophilic" the answer looks; a case perhaps of going "back into the future."

Christopher Trott is a partner and head of sustainability at Foster + Partners. He is a member of the IDCOP Sustainable Facades committee and the London Technology Network Environmental Group.

Redesigning Design

By Lance Hosey

Beauty, as we all know, is in the eye of the beholder. But what if it's not?

In *The Shape of Green: Aesthetics, Ecology, and Design* (Island Press, 2012), I explore whether sustainability changes the face of design or only its content. Typical sustainable design strategies stem from painstaking research and time-tested evidence, and this approach can guide both technical choices and aesthetic choices. For every study demonstrating the benefits hidden inside particular materials and methods, there are other studies showing how certain spaces, shapes, patterns, textures, or colors can create extraordinary social, economic, and environmental value—the aim of sus-

tainability. Can we be as smart about how things *look* as we're becoming about how they *work*?

A good place to start is the workplace. People spend 90 percent of their time indoors, much of it at work. Over 90 percent of a workforce-dependent company is in personnel, and stress can be significant, so the stakes are high. Yet, more and more research shows that smart design can alleviate stress and improve productivity, absenteeism, retention, and morale.

Biophilia theory suggests that people are hard-wired to enjoy certain environmental conditions more than others. Sociobiologist E. O. Wilson, whose book, *Biophilia* (1984), is the standard reference on the topic,

> Growing research reveals a universal, biological basis for visual preferences that often transcend individual and cultural differences.

was among the first to propose that because for the first 98 percent of our history the human brain evolved in a particular environment—namely, the African savanna—we unconsciously have sought out similar aesthetic cues everywhere since leaving that place some 50 thousand years ago. Growing research reveals a universal, biological basis for visual preferences that often transcend individual and cultural differences. Some call it "neuro-aesthetics" and "bio-aesthetics." Beauty is in the genes of the beholder.

Now more than ever, designers have access to an incredible wealth of evidence about what people crave in their surroundings—the mechanics of attraction. For example, environmental psychologists identify five basic needs for people in interior spaces:

- The need for change (comfortable variations in light, air, temperature, and so forth)
- The ability to act on our environment and see the effects of our actions

- Meaningful stimuli (since stagnant, inert environments can cause chronic stress)
- Places of refuge
- Positive views to the outside

With such simple rules of thumb, we can utterly alter the purpose, process, and products of design. Because designers often dwell on fleeting fashions and personal preferences, we often give the impression that design is a luxury—the icing, not the cake. But we have unprecedented opportunities to transform the workplace. Last year, *Forbes* reported that workplace stress is responsible for up to $190 billion in annual health care costs in the United States. Various visual and spatial conditions have been shown to reduce stress by as much as 60 percent. Reshaping every American office around this knowledge could be worth $114 billion a year in healthcare costs alone.

That's the potential power of design.

Architect and designer **Lance Hosey, FAIA, LEED Fellow,** is a principal and chief sustainability officer with the global design firm Perkins Eastman. He chairs the LEED Advisory Committee for the U.S. Green Building Council and serves on the national Advisory Group for the American Institute of Architects Committee on the Environment.

The Use of Biophilic Strategies in the Workplace

By Kendall Wilson

Many of us spend the majority of our waking hours in the workplace and if we look around, very little of what we see or experience is natural. We are likely surrounded by painted drywall, carpet, acoustic ceiling tile, plastic laminate work surfaces, and so forth. This is not the environment that our bodies and our minds were designed for and this is why we often feel a sense of euphoria when we get the opportunity to be surrounded by nature.

Biophilic strategies can bring to an office setting a sense of what makes us feel good when we are in nature. There is also a significant crossover between biophilic design and current thinking on design for improved collaboration and productivity. We all know happy employees are better employees. Informed by research and our

> We often feel a sense of euphoria when we get the opportunity to be surrounded by nature.

own sense of what feels right, we have learned to weave biophilic strategies into every workspace project and the response has been extremely positive.

Our first project to have a strong focus on biophilic strategies was the U.S. Green Building Council headquarters in Washington, D.C., which was completed in 2009. The project had aggressive energy reduction goals and part of that strategy was to maximize natural light which is, of course, abundant in nature. The office plan was largely open and transparent allowing the staff views to the outside as well as the ability to see both long and short distances. This simple approach not only helps sync everyone with their natural circadian rhythms while offering a sense of what the weather is doing, but it also provides a sense of safety in being aware of one's surroundings.

The use of natural materials is also beneficial. In the USGBC's main public area there is a two-story waterfall that brings movement and the sound of water to a space that everyone passes through. The walls surrounding this space are clad with wood with pronounced grain and color variation that helps add another layer of a natural-feeling material.

Plants and even images of nature provide additional benefit. The use of plants needs to be carefully considered during the design process. Randomly placed potted plants

always look like an afterthought and can interfere with the functionality of the space. It is also important to consider the amount of light a particular plant requires and how it will be maintained. In addition to plants, we included images of nature at every workstation throughout the USGBC offices. These images vary in scale and color. Some are not immediately recognizable but the viewer instinctively knows the image is of something natural.

More recently, we have included indoor planting on a larger scale with a 36-foot tall living wall at the law firm Nixon Peabody in Washington, D.C. The Nixon Peabody space also includes many other biophilic strategies. Regarding the biophilic approach, Herb Stevens, Nixon Peabody's chief innovation officer said, "I don't think we properly understood the positive effect that design elements could have on our lives and our work. Honestly, we are better here as people and as lawyers because of this space."

Our design for the headquarters of the American Society of Interior Designers (ASID) is currently under construction and perhaps includes our most involved use of biophilic strategies to date. Included in the design are elements of prospect, refuge, mystery, and dynamic lighting, among many others. The project is seeking not only LEED-CI Platinum certification, but also Well Building Standard certification. ASID hopes to use their office as a living laboratory and will compare pre- and post-occupancy evaluations that measure a number of criteria associated with human health and well-being. ■

Kendall Wilson, FAIA, FIIDA, LEED Fellow, was the founding principal of Envision, a design firm focused on environmental responsibility acquired by Perkins+Will in 2012. His projects have been published internationally and have received more than 90 design awards. In 2005, he was the recipient of the prestigious Designer of the Year award, one of the design industry's highest honors. Ken was a key participant in the development of the original LEED Rating System, and he founded the IIDA's Sustainability Advisory Council.

LEARNING GUIDE

Point Counterpoint II: 4.2

The Science Behind Happy Spaces

DISCOVERY QUESTIONS

- What are you dealing with in your organization today that relates to this content area?
- What emerging sciences indicate that it is possible to design spaces that improve employees cognitive function, reduce stress, and enhance creativity?
- What is the biophilic design trend in workplace architecture?
- How does biophilic design connect to the already strong sustainability movement in corporate organizations?
- What are 14 design elements, or spatial patterns, that support biophilic design?
- How does biophilic design help reduce stress, improve productivity, and elevate employees' moods?
- What companies are already implementing biophilic design?

SELECTED FACTS

What new facts that were presented got your attention?

- Biophilic design, or built environments that connect people with experiences of nature. Positive experiences of nature elicit beneficial psychological and physiological responses, such as lowered blood pressure and heart rate, reduced muscular tension, better mental focus, lowered levels of stress hormones, and enhanced creative problemsolving abilities.
- Attention Restoration Theory (ART) posits that when you are experiencing nature rather than navigating the built environment, the brain shifts to a different mode of processing.
- The 14 patterns of biophilic design are not new inventions, but a codification of the science behind why we respond to certain design elements in specific ways.
- A number of global organizations are developing extensive biophilic workspaces. These new biofilic features include spaces include natural ventilation, radiant cooling systems, dynamic lighting capable of circadian programming with diffuse appearance, and ceiling systems with textured appearances, all of which mimic conditions found in nature.

KEY DISCUSSION POINTS

- Explain the 14 patterns of biophilic design. They are clustered into three sets of experiences: **Nature in the Space,** which refers to direct experiences of nature, **Natural Analogues,** which are representations of nature, and **Nature of the Space,** which replicate preferred spatial experiences found in natural settings
- People spend 90 percent of their time indoors, much of it at work. ΩHow does design help elevate their experience?
- What were the key points being made in this presentation?
- How do we become "smart" about creating spaces that make us happy, enhance productivity, reduce stress, and motivate us to collaborate and innovate for the longest possible time?
- Biophilic design is an evidence/science-based design principle. How does it fit in with the larger trend toward evidence-based HR?
- Discuss: The more we learn about how buildings and our brain are linked, the more "biophilic" the answer looks; a case of going "back into the future."
- More and more research shows that smart design can alleviate stress and improve productivity, absenteeism, retention, and morale.
- Environmental psychologists identify five basic human needs for people in interior spaces. Discuss how our current workplaces do not meet these expectations and what is changing:
  1) The need for change (comfortable variations in light, air, temperature, and so forth)
  2) The ability to act on our environment and see the effects of our actions
  3) Meaningful stimuli (since stagnant, inert environments can cause chronic stress)
  4) Places of refuge
  5) Positive views to the outside

People + Strategy 39.2 Point Counterpoint:

The Science Behind Happy Spaces

REVIEW OF SOLUTIONS

- Identify two to three "big ideas" worthy of exploring in your organization.
- Review and discuss solutions for stress reduction offered through biophilic design.
- Review and discuss solutions for improving cognitive performance enhancement offered through biophilic design.
- Review and discuss solutions for improving mood and emotional states offered through biophilic design.
- Discuss the case of design for the headquarters of the American Society of Interior Designers (ASID) and what they are trying to achieve through the new design.

IDENTIFYING THE PARADOX

- How is it that a solution appropriate for yesterday's organization is no longer valid?
- Consider how very different perspectives might be correct given different situations.
- Is your workplace making you smart or dumb? Explore the complex interrelationship between environment and productivity.
- Given what we have learned from the science, does this saying stand up: "Beauty is in the eye of the beholder"? But what if it's not?
- The workplace experience is determined by much more than its design. Management, technology, processes, and engagement are crucial for supporting employee productivity, health, and wellbeing. Where does they belong?

LEARNING OUTCOMES

- What one new piece of information did you learn that will be important to you in the future?
- Identify one thing that you will do differently based on what you learned.
- By leveraging scientific findings,we can create better workplaces for healthier, happier employees.
- Conscientious and targeted implementation of the 14 biophilic patterns in a workplace can achieve desirable health outcomes for employees, a minimal investment that results in high productivity savings.
- With simple evidence of how humans are hard wired, we can alter the purpose, process, and products of design. We often give the impression that design is a luxury—the icing, not the cake. But we have unprecedented opportunities to transform the workplace. Explain how.

PART 5: ORGANIZATIONAL PURPOSE AND HEALTH

Purpose Fosters Engagement

By Marc Sokol

Purpose. Ask any leader who thinks about employee engagement and its impact, or any leader who thinks about the Millennial generation at work or the aging baby boomer population, and they know that purpose matters in the workplace. But how do we foster purpose?

Aaron Hurst, author of our lead Perspective, has devoted more than a decade to fostering purpose, first through Taproot Foundation, a non-profit focused on making business talent available, pro bono, to organizations working to improve society, and then by creating Imperative, an organization focused on enhancing purpose in all lives. Author of *The Purpose Economy*, Aaron writes about a fundamental shift in our desire for purpose, and how this can affect the ways we choose to work, spend our money, and engage our time.

In the lead Perspective, Aaron reminds us how small organizations, once filled with purpose, can lose that spark as they grow; he offers advice on how to regain a sense of purpose, no matter how large your company is.

In the six commentaries that follow, other leaders share ways to foster purpose, despite the pitfalls of good intentions gone awry. One thing is clear. There are many ways you and your organization can take steps to promote purpose where you work.

Steve Schloss provides the perspective of a chief people officer. Being the steward of purpose is different at a founder-led, fast-growth, high-tech company than it is at a mission-driven legacy association, yet each requires a tailored approach. The question remains, how?

Jane Dutton, with that very question in mind, shares how high-quality connections and the ability to craft

aspects of our own jobs, are among the keys to experiencing purpose on a day-to-day basis.

For **Shannon Schuyler,** the key is flexibility, especially in large companies, along with the alignment of individual and company purpose.

Jennifer Benz wonders if purpose will rebalance the employee value proposition, especially as changes in healthcare impact the traditional sense of what employees most value.

Bob Rosen expands the focus, arguing that as leaders, we can't sustain purpose in work if we aren't grounded in who we are and living in alignment with our core values. The opportunity goes beyond purpose and job crafting to embracing the whole person and what that means for them and the companies they lead.

Finally, **Ronald Capelle,** an authority on the technology of organizational design, warns of two common pitfalls that can inhibit sense of engagement and purpose, no matter how large or

small you design your business.

If purpose matters to you, your employees, and to those who choose whether to do business with your firm, then this installment of Perspectives is for you.

Marc Sokol, Ph.D., is Perspectives editor.

When Purpose Evaporates, Think Small

By Aaron Hurst

Employees who are starved for purpose will often look outside an organization to find it. This is particularly evident when small companies, previously united by a shared sense of purpose and underdog mentality, grow into behemoths.

> So many companies yearn for more innovation and creativity, but they don't take the very first critical step—thinking of their employees as artists.

The challenge for human resources becomes how to attract, retain, and engage these professionals by advancing purpose alongside the ambitions of the organization.

When David Becomes Goliath

David Hahn, vice president of Product Management at LinkedIn, shared this insight regarding small Silicon Valley start-ups. He observed that employees at single-product, first-generation companies feel rich in purpose. They are trying to disrupt the status quo and have a strong sense that their work matters. They have a sense of impact greater than themselves, are growing quickly, and are part of a vibrant tribe—which are the three core ingredients of purpose.

When working in the early stages of the start-up HomeShark.com, I felt that deep sense of purpose. By the time I was 24, I had designed, built, and launched multiple products. I had helped acquire another company and integrated its product line, which I was then responsible for managing.

But what happened at HomeShark is what happens at most growing companies: They transform from David into Goliath. That is, as a company starts to become a leader in the market, it becomes a struggle for employees to find purpose simply by "fighting the establishment." If you look at the Silicon Valley companies that are philanthropic and have volunteer programs, they are nearly always past the "David" phase and are now "Goliaths." They are too big to be tribes and typically haven't found ways to take the key evolutionary step to become communities.

When a company becomes a "Go-liath," they usually start corporate foundations and volunteer programs. They need to supplement purpose, as they are no longer consistently delivering it to employees. Jessica Rodell at the University of Georgia found that "when jobs are less meaningful, employees are more likely to increase volunteering to gain that desired sense of meaning."

As the organization grows, this becomes more acute. Goliaths like Hewlett-Packard or Wells Fargo, who long ago lost their David-like mojo, grew so large that employees struggled to find opportunities to grow and challenge themselves. Job growth is one of the core drivers of purpose for people, and when this too is limited, it's an uphill battle to find purpose.

Yearning for Purpose

One designer from Hewlett-Packard who had been at the company for about a decade summed it up beautifully. He had steady income, worked with good people, and always had access to the best technology and tools. But there was one thing that got him thinking about leaving: He was tired of only designing in blue and white. As a designer, he craved a broader palette; he wanted to be able to use red, green, and purple, too.

In my work at the Taproot Foundation, a nonprofit that enrolls thousands of professionals in pro bono service and builds pro bono programs for companies, I saw how this lack of opportunity for self-expression motivated many of our pro bono consultants. Some were designers, but others were different kinds of artists—marketing managers, project managers, engineers, photographers, and so on. They were passionate about their craft, but working at a single company was forcing them to always choose from the same palette.

While consistency is critical to running a large company efficiently and effectively, for talented and creative professionals, it can be deadening. So many companies yearn for more innovation and creativity, but they don't take the very first critical step—thinking of their employees as artists.

Toward a Human-Centered Workplace

Purpose not only enables attracting, retaining, and engaging employees—as research from the University of Pennsylvania's Adam Grant shows—it also improves productivity. In his experiment, Grant divided university fundraising call center employees into three random groups. The first group was read stories from previous call center employees about how the job had helped them develop their sales skills. The second set was told stories about how alumni had benefited from the donations raised by the call center. The third, the control group, had unrelated stories read to them.

He replicated the study five times and found the same results. Those who were read the second story, the one about purpose, more than doubled the dollars raised. By sharing a five-minute story, he doubled their impact. He had purpose-powered them. More importantly, he had demonstrated just what middle management and human resources in large companies needed: low-cost small steps to create immediate results.

Moving from a human-resourced organization to a human-centered workplace requires that employees' desire for purpose be addressed. Human resource professionals may lead this movement by designing a new approach. Look at the "Davids" and start small—with conversations around purpose to help employees find opportunities for self-expression and personal growth and to show employees that their work matters.

Aaron Hurst is founder and CEO of Imperative, an organization that helps people find purpose and meaning in their work. He is the author of *The Purpose Economy*.

COUNTERPOINT

Purpose Is Here to Stay

By Steve Schloss

Organizations, big and small, have discovered that helping employees find or achieve purpose at and through work is a mutually beneficial arrangement. But is this push for purpose authentic or just a new form of corporate opportunism?

Stripped bare, a culture of purpose is an outcome of great leadership; it is experienced through an inspired mission, core values, the culture of possibility and transparency, and the fostering of a community where people can connect on a personal level and bring their whole self to the workplace. Purpose drives engagement and retention. Just consider Starbucks and the way they provide a true framework for purpose, giving significant leeway to individual stores to operate small and become a place where passion, purpose, community, and staff all converge.

As a senior leader who has led for-profit and non-profit organizations with extremely different workforces, the application of purpose can create true advantage, but the challenge, as Aaron Hurst suggests, is a function of scalability and culture. As the top HR executive in a fast-growing, founder-led software company, we employed young and highly motivated staff. We created a purpose-driven culture supported by a connected system of programs and processes. From

Stripped bare, a culture of purpose is an outcome of great leadership; it is experienced through an inspired mission, core values, the culture of possibility and transparency, and the fostering of a community where people can connect on a personal level and bring their whole self to the workplace.

onboarding to feedback to leadership development experiences, it was each employee's role to own and find their purpose and help others achieve the same. Our challenge was scalability. How could we sustain purpose under significant pressure to innovate and grow revenue and headcount? Our answer could be found in two ways: through formal and informal recognition of individual achievement and the ongoing celebration and storytelling of our shared journey.

Juxtaposed with high tech, I am now helping to lead and transform a 120-year-old premier non-profit organization steeped in tradition, certainty, and purpose. The United States Golf Association's (USGA) mission is to serve the game of golf on a global level through championships, governance, and services. Longer tenured and older on average, employee belief in our mission and purpose is very strong. Growth is not the challenge. Our mission and purpose engenders a sense of community. Our challenge is to sustain a higher purpose (which creates stability) while transforming and rethinking our culture and values. All of this occurs while simultaneously becoming leaders of the game while serving our historic responsibilities of stewardship. Successful purpose-led organizations like the USGA must stay true to their calling, even as they smartly and regularly reevaluate their direction and focus.

Purpose as an outcome and lever of leadership is here to stay. Regardless of size or status, purpose-led organizations will reap the benefits when they are led with integrity and inspire employees, customers, and the community.

Steve Schloss is chief people officer of the United States Golf Association.

Creating High-Quality Connections as a Pathway for Cultivating Purpose

By Jane E. Dutton

The workplace is a site for daily connection and disconnection with others. When connections are high quality, people experience a sense of energy, mutuality, and positive regard. The great fact about high-quality connections at work is that they strengthen people and make them more resourceful, while at the same time affirming a sense of value and worth. I have spent 10 years researching and teaching about the power of momentary positive connections with other people at work. High-quality connections (HQCs) are a potent means for creating and building meaning at work. In our new book, *How to Be a*

Positive Leader: Small Actions, Big Impact, we (coauthors Gretchen Spreitzer and Shawn Achor) outline the different ways that leaders accomplish this form of purpose building.

How Small Actions Can Foster Purpose

Consider the following examples of how people craft their jobs to foster high-quality connections. A hospital cleaner crafts his job so that he has more high-quality connections with patients' families. In interactions with family members, he senses his job is having a positive impact on others. He knows that by providing care for families, he is supporting the healing of the patient. High-quality connections with patients' families infuse him with a sense of significance beyond the care of physical space.

A teacher crafts her job in ways that allow for more one-on-one time with each student. Each day she asks two students to come in 10 minutes before class to help her set up the classroom. In those 10 minutes, she communicates and connects with the students in ways that inspire and excite her for the day. In those 10 minutes of connection, both teacher and students mutually affirm a sense of value and positive regard.

Finally, a middle-level manager makes it a point to end her day by sending an email to at least one subordinate about the difference that person has made in helping her and contributing to the organization. These emails are daily investments in the quality of connection as they clearly communicate the significance of the contributions that people are making. Small actions that connect people in meaningful ways infuse purpose.

Three Steps You Can Take

How can HR managers and other leaders act to foster high-quality connections and purpose? First, believe it is possible. Purpose building through high-quality connections means believing that short-term interactions with others have the power to infuse purpose. Second, take small actions that encourage each of us to be psychologically present in virtual and in-person

meetings. Finally, cultivate cultures, reward systems, and reporting structures that encourage respectful engagement, trust, and mutual help. All are vital pathways for cultivating HQCs.

Jane E. Dutton is the Robert E. Kahn Distinguished University Professor of Business Administration and Psychology, Ross School of Business, University of Michigan, and a faculty member of the Center for Positive Organizations.

If Purpose Is Paramount, Flexibility Is Key

By Shannon Schuyler

Gallup estimates the cost of disengaged workers to U.S. businesses at more than $350 billion per year. But

> Purpose building through high-quality connections means believing that short-term interactions with others have the power to infuse purpose.

what are the costs to individuals? What is the cost of not feeling fulfilled? Not feeling like what you do matters?

Company Flexibility Is Key to Fostering Purpose

I agree with Aaron Hurst; many who are disengaged have lost sight of the company's sense of purpose and community. How well does the company allow individuals to find their own fit in the organization and unique way of contributing? Flexibility is the key, but this can be difficult for large companies that need policies and systems in place to provide for quality, productivity, and efficiency.

Addressing this challenge, Price-

waterhouseCooper's (PwC) flexibility leader, Anne Donovan, said: "For flexibility to work in any size organization, it requires buy-in from leadership and 'execution on the ground.' Millennials are leading the charge in demanding flexibility, and we've learned that more flexibility increases employee engagement in all generations. No organization can afford to lose top talent because they didn't address this important issue."

Aligning Personal with Company Purpose

Beyond flexibility, it is critical that leaders understand the role of purpose in our lives and what their company can do to help employees find their own purpose and connect that to the company purpose.

Whether you call it purpose, meaning, passion, or calling, I believe we all long to find work that satisfies us—work that is more than "something to do" or "a way to make ends meet." Hurst states that for us to find purpose in our work, we need to know whom we serve, why we serve them, and how we serve them. Allow me to illustrate how my sense of purpose as a Corporate Responsibility leader aligns with PwC's purpose as a company:

Here at PwC, our purpose is to build trust and solve important problems. I serve PwC staff, partners, clients, and the communities in which we operate. Why and how do I serve them?

I serve them because I believe the private sector is a powerful force for good in the world; I am passionate about leveraging the power of companies like PwC to help build trust and solve important problems, like accelerating urbanization, resource scarcity, demographic shifts, and other megatrends.

I serve them by working inside and outside PwC to create opportunities for our partners and staff to connect with each other and our stakeholder community in making a difference, both in their client engagements and in programs like PwC's Earn Your Future, "green teams," and pro bono work.

These are my answers. Each PwC staff and partner has to craft his or her own. In fact, we all have to craft our own purpose. What are your answers?

Shannon Schuyler is a principal and corporate responsibility leader at PricewaterhouseCoopers, a member of PwC's Global CR Board, and an officer of the board of the PwC Charitable Foundation. To learn about PwC's approach to fostering employee engagement to drive Corporate Responsibility, see "The Keys to Corporate Responsibility Employee Engagement."

Will Purpose Rebalance the Employee Value Proposition?

By Jennifer Benz

The opportunity to pursue purpose clearly adds to the employee value proposition (EVP) for many people. This is especially important as more traditional components of the EVP evolve and, ultimately, lose value.

Health care benefits have long been a key differentiator for mid-size and large companies. They are a key feature in recruiting materials and are often cited as a reason people stay with a company.

But health insurance isn't an exclusive piece of the employee value proposition like it once was. The Affordable Care Act puts health insurance into the hands of anyone who needs it, regardless of his or her employer or employment status. At the same time, the desire to control health care costs through ever-more-aggressive wellness programs and health plan design lowers the perceived value of this "key benefit."

Prior to the ACA, HR professionals tended to overestimate the value of health benefits. In a 2011 McKinsey study, 85 percent of people said they would not leave their job if their company dropped health insurance. Yet, even today, the idea of changing health benefits can make the most seasoned HR professional squirm. The reality is that health benefits will change—and dramatically so.

As health benefits evolve—decreasing in value, becoming a commodity, and ultimately no longer being a reason to join or stay at a company—organizations of all sizes need to reevaluate and rebalance the employee value proposition. What will fill the gap left by once-scarce health insurance?

It could be purpose that rebalances the employee value proposition.

Purpose is a logical extension of the work done to promote well-being and productivity, already key parts of the EVP at leading companies. There are numerous opportunities to elevate purpose through benefits, HR programs, and company communications, both internal and external.

Savvy companies will look for ways that a holistic benefits package can reinforce and cultivate a strong, resilient, and desirable corporate culture. Those who also help employees understand, act on, and fully enjoy purpose in their work may find themselves far ahead of the rest.

Jennifer Benz is CEO and founder, Benz Communications, a firm that specializes in employee benefits communication.

A New Consciousness Is Emerging

By Bob Rosen

We are entering a time where our search for meaning—in both life and work—converge, and where meaning becomes the new capital. This reflects a broad new consciousness emerging in the world, where there is a radical rethinking of the meaning of work, the definition of success, and the role of leadership at all levels of organizations and society.

Having researched the foundations of great leadership for many years, we believe that human resources leaders have an unprecedented opportunity to champion a more holistic leadership model that improves the health and effectiveness of both individuals and organizations.

This opportunity is amplified by the increasing crisis we observe in leadership. The highly visible failings of some have cast a shadow on all. The credibility of leaders is at an all-time low, leaving employees, consumers, and the public cynical and disengaged.

In contrast to those failings, our research reveals fresh data and insights about how great leaders actually develop deep, personal roots that allow them to stay healthy and fulfilled, maintain perspective and make sound judgments, and execute effectively in the most challenging circumstances. Even more important than fundamental skills and competencies is having a vision of who you are and staying true to that vision, as this determines your true leadership capability. Deeply held aspirations, beliefs, and values are the foundation for effective and sustainable leadership; they are what keep us grounded as leaders and as human beings.

The model, which we refer to as Grounded Leadership, draws upon our own research as well as recent advances in neuroscience, psychology, sociology, and biology. Grounded leaders achieve the balance of being an outstanding and sustainable leader, while also finding ways to be outstanding and sustainable as a human being. To be grounded, we must excel in the following ways:

- **Physically.** How we live, including body/mind awareness, energy management, and a peak performance lifestyle.
- **Emotionally.** How we feel, including self-awareness, positive emotions, and resilience.
- **Intellectually.** How we think, including deep curiosity, adaptive mindset, and paradoxical thinking.
- **Socially.** How we interact, including authenticity, mutually rewarding relationships, and nourishing communities.
- **Vocationally.** How we perform, including a meaningful calling, personal mastery, the drive to succeed.
- **Spiritually.** How we view the world, including higher purpose, global connectedness, and generosity of spirit.

By identifying and nurturing our own roots, we are in a better position to create teams and organizations that allow everyone to discover their own unique purpose—and in turn, nurture their own roots. And everyone benefits from the greater good.

Bob Rosen is founder, chairman, and CEO of Healthy Companies International, a leadership development firm dedicated to transforming the world, one leader at a time. He is the author of *Grounded: How Leaders Stay Rooted in an Uncertain World.*

Designing Organizations to Enable Purpose: The Promise and Pitfalls of Alignment

By Ronald Capelle

While smaller work units may seem key to achieving purpose, all organizations can be designed to better foster purpose. We have seen this across 100 large-scale projects and 24 research studies; optimizing organizational design leads to better employee engagement, as well as increased customer satisfaction and financial performance.

In fact, alignment of the manager-direct report relationship, by itself, leads to better employee engagement (as well as the other two outcome measures). There is a key to increasing alignment and two pitfalls to avoid.

The Key to Manager–Direct Employee Alignment

Every employee should have a manager exactly one level above, both in the complexity of work done and the capability to work at that level. Our research shows that, in a well-designed manager-direct report relationship, each level in an organization is different in the nature of work, the complexity, and the capability required to perform at that level. We calibrate this with measures of time span analysis and information processing capability; yes, there actually is a science to organizational design with predictable results. Those

results include increased employee engagement and the opportunity to experience higher purpose or meaning in one's work.

Pitfalls of Poor Alignment

One common pitfall is compression, when the manager and the direct report are actually operating at the same level. Organizational charts don't tell you this, but employees can tell you when they are doing essentially the same job as the boss, and how that makes them feel.

In compression situations, managers tend to micromanage and not add sufficient value. Direct reports, in turn, cannot work to their full capability. Can you see how this sets the stage to stifle employee engagement and purpose?

Another common pitfall is the gap, when a manager and a direct report are operating more than one level apart, leaving a vacuum of focus and work to which neither attends. As a result, the manager feels "pulled down into the weeds" or sees the direct report as having "no initiative." The direct report sees the manager as not providing appropriate guidance or setting them up

to fail. It's hard to feel purpose when the employee and the manager are unintentionally at odds figuring out who should do what.

Purpose Emerges in the Power of Proper Alignment

If manager, direct report alignment is so important, how well do organizations rate on this dimension? We have a database of more than 59,000 relationships in 76 organizations. Manager-direct report alignments are correct 55 percent of the time; compression exists 36 percent of the time; and gaps exist 9 percent of the time. Imagine the cost of compression and gaps, in wasted time and in lost opportunity to foster purpose.

Creating appropriate positions and matching people to them is an underlying key to enabling purpose. If you want to foster increased purpose, focus on the promise and pitfalls of organizational design. ▓

Ronald Capelle, president of Capelle Associates, is the author of *Optimizing Organization Design: A Proven Approach to Enhance Financial Performance, Customer Satisfaction and Employee Engagement.*

LEARNING GUIDE

Point Counterpoint II: 5.1

Purpose Fosters Engagement

DISCOVERY QUESTIONS

- What are you dealing with in your organization today that relates to this content area?
- How is purpose defined? What makes it a powerful cultural driver in organizations today?
- Why is purpose becoming central to organizational success?
- Why is it so hard to maintain purpose in fast-growing organizations?
- What areas of Talent Life Cycle does "purpose" affect?
- What is meant in this Perspectives by "David" and "Goliath" companies?
- What is involved in the move from human-resourced to human-centered workplaces?
- What makes the workplace a community?
- What makes a purposeful (grounded) leader?
- Why is organizational alignment key to deliver on purpose?
-

SELECTED FACTS

What new facts that were presented got your attention?

- Gallup estimates the cost of disengaged workers to U.S. businesses at more than $350 billion per year. But what are the costs to individuals?
- Millennials are leading the charge in demanding flexibility, and we've learned that more flexibility increases employee engagement among all generations. No organization can afford to lose top talent because they didn't address this important issue.
- PWC employees have the opportunity to make a difference both in their client engagements and in programs like PwC's Earn Your Future, "green teams," and pro bono work

KEY DISCUSSION POINTS

- What were the key points being made in this presentation?
- Hurst states that for us to find purpose in our work, we need to know whom we serve, why we serve them, and how we serve them.
- Do you agree that a purpose centered organization is an outcome of great leadership?
- Grounded leaders achieve the balance of being an outstanding and sustainable leader, while also finding ways to be outstanding and sustainable as a human being.
- Does alignment of the manager-direct report relationship, by itself, lead to better employee engagement?
- Describe what it takes to build and sustain a purpose driven organization. Do you agree with the statement that, "The credibility of leaders is at an all-time low, leaving employees, consumers, and the public cynical and disengaged."
- Review and then explain the outcomes of the psychological experiment conducted by Professor Adam Grant at the fundraising call center at University of Pennsylvania.
- How well do organizations rate on manager–direct report alignment? (Given the database of more than 59,000 relationships in 76 organizations, manager-direct report alignments are correct 55 percent of the time; compression exists 36 percent of the time; and gaps exist 9 percent of the time. Imagine the cost of compression and gaps, in wasted time and in lost opportunity to foster purpose.)

Point Counterpoint II: 5.1

Purpose Fosters Engagement

REVIEW OF SOLUTIONS

- Identify two to three "big ideas" worthy of exploring in your organization.
- How can HR managers and other leaders act to foster high-quality connections and purpose?
- How many
  a) Believe it is possible?
  b) Take small actions that encourage each of us to be psychologically present in virtual and in-person meetings?
  c) Cultivate cultures, reward systems, and reporting structures that encourage respectful engagement, trust, and mutual help?
- Flexibility at work is critical to inviting individual to discover their purpose. For flexibility to work in any size organization, it requires buy-in from leadership and "execution on the ground." Describe the case of PwC.
- Do you agree that the private sector is a powerful force for good in the world? It is important to leverage the power of companies like PwC to help build trust and solve important problems, like accelerating urbanization, resource scarcity, demographic shifts, and other megatrends? Why or why not?
- If you want to foster increased purpose, focus on the promise and pitfalls of organizational design. Yes or no?
- For leadership to create and lead purpose driven organizations, they need to be grounded. To be a grounded leader, one must excel in the following ways:
  - › **Physically.** How one lives.
  - › **Emotionally.** How one feels, including self- awareness, positive emotions, and resilience.
  - › **Intellectually.** How one thinks.
  - › **Socially.** How one interacts.
  - › **Vocationally.** How one performs.
  - › **Spiritually.** How one views the world, including higher purpose.

IDENTIFYING THE PARADOX

- How is it that a solution appropriate for yesterday's organization is no longer valid?
- Consider how very different perspectives might be correct given different situations.
- While consistency is critical to running a large company efficiently and effectively, it often becomes deadening for high-potential and creative professionals. Why is it the case?

Leadership Lessons Reverberate Down the Line

By Marc Sokol

Imagine a string that connects the CEO of your company to every employee in the field, and the way that string is pulled is somehow felt by every single employee. Now imagine that the executive team and even the leaders a level below also touch that string and have their own impact on employees.

This will be helpful if the string vibrates in the right way, sending clear messages that drive productive and healthy behavior. It can also be confusing, even damaging, if the messages are inconsistent or counterproductive.

All of which assumes the CEO and other leaders actually know when they are tugging on the string and what messages they are conveying with their actions.

Robert Hogan, author of our lead Perspective, *Six Lessons on Leadership*, is one of the world's foremost authorities on that string that connects leaders to the rest of the organization. His research and its practical application have helped articulate the value chain of executive personality and information processing, leading to engagement and business unit performance. Ultimately, this connects to organizational health and wellness—or the lack thereof.

To amplify and expand on Dr. Hogan's perspective, we invited commentary from five other thought leaders:

Dave Winsborough highlights attributes of leaders who mark dysfunction and eventual peril for followers. If you can recognize them, steer clear of these types of leaders.

Rob Kaiser writes about the contrast of attributes that help some ascend to executive roles versus a different set of attributes that reflect leaders' real effectiveness. Can you spot the difference among your executives?

Adrian Furnham takes issue with

the assertion that leaders can drive positive and negative engagement, as there exists a different set of factors underlying each.

If the first three commentaries are cautionary about leaders and their impact, the next two are optimistic.

Allan Church describes how one global firm helps its leaders leverage awareness of personal tendencies and provides a process to help their behavior not be dominated by the presence or absence of particular tendencies.

Joshua Ehrlich closes the set, arguing that through mindful self-acceptance leaders actually can manage their own personal tendencies and in the process contribute to wellness in the workplace.

If you believe leaders can impact the health and wellness of the workplace, then this installment of Perspectives is for you. After reading the lead Perspective and the commentaries that follow, you can contact any of the authors directly, or let me know how you

are addressing leadership and organizational health in your company.

Marc Sokol, Ph.D., is Perspectives editor.

Marc Sokol, Ph.D., is Perspectives editor.

POINT

Six Lessons on Leadership

By Robert Hogan

I am obsessed with the topic of leadership. Organizations need leaders to make key decisions, anticipate and manage changing market trends, and set strategic vision. When competent leadership prevails, people and companies prosper. Bad leadership almost always gives rise to disengaged workers, corporate chicanery, and, eventually, business failure.

The problem with most leadership competency models is they fail to distinguish between successful managers—people who are rapidly promoted in their organizations—and effective managers—people whose subordinates are committed and whose organizational units perform well. If we distinguish between these groups and review the leadership literature from the perspective of team effectiveness, we find six useful generalizations.

1. What Followers Want from Their Leaders

The first concerns the characteristics that people want to see in their leaders. Kouzes and Posner (2010) devised a simple paradigm for studying this: Ask people to describe the best and the worst managers they have ever had using a standardized format. This research reveals that people evaluate leaders in terms of four broad categories:

Integrity. Followers want to know that the people in charge won't take advantage of their positions—they won't lie, steal, play favorites, or betray their subordinates.

Judgment. The success or failure of organizations depends on decision-making. Some leaders make better decisions than others.

Competence. To be competent in the team's business, good leaders seem to know what they are talking about. Subordinates see leaders who lack business acumen as empty suits, and are unwilling to follow them.

Vision. Good leaders can explain how their mission fits into the larger scheme of things. This vision clarifies roles, goals, and the way forward, thereby facilitating team performance.

These four themes emerge in descending order—with integrity being the most important attribute and vision the least important—but all four are crucial components of leaders' reputations. Conversely, leaders who lack integrity, good judgment, competence, and vision will surely fail.

2. Personality Predicts Leadership

The second lesson concerns personality and leadership. The data are clear: Personality is the best single predictor of leader performance that we have. For example, Jim Collins published a milestone study of 11 Fortune 1000

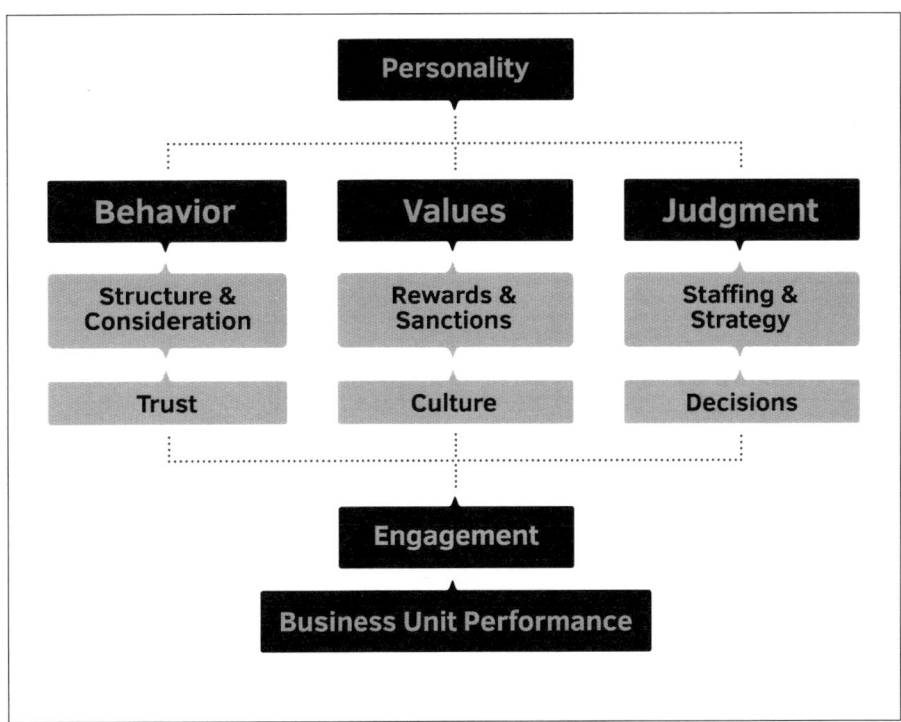

companies that had 15 years of below average performance, followed by a transition year, and then 15 years of performance substantially above their industry average.

Collins found that in each case a new CEO had turned the company around and that these 11 highly effective CEOs combined extreme personal humility with a fierce and relentless drive to win. This contrasts with their high-profile, publicity-seeking counterparts in poorer performing companies. While personality is important in both cases, we can also reject the view that CEOs need charisma to be effective.

3. Leadership Drives Engagement; Engagement Drives Performance

The third lesson concerns leadership and employee engagement. Engagement is "…a persistent psychological state associated with behaviors that are beneficial to an organization" (Macey & Schneider, 2008). In major separate studies, Huselid (1995) and Harter, Schmidt, and Hayes (2002) show that: a) managers' behavior predicts employee engagement; and b) employee engagement predicts business-unit performance. Engagement is a function of how people are treated by managers. Specifically, the quality of the relation-

ship between leaders and followers creates engagement.

4. Leaders Drive Financial Performance

The fourth lesson concerns the financial consequences of good and bad leadership performance. Collins' research shows that well-led companies are more profitable than those with average leadership. Although the estimates vary from 14 percent to 40 percent, several studies conclude that CEOs account for a significant proportion of variance in the financial performance of large organizations.

5. There Are More Bad Leaders than Good Ones

The fifth lesson concerns managerial incompetence. In another milestone paper, Bentz (1967; 1985) reported on a 30-year study of managers at Sears. His research showed that the failure rate for managers in American business is substantially higher than expected. How many bad managers are there? We identified 12 published estimates of the frequency of management failure, which range from 30 percent to 67 percent, with an average of about 50 percent. Note that these estimates concern the number of managers who are actually fired. I believe that about two-thirds of existing managers are ineffective, but fewer than half will be caught because they are good at internal politics. The misery that bad managers create for their staff has consequences on morale. About 75 percent of working adults say the most stressful aspect of their jobs is their immediate boss.

6. Bad Managers Lead from the Dark Side

Finally, bad managerial behavior originates in the dark side of personality. As Bentz (1967) noted, most managers fail for the same reasons: emotional immaturity, arrogance, micro-management, dishonesty, indecisiveness, poor communication skills, and so forth. Hogan and Hogan (2001) proposed a taxonomy of the most common counterproductive managerial behaviors. Although the behavior patterns are different, they have the same effect on employees: They erode trust, increase stress, and degrade performance.

The foregoing discussion leads to the question, "What is the profile of an ideal leader?" I start with Peter Drucker's observation that leadership is really about followership, that leadership should be understood in the context of what the followers expect from their leaders. The points presented above suggest that followers want to see six characteristics in their leaders—integrity, good judgment, competence, vision, humility, and fierce ambition for collective success—and those characteristics provide a guide to an optimal assessment profile.

References

Kouzes, J.M., & Posner, B.Z. (2010). The Truth About Leadership: The No-Fads, Heart-Of-The-Matter Facts You Need to Know. San Francisco, CA: Jossey–Bass.

Macey, W. H. and Schneider, B. (2008). The meaning of employee engagement. *Industrial and Organizational Psychology*, 1: 3–30. doi: 10.1111/j.1754-9434.2007.0002.

Delaney, John T. and Huselid, Mark A., The impact of human resource management practices on perceptions of organizational performance. *The Academy of Management Journal*, Vol. 39, No. 4 (Aug., 1996), pp. 949–969.

Harter, J. K., Schmidt, F. L., & Hayes, T. L. (2002). Business-unit-level relationship between employee satisfaction, employee engagement, and business outcomes: A meta-analysis. *Journal of Applied Psychology*, 87(2), 268–279.

Bentz, V. J. (1967). The Sears experience in the investigation, description, and prediction of executive behavior. In F. R. Wickert & D. E. McFarland (Eds.), *Measuring Executive Effectiveness* (pp. 147–205). New York: Appleton-Century-Crofts.

Hogan, R. and Hogan, J. (2001), Assessing leadership: A view from the dark side. *International Journal of Selection and Assessment*, 9: 40–51. doi: 10.1111/1468-2389.00162.

Dr. Robert Hogan defied decades of conventional wisdom and academic tradition by proving that personality predicts performance. Thirty years later, Dr. Hogan's theories on personality and leadership continue to challenge mainstream thinking and have been adopted by some of the largest and most successful companies in the world.

Getting Leadership Back to Its Purpose: And It's Not About You, Cupcake

By Dave Winsborough

Bob Hogan is obsessed with leadership, and has done more than most to highlight the idea that the person in charge is profoundly consequential to the well-being and lives of those who follow. The characteristics of integrity, judgment, competence, vision, humility, and ambition he describes have a timeless quality to them.

As they should, for Hogan's thinking is rooted in evolutionary biology and locates the importance of each element in our profoundly group-oriented nature. Humans live in groups, and there is always a status hierarchy in the group; being closer to the top of that hierarchy confers greater rewards, be they food, money, sex, or attention.

This also means that followers always hold out hope that the people who climb to the top will have their interests at heart, be competent, and behave benevolently towards them. Sadly, the evidence in human society shows that good leadership and occupying the top job are simply not one and the same. There is no shortage of self-aggrandizing leaders who prove to be inept or corrupt, or both. A partial list might include Robert Mugabe, Bashar al-Assad, Kim Jong-un, Robert Fuld, Carly Fiorina, and Bernie Ebbers. If you notice a trend in the list, it's very likely causal: recent experimental work by John Antoniakis[1] shows that access to power and testosterone interact and lead to corruption, even among individuals who are otherwise honest.

Consider descriptions of the bad and incompetent against Hogan's list. Barbara Kellaway describes "rigid," "intemperate," "callous," "corrupt," and "insular" as markers. Sidney Finklestein describes "dominant," "over-identified," "overconfident," "ruthless," "slick," and "tried-and-true." Don't these look a lot like the opposite pole of the features described by Hogan?

But there is a conundrum: While few would argue with the list, how does anyone who does not embody the attributes described by Hogan make it into a leadership role? This is a real, practical, and consequential question.

There are five classes of problems when it comes to leadership.

First, the hierarchical nature of human society means subordinates defer to leaders. That is, they create distance around them, tend to provide only good news, and tell them what they like to hear.

Second, many of the traits that seem attractive when one is young and showing potential can ossify or become overused when the reins of power are handed over.

Third, evidence suggests that leaders tend to hire in their own image—and some firms like Goldman Sachs are obsessive about ensuring the fit is very tight.

Fourth, the study and practice of leadership and leader development are premised on a tautology—by studying only those in charge, the picture that emerges is going to look a lot like the people who are already in charge.

Finally, leadership has become an end in itself. Our obsession with leadership inside companies typically means that leaders are trained as individuals in a pampered and often expensive manner. As Rob Kaiser has pointed out, the nearly $15 billion spent on leadership training and development hasn't impacted trust in leaders as measured by the Harris Poll. Leadership seems decoupled from its biologically determined purpose—to act as a resource for the good of the group.

So a plea to the readers of this journal: Use the six characteristics that Hogan outlines only as a screen, a selection tool, and an ongoing index of suitability as you choose leaders for your own enterprise.

Reference

[1]Bendahan, S., et al., (2014). Leader corruption depends on power and testosterone, *The Leadership Quarterly*, http://dx.doi.org/10.1016/j.leaqua.2014.07.010.

Dave Winsborough is managing director of Winsborough Limited, a leading New Zealand consultancy. An expert on leadership at the top of organizations, he is recognized for his skills in building high-performance senior-level teams.

Leaders Must Look Within to Create a Healthy Workplace

By Robert B. Kaiser

In his characteristically incisive and iconoclastic way, Robert Hogan has cut through the hype and hoopla to get to the heart of what we know about effective leadership. His secret is to turn the leadership equation around by starting with the people being led.

From this view, Hogan makes a crucial distinction: the difference between successful managers (who get ahead in their careers) and effective managers (whose people are engaged and get

great results). We'd like to think that effective managers are also those who get ahead, but this is not normally the case.

Research on the topic suggests that only about one in 10 managers are both effective and successful (Luthans, Hodgetts, & Rosenkrantz, 1988). Look around at the people at the top of most organizations and consider which qualities best describe them: 1) good at self-promotion, well-connected, and politically astute, or 2) able to bring out the best in others, influential at getting people to set aside their personal agendas and work together, and utterly committed to the vision.

The first set of qualities is table stakes: Without them, you aren't likely to get very far. But having them does not mean you will have the second set of qualities. In fact, the more a manager emphasizes the first set, the less likely he or she is to emphasize the second set. That's because they represent two distinct—and sometimes conflicting—motivations: self-interest and collective interest. Unfortunately, self-interest usually trumps the collective interest.

It is unfortunate for two big reasons. First, it means that most people who aspire to positions of leadership do so for self-interested aims: the compensation, status, and prestige of upper management. The welfare of employees and the performance of the organization may only be an afterthought, if they are given any serious thought at all. Second is the irony that their selfish behavior is unlikely to bring them satisfaction. Spiritual teachings from the Buddha to the Bible emphasize that the best way to be happy is to make other people happy. And indeed, empirical research shows that doing good for others, investing in them, and helping them to succeed leads to greater personal satisfaction (Dunn, Aknin, & Norton, 2008).

If managers are to create a healthier workplace, they must start by looking within, at their motivation for aspiring to a position of leadership. If they are more driven by the trappings of status and other self-gratifying desires, then you can expect little benefit to workplace health. Those who seek to serve a greater good are the ones more likely to create the

kind of culture that takes care of people and performance. And in a karmic turn of justice, those same managers are likely to achieve a greater sense of fulfillment and peace of mind for themselves.

References

Dunn, E.W., Aknin, L. B., & Norton, M. I. (2008). Spending money on others promotes happiness. Science, 319, 1687–1688.

Luthans, F., Hodgets, R.M. & Rosenkrantz, S. A. (1988). Real Managers. Cambridge, MA: Ballinger.

Rob Kaiser is president of Kaiser Leadership Solutions, a provider of cutting-edge tools for the assessment and development of leaders, and the editor of *Consulting Psychology Journal: Practice and Research.*

Leaders Can Drive Disengagement, But Not Engagement

By Adrian Furnham

Bob Hogan is a courageous academic and clear thinker, willing to go against the tide when he believes the consensus is flawed. He helped "resurrect" personality theory in the 1980s and '90s and has made a major contribution to understanding leadership derailment.

Few academics can claim to have started a highly successful, international, multimillion dollar company based on sound research findings. He is a "one off" and should, I believe, be seen as a "national treasure" for American psychology.

One of the great attractions of reading or hearing Bob is seeing him cut through the Gordian knot of tangled theories or research findings. He has a knack for getting to the heart of the issue, which he always summarizes in a few memorable points. He has done this in his "Six Lessons" piece, which is classic Hogan.

While I agree with points one, five, and six, and would commend anyone to read his work on the dark side, I take issue with point three, that leaders drive engagement, and engagement drives performance. In past presentations, Hogan has noted the change in concept from job satisfaction to involvement to commitment and then to engagement, which seems the new flavor of the month. Despite the enthusiasm for the concept and claims, the evidence remains weak. There is both an absence of evidence and evidence of an absence with regard to the idea that leaders (alone) drive engagement, which (alone) drives performance.

In even the best studies and sound meta-analyses, the size of the correlations suggests that a manager's ability, personality, and motivation does relate to performance, but that the correlations are low (typically around r=.2).

Too many things drive performance; I prefer the idea that leaders drive disengagement. This is a bit like the Herzberg two-factor theory, in which the factors that drive satisfaction are not simply the opposite of those that drive dissatisfaction. Similarly, the opposite of engagement is not disengagement. They are different processes. We observe that leaders can quickly and dramatically cause staff disengagement on their own. The drivers of sustained engagement, however, are broader than the pull, presence, actions, or any leader just on his or her own.

Adrian Furnham, Ph.D., is a professor of psychology at University College, London, and the author of more than 1,000 scientific papers and 75 books.

Leveraging Personality to Develop Leaders and the Organization

By Allan H. Church

We are all obsessed with leadership. As talent management (TM) professionals, our mandate is to ensure our organizations have a holistic talent development strategy and set of supporting processes, practices, and tools to achieve the company's business objectives. One of the most critical components of this mandate is to identify and secure (whether through a buy or build model) the right level of leadership to effectively run the business today and meet the succession goals for the future. Thus, for many of us in TM, the key distinction we need to make with respect to leadership competencies is, "do they reflect the success profile of today or those capabilities required for the future?"

Balancing Leadership Development with Organization Development

One of the most effective ways to achieve these goals is by blending the best-of-the-best theories, frameworks, and interventions from different professional disciplines, including industrial-organizational psychology and organization development. Organizations need to ground their talent and leadership succession efforts in:

- Understanding leaders in the pipeline and differentiating them around their individual skills and capabilities, which includes personality
- Enhancing self-awareness and knowledge of the cultural impact of personality characteristics and leadership behaviors on employee outcomes such as engagement, commitment, and performance

The first leads us to enhance the talent management agenda via formal assessment and the identification of high-potentials. The second leads us to support an organization development agenda via feedback and coaching interventions. Achieving this dual emphasis and balance on differentiation and development is critical to having an effective and holistic approach to leadership development.

What Works at PepsiCo

At PepsiCo, our approach to talent management and employee development reinforces this dual emphasis. In general, it is aligned with Bob Hogan's observations, and we have fully integrated both the bright and dark sides of personality along with values orientation within our formal multi-tier assessment and development efforts. Developed and launched in 2010, the Leadership Assessment & Development program (LeAD) provides increasingly intensive integrated assessment and development efforts that are linked to key leadership transitions and targeted at individuals in certain career stages or levels in the organization. The system leverages a multi-trait, multi-method model beginning at lower levels in the organization, with "Checkpoint-0" designed to assess early indicators of potential. This is followed by higher checkpoints (1, 2, 3) which go successively deeper in the assessment process and are supported by higher levels of development "touch" and individual planning support from internal I-O psychologists with expertise in this area.

One of the most critical aspects of the LeAD framework is that it is rooted in the Leadership Potential BluePrint (Church & Silzer, 2014), which includes personality as one of the two key foundational aspects of defining a high-potential leader. Based on the model, we integrate personality measures at every level of our assessment and development efforts—from early identification to senior levels. This step is critical when giving one-on-one feedback to participants because it helps us ensure our leaders have a complete picture of their personality characteristics and how these influence their behaviors as measured through 360-degree feedback (i.e., ratings from their direct reports, peers, and managers).

Interestingly enough, we have found that the participants' personality dispositions are reflected in other aspects of the program, including areas such as attention to detail on our custom simulations, executive presence in critical incident interviews, and even compliance with timelines and various deliverables related to the process in general.

As a consequence, when delivering feedback, our internal team in the assessment and development Center of Excellence almost always starts with the personality tool, given that so many other aspects are influenced by how leaders perceive their world. In sum, we would argue that personality is a foundational component of both effective leadership—and future leadership potential—and that enhancing managerial self-awareness is a key means to achieving one's potential.

References

Church, A., and Silzer, R. (2014). Going behind the corporate curtain with a blueprint for leadership potential: An integrated framework for identifying high-potential talent. *People + Strategy*. 36.4.

Allan H. Church, Ph.D., is vice president, OD Global Groups and Executive Assessment at PepsiCo.

Mindful Self-Acceptance: The Heart of Healthy Leaders

By Joshua Ehrlich

Leaders perform well when they feel good about themselves. Few are able to do so, though, because they try to grow from the outside in (building self-esteem) instead of from the inside out (cultivating self-acceptance).

Building Self-Esteem vs. Self-Acceptance

Society teaches us to build self-esteem from:

- Stuff ("I have a lot of money.")
- Approval ("I get recognition.")
- Accomplishment ("I am winning.")
- Fantasy ("I am great!")

Yet this only makes leaders vulnerable to market forces, which are inevitably uncontrollable and take away these sources of false satisfaction. We add to this by telling leaders they are never good enough ("You saved the company $40M this year? Great. Next year save $50M.") The result is battle-weary leaders who reveal their immaturity and survive by depending on their dark side.

Contrast this with ways we can develop self-acceptance:

- Alignment ("I am in sync with my values and purpose.")
- Self-regulation ("I can manage emotional ups and downs.")
- Facing reality ("I can look myself in the mirror.")
- Self-support ("I can treat myself with kindness instead of self-criticism.")

These factors are intrinsic and controllable, and when we lead from this basis we are energized and passionate. Self-acceptance does not lead to self-indulgence, complacency, or arrogance. It enables us to be open to feedback and care about our impact. It helps leaders build true self-confidence and to demonstrate integrity, humility, and stability.

Look around your organization for a moment and ask yourself, would you prefer to follow leaders who try to build their self-esteem or leaders who work at developing their self-acceptance?

The Benefits of Mindful Self-Acceptance

Mindfulness is present, open, and engaged attention with a quality of kindness and warmth towards oneself. We can develop self-acceptance by teaching leaders to be mindful in six areas:

- **Body.** Paying attention to physical health, especially exercise, diet, and sleep.
- **Mind.** Learning to stay focused and setting boundaries to ensure time to think.
- **Emotion.** Cultivating gratitude, empathy, and positivity.
- **Spirit.** Staying connected to sources of meaning, values, and purpose.
- **Connecting.** Giving and getting support to form strong, lasting relationships.
- **Inspiring.** Energizing others with your vision and passion.

Research on the benefits of mindfulness continues to mount in the same six areas (Wallace & Shapiro, 2006; Langer, 2009; Davis & Hayes, 2012). Benefits include:

- **Body.** Lower stress, fatigue, burnout; higher immune response, life expectancy, resilience, and energy.
- **Mind.** Enhanced focus, job performance, accuracy, clarity, flexibility, objectivity, perspective, learning, memory, creativity, and problem solving.
- **Emotion.** Higher empathy, stability, positivity, psychological and moral maturity; tolerance for anxiety, ambiguity, and uncertainty.
- **Spirit.** Increased motivation, engagement, empowerment, career development, job and life satisfaction; customer loyalty; decreased absenteeism and theft.
- **Connecting.** Improved listening and empathizing, clearer communication and stronger relationships; employee retention.
- **Inspiring.** Increased innovation, new product development, sales, quality performance, leadership presence, and attractiveness.

Companies such as Google, BlackRock, and McKinsey are teaching mindfulness as both a wellness and a productivity tool. Human resources professionals can create mindful environments by leveraging performance management, engagement, recruiting, and assessment processes. And leaders can build mindful teams by establishing simple routines, such as exchanging the breathless back-to-back 60-minute meeting schedule for a 45-minute norm.

At the heart of healthy companies are healthy leaders. We can grow healthy leaders from the inside out, not only by treating them well, but by teaching them to treat themselves well. ⚏

References

Davis, D. and Hayes, J. (July 2009). What are the benefits of mindfulness? *Monitor on Psychology*. American Psychological Association, Vol. 43, No. 7, page 64.

Langer, E. *Counterclockwise*. (May 19, 2009). Ballantine Books; 1st edition.

Wallace, B. Alan, and Shauna L. Shapiro. (2006). Mental balance and well-being: Building bridges between Buddhism and western psychology. *American Psychologist* 61: 690–701.

Joshua Ehrlich, Ph.D., founded the Global Leadership Council, an international network of experts in mindful leadership and organizational transformation. He is the author of *Mindshifting: Focus for Performance.*

LEARNING GUIDE

Point Counterpoint II: 5.2

Leadership Lessons Reverberate Down the Line

DISCOVERY QUESTIONS

- What are you dealing with in your organization today that relates to this content area?
- How do you see Hogan's view of effective leadership applying to your organization?
- Winsborough's article describes the "flip side" of effective leadership. Do you see these behaviors in your own organization?
- What kinds of leader behaviors have you observed in your organization that lead to employee disengagement?
- Given everything you learned about leadership purpose, what recommendations would you have for your organization?
- What programs does your organization have for identifying "high potentials"?
- In your organization, what differentiates effective and ineffective leaders?
- What assessments have you personally experienced, and what did you learn?

SELECTED FACTS

What new facts that were presented got your attention?

- People evaluate their leader based on four qualities: integrity, judgment, competence, and vision.
- The most effective CEOs combine extreme personal humility with a relentless drive to win.
- It is estimated that $15 billion is spent annually on leadership training and development.
- Only one in 10 managers are both successful and effective.
- Characteristics of the manager correlate with performance outcomes, but low (around .20).

KEY DISCUSSION POINTS

- What were the key points being made in this presentation?
- What is the difference between successful managers and effective managers?
- Kaiser describes self-interest versus collective-interest; why does that matter?
- What do Buddha, the Bible and Karma have in common with effective leadership?
- What do you think of Furnham's point that the factors creating disengagement are not the opposite of those that cause engagement?
- How would you describe Church's dual process of differentiation and development?
- What do you think about the PepsiCo development process that focuses on career transition levels?
- What is the difference between building self-esteem and cultivating self-acceptance?
- What are the six areas of "mindfulness," and what are the benefits of each?

REVIEW OF SOLUTIONS

- Identify two to three "big ideas" worthy of exploring in your organization.
- What would you change in your organization to more effectively identify effective leaders?
- What content from these articles would you most want to apply in your organization?

IDENTIFYING THE PARADOX

- How is it that a solution appropriate for yesterday's organization is no longer valid?
- Consider how very different perspectives might be correct given different situations.
- Is an "effective leader" effective in every different situational or business context?

LEARNING OUTCOMES

- What one new piece of information did you learn that will be important to you in the future?
- Identify one thing that you will do differently based on what you learned.

Ensuring the Secure Enterprise

By Marc Sokol

The challenge of enterprise security, at first glance, seems one of having the right technology, a more consistent process, and avoiding others with bad intentions. Then again, perhaps you have come across the Pogo cartoon phrase, "We have met the enemy and he is us." The author of our lead perspective, as well as the other thought leaders providing commentary, tell us that in the end we are responsible for what happens. It comes down to awareness of our own human nature, our habits, and the unintended consequences of structures we create in pursuit of specific objectives. It also comes down to enabling choice and the capacity to act in the face of difficult decisions. Building this into your organizational culture and preparing teams to think together—before, during, and after a crisis—this is the real opportunity for HR professionals.

Mary Gentile, author of the book and program, *Giving Voice to Values*, is a global authority on why people choose not to speak up, and what we can do to foster speaking up when it matters most. In her lead perspective, Gentile shares a view on the human factor in enterprise security, along with research that tells us it's more than building a better mousetrap.

The commentaries that follow each build upon the initial perspective.

Malcolm Harkins, a deeply experienced chief information security officer, provides concrete example of how people are both the cause and cure for information security issues.

Ron Sanders, former chief HR officer for the U.S. Intelligence Community, the IRS, and the Defense Department's civilian workforce, shares his observation of habit and response as the critical human factors that impact enterprise security. Ron also sees effective response coming from human resources, and how we can access the levers of orga-

nizational DNA to enhance enterprise security.

Judy Docter, the chief human resources officer for a financial institution, provides a final commentary, showing how we put intention into action, and how an HR team comes together to build that culture of risk management called for by other thought leaders. Culture, in this case, isn't just a lofty concept; it's a set of tangible tactics that give voice to individuals and teams across the organization.

If you believe effective enterprise security and risk management requires intentional action before, during, and after critical events, then this issue of Perspectives is for you. After reading the lead perspective and commentaries that follow, you can contact any of the authors or me directly. Let us know what your company is doing to ensure a secure enterprise.

Marc Sokol, Ph.D., is executive editor of *People + Strategy*.

The Human Factor in Enterprise Security

By Mary C. Gentile

At its heart, enterprise risk and enterprise security come down to the human factor. This includes tangible and critical arenas for HR risk management, such as working with risks potentially associated with engaging third-party service providers, protection of company data, outright fraud, issues of physical safety, and numerous but less tangible risks to good organizational decision-making that arise from false or incomplete information. In all of these cases, ensuring enterprise security requires more than systems of data flow, approval processes, and monitoring systems.

The most logical and well-communicated control system is useless if it is not observed, and employees can find ways to circumvent the most complete monitoring process, whether they are driven by nefarious intent or merely acting upon a desire to simplify their workload. In the end it comes down to a human factor, how conscious we are of the choices we face, whether we choose to act on this awareness, and the ability to act effectively.

Even within institutions where we assume heightened attention to security and risk, this can be an issue. A recent study by professors at the Army War College illustrates this point. Professors Leonard Wong and Stephen J. Gerras found that lying and untruthfulness are not only very common in the military, but that the proliferation of requirements and systemic assurances demanded of personnel have actually contributed to this phenomenon ("Lying in the Military is Common, Army War College Study Says" *Washington Post*, Feb. 18, 2015,). Individuals feel pulled in seemingly conflicting directions—speed and productivity on the one hand, and compliance with checks and regulations, on the other—and this too often results in a "let's-not-and-say-we-did" type of response to comply with risk management protocols.

Building "Moral Muscle Memory"
The point here is not to say that the careful design, clear communication and consistent monitoring of risk management protocols is unnecessary or useless, but rather that it is not sufficient by itself. What becomes critically important is an organizational culture and leadership development training that builds the capability, the confidence and the "moral muscle memory' needed to really act on these protocols.

The most effective way to build this muscle memory is through pre-scripting, rehearsal, and peer coaching. Yes, there are those employees who intentionally flaunt rules and regulations, but this is not the largest group. More often, we see individuals who feel caught in the type of conflict mentioned above (time pressure vs. compliance) or who feel pressured by colleagues or managers similarly caught in what looks like a no-win dynamic. To resist this sort of very real, intense pressure, organizations

are beginning to see the value of going beyond communicating the guidelines to actually creating opportunities for employees to practice how they can respond to these pressures, and in a manner that is likely to be effective.

Responding to Pushback
The elaborate speeches that we might craft in our heads are often difficult to deliver and not often effective. What is proven to be more effective is for people to think through the tactics and arguments that will enable more of their colleagues to see the value in compliance. This typically means identifying what is at risk or at stake for all parties in an effort to find ways to

> At its heart, enterprise risk and enterprise security come down to the human factor.

mitigate those risks. It also means anticipating the sorts of pushback—the "reasons and rationalizations"—that one is likely to hear when trying to adhere to risk management protocols.

These arguments are actually predictable and therefore, vulnerable to rehearsal for effective response. Rather than engaging in the "preach and pretend" model of compliance training, it is more effective to invite employees to rehearse and peer coach each other, to harness their own creativity in coming up with convincing ways to address challenges, and to hear themselves voice these very responses in front of their colleagues and with their help in enhancing the scripts.

Beyond planning and leading control systems, a key role for HR leaders in enterprise security is building the capacity for effective voice and action in the face of risk. We need to make a conscious choice to build such capacity throughout the enterprise and act on that choice.

Mary C. Gentile, Ph.D., is the creator and director of Giving Voice to Values curriculum and author of *Giving Voice to Values: How to Speak Your Mind When You Know What's Right.*

The Cause Is Also the Cure

By Malcolm Harkins

Consider the following statistics:
- Seventy-five percent of mobile apps will fail security tests.
- Eighty-four percent of organizations who suffered a breach were out of compliance with application security controls.
- Eighty percent of CISOs believed at the beginning of 2014 that their security framework was strong enough to prevent/manage potential breaches.
- Malware used in the Sony attack would have gotten past 90 percent of cyber defenses.
- Seventy-five percent of corporate boards have no part in reviewing security or privacy risks.
- Seventy percent of employees frequently ignore IT policies.
- Fifty-six percent of employees reuse passwords between personal and corporate accounts.
- Twenty percent of employees share passwords with other employees.
- Fourteen percent of employees say they would sell their passwords to a third party.

The common thread across these data points isn't just information security, it's people. People created the web apps that fail security. People manage the systems and applications within their organization. People are the employees who ignore policies including sharing passwords. People are responsible for corporate governance on the boards of directors who have not stepped up to be accountable for corporate oversight. People are the CISO's who mistakenly believed their existing security solutions were strong enough to prevent potential breaches. People are the creators of the malicious code being spread around daily, taking foothold on our systems driving the cycle of information risk we experience.

People are the cause of the information security issues we face, but they are also the cure. Even as computing shifts to mobile and social technology, and as we see an explosion of applications and device types, it remains that people

> The common thread across these data points isn't just information security, it's people.

dynamics determine an organization's ability to manage information risk in the following ways:

Structure drives behavior. If you have the wrong security and a privacy structure that lacks independence from the technology creators or managers, you may not have sufficient tension in the system to effectively deal with information risk. Structures can drive an organizational bias that is siloed and can leave blind spots.

You get what you measure. If your IT organization is managed primarily on cost and the fast deployment of new tools, you will not have adequate information security and privacy in your infrastructure. If your technology product/services team are primarily measured on time to market and margin, then you will likely not have sufficient security development lifecycle and privacy by design to limit vulnerabilities in the technology your organization will release to its customers. If you get the measurements correct you will get movement in improving security.

Culture is the strongest form of control. The top sets the tone for the importance of security. This includes role modeling a "see something say something" approach where we all hold one another accountable for following processes meant to sense, interpret, and act upon risks. This includes the tendency to run toward risky things the organization may want to do to get there early, rather than shape the path of the risk, and be there late or even say no. If the security team isn't working on enabling the business and its employees they will go around the controls meant to manage risk.

The rule of law needs to be applied in the cyber domain. Governments need to cooperate internationally to enhance and protect our digital future. This includes prosecution for those responsible for attacking consumers and corporations.

People may be the cause, but in the end they are also the cure.

Malcolm Harkins is global chief information security officer at Cylance and former chief security and privacy officer, Intel Corporation. He is the author of *Managing Risk and Information Security: Protect to Enable.*

Embedding Cybersecurity into Your Company's DNA

By Ronald Sanders

Today's organizations, both private and public, face a daunting variety of threats to cybersecurity, not just from criminals and hacktivists, but also from state and non-state actors who are after their intellectual property. A cyberattack can threaten the very existence of an organization (not to mention the jobs of some of its C-suite officers), but the response doesn't rest solely on a building a better technical solution.

It's all about the people, and that means it's HR's business. It is not just about assuring the skill and trustworthiness of an organization's cyber talent, or mitigating any impact a cyberattack may have on the organization's workforce. Those are relatively obvious. HR also has a strategic role to assure the cyber-efficacy of the organization's culture and its leaders; that role is just as crucial to preventing, detecting, and responding to an attack as your network operations center.

Creating a Cyber-Secure Culture

Ironically, many cyber breaches are the result of nothing more than poor "cyber hygiene"—that is, an insider who unwittingly responds to a spear phishing attack, lets slip a confidential passphrase, or plugs an infected device into the network. These individual behaviors, many of them almost second nature to today's digital natives, can put an entire organization at risk. While this most common attack vector can be slammed shut with nothing more than good, commonsense cybersecurity practices, when it comes to organizational behavior, that's always easier said than done.

Cyber insecurity comes down to an organization's culture…something squarely in the chief HR officer's job jar. The CTO or CISO shares that responsibility, but at the end of the day, good cyber hygiene comes down to ensuring individual employees understand, internalize, and behave according to a set of commonsense cybersecurity standards—just as we would expect them to comply with standards of conduct, ethics, nondiscrimination, and the like.

Good cyber hygiene is more than just providing mandatory annual online training. Like other core values, it must be embedded in an organization's DNA,

> HR has a strategic role to assure the cyber-efficacy of the organization's culture and its leaders; that role is just as crucial to preventing, detecting, and responding to an attack as your network operations center.

and since HR holds sway over most of the levers that shape that DNA, we have to be as much a part of an organization's cybersecurity strategy as the CTO.

Preparing Senior Leaders for the Worst

While shaping a cyber-secure culture is important, HR's most critical contribution is helping leaders prepare for that almost-inevitable worst case. That too is a shared responsibility with the chief risk officer, the COO, or whoever is responsible for an organization's emergency management protocols. Since no contingency plan survives contact with reality, it cannot stop there; effective cyber response requires leadership practice. Just as the military uses war games and exercises to practice for war, so too must any organization in someone's cyber crosshairs…and that's just about everyone!

My firm is in the business of helping organizations prepare for and respond to cyberattacks (just as my agency was when I served in the Intelligence Community). We've found that war games can be one of the most powerful ways to prepare for the worst, and have conducted dozens of them for commercial and government clients. They can be especially valuable for senior leaders who have not lived through the intensity of a cyberattack, when they must act quickly and collaboratively for the survival of the enterprise. Experiencing that intensity as a leadership team, in the relative safety of a mock attack, can be invaluable when it comes to the crucible of the real thing.

When we take C-suite leaders through these exercises, they often find that placing their organization's technical experts in charge of managing the crisis can be risky. A firm's technical response to an attack is only one piece of the crisis puzzle, and often a relatively small one compared to the risks inherent in dealing with the media, shareholders, suppliers, bankers, customers, regulators, and boards of directors. To successfully navigate through such a crisis, an organization requires C-suite leaders who understand the *strategic business implications* of a cyberattack, and who, like a championship athletic team, have trained to collaborate and connect *all* of the dots—not just the technical ones—in the simulated heat of that crisis.

Think of it as leadership teambuilding on steroids, and that's HR responsibility too.

Ronald Sanders, Ph.D., is a vice president and fellow at Booz Allen Hamilton where he is a leader in the firm's human capital, war gaming, and organizational transformation practice areas. He was the former chief human capital officer for the U.S. Intelligence Community, the chief human resources officer for the Internal Revenue Service, and the director of civilian personnel for the Department of Defense.

Build a Culture of Risk Management

By Judy Docter

As an HR department, do you consider yourself in the risk management business? If not, it may be time to rethink that position. The 2014 "Report to the Nations on Occupational Fraud and Abuse" by the Association of Certified Fraud Examiners, which bills itself as the world's largest anti-fraud organization, shows that employee fraud is on the rise. The report estimates the typical organization loses five percent of its revenue each year to fraud. That works out to a global impact of $3.7 trillion, according to the report. With this type of revenue drain as a result of employee behavior, we must determine appropriate actions.

Tangible Tactics to Give Voice

As Mary C. Gentile says, "What has proven effective is for people to think through the tactics that will enable more colleagues to see the value in compliance and build capacity for effective voice." She is right on with this thinking. As we know, what gets measured gets managed. There are several approaches to developing risk management tactics, particularly for human resources departments.

Give voice to those close to the action. Give voice to those who are actually responsible for managing risk—colleagues on the front line of HR. Imbed a risk management officer into HR's organizational chart, someone that gets up every morning and thinks about identifying, measuring, and managing people risk.

Sponsor the collaboration of HR professionals from across the organization. Next, create a larger HR Risk Committee to broaden the responsibility both within and outside the department. Ensure representation from all areas of HR. The talent acquisition group will likely see risk from a different perspective than the benefits design team. Getting all voices to the table is an important part of the exercise.

When awareness is coupled with proactive detection measure at the front line, it builds a powerful defense against those who may consider fraudulent actions.

Define levels of risk and what that looks like. Have the Risk Committee create a definition for different levels of risk. We know that the risk of an employee violating the dress code (assuming you still have one), or not protecting customer data is not the same. Some risks are greater than others. Build language that defines the difference.

Measure, report, and widely communicate risk levels to drive ongoing risk mitigation. Provide the Risk Committee with the responsibility and accountability to identify and rate the risks within HR, and importantly, determine actions for mitigation. Then, broadly communicate the action plan.

This approach helps to build a culture of risk awareness. When awareness is coupled with proactive detection measures at the front line, it builds a powerful defense against those who may consider fraudulent actions. ▪

Judy Docter is chief human resources officer at Associated Bank.

LEARNING GUIDE

Point Counterpoint II: 5.3

Ensuring the Secure Enterprise

DISCOVERY QUESTIONS

What are you dealing with in your organization today that relates to this content area?

- What facts about the lack of security or risks to enterprise security caught your attention?
- How many different views can you find regarding who is responsible for enterprise security?
- What differences did you notice about the responsibilities of the CIO, Chief Information Officer, and the CISO, Chief Information Security Officer?
- What role do HR professionals play in information security?
- What does organizational culture have to do with information security?

SELECTED FACTS

What new facts that were presented got your attention?

- One research study illustrated that people feel pulled in conflicting directions, speed and productivity on one hand, and compliance checks and regulation on the other hand.
- Pre-scripting, rehearsal and peer coaching are techniques to prepare for challenging situations and conversations.
- Eighty-four percent of organizations that suffered a security breach were out of compliance with application security controls.
- Seventy-five percent of mobile apps fail security tests.
- The malware used in the Sony attack would have gotten past 90 percent of other company cyber defenses.
- Seventy percent of employees frequently ignore IT policies.
- Fifty-six percent of employees reuse passwords between personal and corporate accounts.
- Seventy-five percent of boards have no part in reviewing security or privacy risks.
- Twenty percent of employees share passwords with other employees.
- According to the Association of Certified Fraud Examiners the typical organization loses five percent of its revenue each year to fraud.

KEY DISCUSSION POINTS

- What were the key points being made in this presentation?
- One commentary raises the view that the roles of CIO and CISO may be inherently in conflict. Why do you agree or disagree with that statement?
- One of the commentary authors refers to employees needing to have good "cyber hygiene." What does the author mean by that term? What would be the contrast of good versus poor cyber hygiene?
- How have you observed IT and HR to collaborate around enhancing information security?
- Why does the lead author suggest enterprise security requires intentional action before, during, and after breaches in security?
- What might organizational culture look or feel like in a company with a very strong focus on enterprise and information security?
- In contrast, what might an organization culture look or feel like in a company with a very weak or lax focus on enterprise and information security?
- What would be an example of an organization having a blind spot with respect to information security?
- What might be the role of government in ensuring enterprise information security?
- What could be the strategic business implications of a cyberattack? How could it impact employee engagement, customers, suppliers, and even the board of directors?

Point Counterpoint II: 5.3

Ensuring the Secure Enterprise

REVIEW OF SOLUTIONS

- Identify two to three "big ideas" worthy of exploring in your organization.
- How would you design the role of the CISO to maximize enterprise security?
- How can HR professionals impact information security in the ways they hire, on board, train, and design performance management systems for the organization?
- How might the simulation of a security breach help company leaders better prepare for a real breach in security?
- How would you help an organization define levels of risk and actions that can be taken in response to these levels of risk?
- How could a cyberattack simulation contribute to team building and organization development?

IDENTIFYING THE PARADOX

- How is it that a solution appropriate for yesterday's organization is no longer valid?
- Consider how very different perspectives might be correct given different situations.
- How is it that the CIO and CISO could both be partners and at odds with each other with respect to their organizational roles?
- How might having employees talk openly about lapses on security make the company more secure?
- How is it that people can be both the cause of information security issues and also the cure?
- If the CIO is one of the most knowledgeable leaders with respect to information technology, why might he or she be the wrong person to speak to the media after a security breach?

LEARNING OUTCOMES

- What one new piece of information did you learn that will be important to you in the future?
- Identify one thing that you will do differently based on what you learned.
- What steps can HR take to promote better cyber hygiene among employees?
- What is the difference between the role and focus of the CIO and the CISO?
- One of the commentary authors reminds us, "What gets measured gets managed." What would you measure to help improve information security?

The Transparency Paradox at Work

By Anna A. Tavis

This Perspective shines new light on the evolution of the transparency and privacy debate in the age of artificial intelligence (AI), also known as "machine learning." Whether we call it "people analytics," "HR metrics," or any other data-related name, we are still talking about human behavior—recorded, aggregated, broken down, and served back to us as data. With the ubiquity of mobile devices and the always-on Internet, the moment of truth comes with the question of who is seeing our data and how it is being used. Take HR or management, what data should be used to recruit, appraise, promote, or dismiss employees? Take employees, how much of our private lives do we want our employers to know about and judge us by?

Ethan Bernstein opens the debate noting that with machine learning the very notion of "transparency" in management has taken on a new paradoxical dimension. "People say they value their privacy, but they don't act that way." He draws a distinction between "data fusion" that feels more like surveillance and top-down control and "personal data fusion," which is about employees using their own data to improve their performance. The real ethical question for 21st century management becomes whether managers, peers, or HR teams can actually decide how much data they are willing to "*not* access for the sake of productivity."

The Hogan Assessments team offers their psychological angle on the debate. Online behavior is still fundamentally human behavior, they argue, and "the difference between the 20th and 21st centuries lies in the ubiquity and volume of behavior," broad access to data, and "the sophistication of tools to interpret the results." The authors argue in favor of human nature that is "inherently social." They are optimistic that humans

will continue to "swim best in a world of connection, relationships, status hierarchies, and groups." The introduction of increasingly more powerful tools will help us tame technology in the service of even greater humanity.

Doug Cunningham, a developer who runs his own HR technology business, knows first-hand the power of data and the possibilities it offers. He cautions on the efficacy of the decisions that could be made deploying AI. We should not get carried away with what is technically possible, but rather focus on the boundaries that need to be placed on the data used. Cunningham calls on managers and HR professionals to join in national and global community conversations to collectively anticipate the future evolution of AI and be prepared to address the consequences.

Robin D. Richard adds to the exchange a compelling illustration of how the solution to the transparency paradox could be found in the human-cen-

tered design. Take the case of his company, CareerArc, which provides personalized and on-demand outplacement services correcting for the fatal flaws of the brick-and-mortar outplacement firms, lack of privacy, and availability of choice. With the ubiquitous technology available to us, the service is scalable and democratic, addressing the need of the new economy for the ongoing career development options. The solution to the transparency paradox will be possible only when "products are designed to respect, not correct, the human instincts for privacy and safety."

The final word in this discussion comes from **Christine Congdon** of Steelcase, an innovator in smart workspace design. Steelcase is optimistic about technology and sees it as an enabler that will take human performance to the next level of productivity and excellence. Taking its cue from the latest car design, she argues that if cars could actually help people be better drivers, then tech-enabled offices will help people be more productive and more connected workers.

This Perspectives comes full circle to conclude that technology is on its way to help humans be better humans, depending on how we use it and why.

Anna A. Tavis, Ph.D., is Perspectives editor and an associate professor at New York University. You can connect with her on LinkedIn at annatavis.

The Evolution of "Transparency" in Management

Get Me Everything You've Got on ... Me

By Ethan Bernstein

It's startling—but no longer science fiction—how much information can be and is being gathered about employees at work. Fifty years ago, a typical manager might have periodically tracked a few numbers—revenue, expenses, customer satisfaction. Today, the workplace is bristling with monitoring software, sensors, and cameras. We label our workplaces "smart" because they are always observing us: a cocktail of smartphones, computers, fixtures with embedded sensors, and cameras collectively contain enough locational, audio, video, text, and activity data to produce an unfathomable set of digital breadcrumbs. And the more information management gets, the more it realizes it needs.

More Is More

More information not only calls for even *more* information, it also demands more information-processing power. No person or HR team could ever parse so much data, but people no longer have to. That's why we have artificial intelligence (AI), or machine learning. AI can filter floods of information—from our email, apps, calendars, social media, Web browsers, news services, enterprise workflow apps, systems of record, mon-

itoring devices, wearable sensors, video camera feeds—and *make sense of it*. All in real time. While we humans can only handle so much data, AI systems get smarter with more information.

Our work lives are now full of examples. Google can use your past location and calendar data to predict your next client visit and help you avoid traffic jams on a trip you haven't even told it you will be making. Siri can answer your questions with much greater ease and accuracy because she knows everything you have ever done with—or near—your iPhone (and its apps, microphone, accelerometer, GPS sensor, Bluetooth, WiFi, and so on), and when she hears you curse or sees you frown, she can ask you if she can help. Cortana can tell you to "ask me anything" because, chances are, the answer lies somewhere in the gigabytes of information flowing through—or stored in—your work computer. Even your office bathroom's hand soap dispenser (enabled with RFID sensors which read your ID badge) can remind you, by name, to wash your hands before you return to work. This is not science fiction. Even in ordinary workplaces, substantially increased use of observation—"the act of careful watching and listening, or paying close attention to someone or something, in order to get information" (as the Merriam-Webster Online Dictionary defines it)—has become widespread over the last 15 years.

As I explain in my forthcoming article in the *Annals of Management,* these Big Data developments, while viewed as cutting-edge, are in fact the latest phase of a long evolution of observation in management. It's pretty basic: you can't understand, control, or change anything without observing what's going on. During the Renaissance, it was an innovation to keep modern accounting records. Roughly a century ago, it was an innovation to observe scientifically exactly how workers did their work. A few decades later, it was an innovation to observe scientifically how workers worked together. Now it's AI-enabled "transparency." With each innovation, companies have learned more about how they could improve productivity—if they collected the necessary information.

Which Side Are You On?

Studying this history, I noticed that there has long been something one-sided about it. It's all conceived and implemented from the observer's point of view: *We* need to know what *you* are doing. The more we know, the more we can help you do it better. But what about the observed? Are they willing to be so intensely examined? Does it actually help them do better? Or do they now clamor for "privacy"?

Management—including HR—has largely been able to brush these questions aside for two reasons. The law allows them to collect as much information as they can, as long as they let employees know they are doing it. And employees are letting them do it (just click "Agree"). This is actually somewhat puzzling. In what social scientists call the "privacy paradox," people say they value their privacy, but they don't act that way. Think of it. Most of us, even if the offer were made, would not sell our private information to a big, rich company for a paltry $60. Yet Microsoft recently bought LinkedIn and what it bought—at $60 per person—was all that information that 433 million of us put onto our LinkedIn pages. The same thing happened when Facebook bought WhatsApp for all its address books, and Facebook got away with paying only $42 for each one. Not that any of us got a cent. If we value our privacy, why did we put all that information online for free, knowing that companies sell it to each other?

Even so, companies aren't necessarily getting the free ride it appears they're getting. It has long been known—and we know from our own experience—that human behavior may change when we know we're being watched. As I explained in my 2014 *Harvard Business Review* article, "The Transparency Trap," when we feel over-observed at work, our performance suffers. This can take two forms. One response is to just do exactly what the watchers want to see. Observers may get compliance, but they won't get much innovation. We're just not likely to try something different if we're being watched to make sure we're doing our jobs right.

Another response, no more to a company's advantage, is to find ways to hide. Put employees in open offices and they'll work from home—and feel more productive. Track more data, and they'll find a way to stay under the radar. Monitor their work smartphones, and they'll get a second one, as many people do. Make all written work accessible, and people will stop writing things down. Track email, and they'll use Slack instead. These are all real examples. So rather than learning more, management may end up learning less, or even learning things that aren't true.

Let "Us" Have the Data and You Can Have the Results

Must all this incredible data-gathering and data-crunching ability go to waste, then? I don't think so. It just needs to be rechanneled. When entrepreneur David Brunner was conducting his doctoral research at Harvard, he observed that organizations can deploy AI either to help them improve their employees or to help their employees improve themselves. The first approach is standard *data fusion* and to employees, it feels like surveillance and control (even if you might call it "people analytics" or "transparency"). The second approach is called *personal data fusion* and to employees, it feels like coaching, mentoring, and self-improvement. It's for *them*. The company provides AI to gather and process information which *you*, the employee, own and which *you* can use to improve *your own* performance. You become a more valuable employee—which of course can be rewarded by the organization. You are also likely to feel more loyal. Thus, the company gets the results it wanted, not by taking, but by helping its employees give.

In that sense, AI presents an amazing opportunity. Whereas being observed by a person can feel like an invasion of privacy, it doesn't if the "observer" is a machine—the data stays personal so long as another *human* doesn't access it. And if the machine adds value to how we do our work (like with LinkedIn and WhatsApp), we give willingly. But at work, this only works if the data stays personal—i.e., out of the curious hands of another human being.

Yet putting together a business case for privacy is far from easy in a world blindly enamored with transparency. So whether you are manager, peer, or HR team, the real question about transparency in today's workplace is how much data are you willing to not access for the sake of productivity?

Ethan Bernstein, Ph.D., is assistant professor at Harvard Business School and author of *The Transparency Trap.*

Data Fusion Is Unlikely to End Life as We Know It

By Dave Winsborough, Darko Lovric, and Tomas Chamorro-Premuzic

A few years ago, when Cambridge University researchers demonstrated that your Facebook likes could be used to predict your sexual orientation, voting preferences, personality, and even IQ, the world erupted in a frenzy of outrage and concern, and governments everywhere responded with new laws limiting the use and sale of your private data.

No they didn't. Nothing much happened at all. There were news stories, mild wonderment and a smattering of online chat, but the net effect on online behavior was precisely zero. Facebook continued its stratospheric growth, and while a few thousand people may have tightened their privacy settings the net impact of knowing that Facebook could know everything about you was a collective, "meh."

Most users of social media acknowledge that there is a tradeoff between what you give (access to lots of personal data) and what you get (free search, a free platform to follow celebrities, and the largely unfulfilled promise of relevant ads).

Nor do they seem to mind that these data are used to evaluate them. For example, employers and recruiters use social media to evaluate job candidates, and at least one business, LinkedIn, was designed and built to capture user profiles to monetize recruitment

and search at a global scale. Our own research and that of others shows that younger people expect that employers peruse their online lives and are comfortable with being evaluated in that way. Employers regard it as a method for "discovering the applicant's true self." After all, online behavior is still behavior and people take as many pains online to curate an image of themselves as they do offline. When social media users decide what images, achievements, musical preferences, and conversations to display online, the same self-presentational dynamics are at play as in any traditional social setting.

Burnishing one's image online has even been taken as a right, insofar as

> The fragmentation of tools to merge these data, and the changing fashions between applications and formats means that there isn't a master algorithm that binds our fragmentary digital traces into a coherent whole, a digital twin, who contains our thoughts, emotions, and actions.

the European Union allows citizens to hide links to images or posts that do not fit the reputation they want to portray online. Consequently, people's online reputation is no more "real" than their analogue reputation; the same individual differences are manifested in virtual and physical environments, albeit in seemingly different ways. It is therefore naïve to expect online profiles to be more genuine than resumes, although they may offer a much wider set of behavioral samples.

The difference between the 20th and 21st centuries lies in the ubiquity and volume of behavior that is captured, by the breadth of those with access to those data, and by the sophistication of tools to interpret the results. Right now, the fragmentation of tools to merge these data, and the changing fashions between applications and formats means that there isn't a master algorithm that binds our fragmentary digital traces into a coherent whole, a digital twin, who contains our thoughts, emotions and actions.

You can bet good money that in the future our digital selves will have personalities that are accessible to anyone who cares to look. It will be, possibly, an age of true digital transparency.

Yet when Socrates exhorted us to "know thyself," it is doubtful he considered a world where companies (read your employer, or Facebook, or Google) know us better than we can know ourselves. That opens two scenarios for the future.

In the first we lack agency over our digital selves. Our personal data is owned instead by the hardware and software we use and sold to the highest bidder. Anonymity and privacy are in demand but very expensive—but there is no practical opt-out for ordinary people. In this world our every engagement with the digital world creates food for marketing and social engineering of Machiavellian/Orwellian proportions.

In the second scenario, our personal data is ours. New companies have emerged to allow us to "bank" our data and "lend" it to corporations. These companies have the opportunity to allow our digital selves to become our agents and avatars, revealing our preferences for specific purposes. We'll have as many digital selves as required, ensuring fragmentation works for us instead of against us. Importantly, these companies can use our profiles for both self-insight and growth, helping us lead more authentic lives but preventing others from using this information to manipulate or game us.

Humans are inherently social, and we swim best in a world of connection, relationships, status hierarchies and groups. Technologies that emerge from human activity are still fundamentally human. Through history, social technologies have been decried as destructive (cellphones were predicted to destroy face-to-face interaction; rock and roll would usher in the end of days; and video games would stop children from exercising). Personal data fusion is very likely to happen. The world is very unlikely to end.

Dave Winsborough is vice president of innovation at Hogan Assessment Systems and founder of the New Zealand firm Winsborough Limited.

Darko Lovric is a principal at Incandescent and a former fellow of the World Economic Forum.

Tomas Chamorro-Premuzic is the CEO of Hogan Assessment Systems, a professor of business psychology at University College London, and a faculty member at Columbia University.

Applying AI

By Doug Cunningham

The business world is buzzing with visions and promises of how artificial intelligence will radically alter companies. The potential is real. The number of workplace data sources is growing at a breakneck pace, and so is our ability to store, process, and draw conclusions from this data.

The result: an unprecedented opportunity for AI to uncover patterns and associations that yield perspective and insights on our workforce. Areas such as employee engagement, workplace health, talent acquisition, and productivity are all positioned for dramatic change.

Tread Carefully

We have already witnessed rapid developments in the consumer technology market. Apple's Siri, Google Now, and Microsoft's Cortana are becoming smarter every year. Most of us welcome the advancements and gladly yield our privacy in exchange for the benefits.

But applying AI in the workplace exposes companies to a different set of risks, and leaders must take great care to protect their employees and businesses. Companies have a responsibility to protect the privacy of their employees and ensure they are not discriminated against.

Privacy. When sufficiently powerful AI crunches vast quantities of data on web searches, emails, chat messages, calendar events, mobile activity and more, it has the potential to learn personal information that employees never intended to share with their employer. One could argue that employees should take care in using company systems for personal use. But anyone who has worked in a corporate setting knows that consistently separating work and personal is near impossible.

Is it acceptable if AI learns that an employee has financial problems? Is expecting a child? Has a sick family member? With sufficient data, these aren't difficult to figure out. A watchful manager might draw similar conclusions. AI can watch everyone all of the time.

Discrimination. The real power of AI is to do something with what we have learned, and this is where businesses need to be even more careful. Julia Angwin recently presented the results of a study analyzing the output of software in wide use across the country to predict future criminal behavior. They uncovered a racial bias that had previously gone undetected.

Businesses leveraging AI need to approach this with utmost diligence, lest a recruiting chat bot wrongly reject a specific group of applicants or a performance system unwittingly develop a gender bias.

What to Do

So how do we ensure that we don't learn things we shouldn't? Or make decisions we shouldn't? Should we run from AI? Of course not. But we should be very thoughtful and considered in how we build and deploy such systems.

To start, artificially intelligent systems in the workplace must be built not only considering the possible but also the allowed. The vendors behind them must develop safeguards to monitor their results and detect breaches of privacy and unintentional discrimination.

Second, managers and executives deploying such technology need to be cognizant of the risks and how they use the technology. They need to set clear guidelines around acceptable use and communicate these to employees. They need to work closely with vendors to ensure that any technology deployed aligns with the expectations of the business.

Last, we need continued discourse on the challenges and opportunities. The White House Office of Science and Technology Policy this year hosted public workshops to prepare for the future of artificial intelligence. Other efforts are under way as well. Management and human resources executives should participate in these groups to expand their view of the possible, but also understand the risks and concerns.

Doug Cunningham is CEO of Uppercase HR, an agile performance management software company.

The Paradox of Innovation and the Currency of Trust

By Robin D. Richards

Bernstein's writings on privacy and personal data reminded me of the unintended paradoxes that can sometimes result from product innovation and design—much like in his article, *Big Brother Vs. Personal Data Fusion*, where he offers the example of modern CRMs that come with the promise of delivering more useful and transparent data to sales organizations, but may in reality encourage secrecy in the salespeople they were designed to assist. We found a similar paradox in our study on workplace flexibility.

When we surveyed over a thousand working professionals on their work-life balance, telecommuting arrangements, and wellness benefits, we found that one in three working Americans felt obligated to answer work-related calls and emails past regular working hours. With the company-issued smartphone tethering modern-day workers to the virtual desk, it appears that time saved by many employees from using the technology initially designed to make work and life more efficient, often ends up overtaken with more work. However, it is important to note that it is the person who,

shaped by their culture and standards of practice, decides to rededicate those hours to work, and not the innovation itself, that causes the paradox.

As human capital software and service providers, we at CareerArc think about these types of decisions every day. Developing technology for people who manage teams, recruit talent, and transition employees, we build each new product platform or feature with a people-centered approach to design. An area we have applied this focus is one where technology actually *supports* the human instinct for privacy and safety, and that is in our approach to modern outplacement.

Many of today's outplacement services, which are benefit given to laid off employees to support their job search and transition, still follow the brick-and-mortar model born out of the 1960s: They typically include the provision of physical satellite offices where coaches conduct resume and interview preparation in-person. But for companies downsizing, this model can be costly and increasingly underutilized, effectively reserving outplacement for executives and upper-level employees and excluding those in entry-level to middle-management who could arguably most benefit from assistance. We immediately saw the need for a tech solution that could impact more people.

Designing with our end-user—the exiting employee—in mind, we aimed to correct the two design flaws in the brick-and-mortar approach that were similar to the flaws Bernstein found in many data and enterprise tools today: the neglect of the human instincts for safety and privacy, and the omission of choice (forced opt-in, and so forth).

Knowing job loss and career transition can be one of the most challenging moments in a person's life, we learned through customer interviews and feedback that privacy, safety, and autonomy were very important for those undergoing this change. By delivering career assistance content and virtual coaching through an online platform, we strived to create a safe space for these new job seekers to brush up on their resume writing and interviewing skills, take self-assessment tests, explore new career interests, and even video chat with a

coach all in the privacy and convenience of their home. Most importantly, users are given full autonomy over their time and priorities; they decide what to do first, when to do it, and whether to opt-in at all. Through this approach, we are seeing employees land jobs three times

> The core issue here is *trust*—the real currency in today's increasingly connected and surveilled work life.

faster than the national average time it takes to find employment.

Whether it's moving from an offline note-taking system to the sales CRM in the cloud, or transitioning from face-to-face outplacement models to on-demand video sessions with a career coach, the core issue here is trust—the real currency in today's increasingly connected and surveilled work life. Personal data fusion, a system that can strike that perfect balance between data privacy and transparency, is possible only when products are designed to respect, not correct, human instincts for privacy and safety.

Robin D. Richards serves as chairman and CEO of CareerArc, a leading HR technology company powering employer branding solutions that help business leaders recruit and transition the modern workforce.

Technology Drives the Well-Being of People

By Christine Congdon

Offices would be better places to work if they could learn from cars. New car models are embedded with technologies that make driving easier, safer, and more fun. Sensors tell drivers if there is a truck in their blind spot, or if they are about to back into another car when parking. The car doesn't just provide transportation anymore—it actually helps people be better drivers.

People used to think that technology would make offices obsolete—but the opposite is happening. In the near future, technology will be embedded in offices so it actually helps people work better and makes the workplace even more relevant. Like cars, a network of sensors and other technologies in the workplace will help make work a much better—and more humane—experience. Technology will serve individual workers, teams, and organizations. It will help people cope with the sense of being overwhelmed that they often feel as work intensifies and the pace of change accelerates. This data will also help organizations design the kinds of spaces that workers love to work in versus have to work in.

Companies that want to create great workplaces can benefit from this embedded technology to help individual workers and teams, and they can also draw from the data that is generated. Design, facilities, and real estate professionals can make better decisions about where to focus their efforts if they have a data stream to tell them which rooms are always busy and which rooms are ignored. With this information, organizations can better

> The challenge with technology in the workplace is making it meaningful to the employee.

understand what's working and what's not, so they can make the best workspace possible.

The challenge with technology in the workplace is making it meaningful to the employee. It should help them cognitively off-load some of the tasks they have to think about today, and leverage new technologies that will be embedded in the physical environment to make their work lives easier and more productive. When smart and connected spaces are enabled in the office in an intentional way, people can more easily navigate the complexity of work today and reduce their stress.

When objects, like chairs or rooms, can sense the environment and communicate, they become tools for understanding complexity, identifying opportunity and responding to needs swiftly. The work environment itself will become a tool for creating more productive, engaged employees who are in control of their surroundings and able to choose what they need to accomplish their tasks.

Just as technology in today's cars is improving the driving experience, tomorrow's office will harness the power of emerging technologies and allow people to more easily navigate the complexity of work as well as help organizations create better work experiences for individuals and teams. ⏹

Christine Congdon is global director of research communications at Steelcase.

Point Counterpoint II: 5.4

The Transparency Paradox at Work

INTRODUCTION

The more information managers get, the more information they ask for. The more information employees voluntarily give up about themselves, the more concerns they raise about the use of their private data by organizations. The paradox of the new "smart" workplace requires a new skill set from HR managers. Not only is HR expected to have the ability to gather, organize and interpret employee data, it is with introducing and cultivating the new set of values and behaviors with heightened respect for employee privacy. Yet, it is clear that when data fusion becomes personal data fusion, i.e. allowing employees to have exclusive access to their own data, it will open up unprecedented sources of enhanced productivity and performance.

DISCOVERY QUESTIONS

- What are you dealing with in your organization today that relates to the area of transparency and privacy at work?
- How do you see the new "smart" workplace coming to your organization and to the organizations around you?
- Does new workplace transparency line up with the historical precedent of management oversight?
- What is changing now in the treatment of "privacy" in the new workplace that historically was not true?
- What is radically different between "big data," "data fusion," and "personal data fusion"?
- How does human behavior change when we are being watched and feel "overexposed"?
- What is the new data-enabled path to superior human productivity and performance?

SELECTED FACTS

- What new facts that were presented got your attention?
- What were the costs of Microsoft's acquisition of LinkedIn and Facebook's acquisition of WhatsApp? What was the cost of the information per user? Why could it be troubling?
- What was the public's reaction to Cambridge University's research on the use of Facebooks "likes"?
- What paradox was revealed in the study of flexible working?
- Summarize the difference between human behavior in the 20th and 21st centuries.

KEY DISCUSSION POINTS

- What were the key points made in this Perspectives?
- Discuss the pros and cons of "transparency" in the workplace.
- Describe two scenarios for the future of having "digital twins."
- Compare the evolution of technology in outplacement services in the 21st century.
- What is the role of HR in the "smart" workplace?

REVIEW OF SOLUTIONS

- Identify two to three "big ideas" worthy of exploring in your organization.
- What caution needs to be taken when introducing AI in your organization?
- Describe a possible government role in making AI "safe" in organizations.
- Describe what the workplace could learn from the advances in car design.
- What new HR competencies must be developed to support the evolution of technology in the workplace?

IDENTIFYING THE PARADOX

- How is it that a solution appropriate for yesterday's organization is no longer valid?
- Consider how opposing perspectives on workplace transparency might work in vastly different situations.
- Explain what is meant by the statement, "The data stays personal so long as another human doesn't access it."
- What have we learned since we implemented flexible working?
- Summarize the "transparency paradox" as you see it now.

LEARNING OUTCOMES

- What one new piece of information did you learn that will be important to you in the future?
- Identify one thing that you will do differently based on what you learned.
- Commit to learning more about AI and "machine learning," and think about what would need to change if it were to be implemented successfully in your organization.